71/45.

D0349249

Kelly

Kelly

A Memoir

GERRY KELLY
with Don Anderson ∾

Gill & Macmillan

Gill & Macmillan Ltd
Hume Avenue, Park West, Dublin 12
with associated companies throughout the world
www.gillmacmillan.ie

© Gerry Kelly 2008
978 07171 4253 8

Index compiled by Cover to Cover
Typography design by Make Communication
Print origination by Carole Lynch
Printed and bound in Great Britain by
MPG Books Ltd, Bodmin, Cornwall

This book is typeset in Linotype Minion and
Neue Helvetica.

A CIP catalogue record for this book is available from
the British Library.

5 4 3 2 1

CONTENTS

FOREWORD
By Gloria Hunniford

In spite of Gerry Kelly's extensive broadcasting success through-out Ireland, it seems ridiculous that one of my own favourite memories of his career is when he split his trousers on *Good Evening Ulster*—and caused guffaws of laughter all over the coun-try. However, fun and joy is what Gerry has been able to combine, for many years, with a fine technique of conducting interviews and presenting chat shows like KELLY.

When Gerry arrived with us on *Good Evening Ulster* in 1978 he was definitely 'the new boy'. It was his first taste of television, and of course he was given many of the quirky film jobs that allowed his generous personality to shine through. But it was always evi-dent that he had, as my mother would have said, 'a good brain' and was a highly intellectual man. After all, he had been a teacher for a number of years. It's this enviable combination that led Gerry to become one of the best chat show hosts in Ireland. His incredibly successful show KELLY ran for sixteen years and is still sorely missed.

In London, when I was interviewing star names for Radio 2 or television, they would always say, 'Oh, I had a fantastic night in Belfast on the KELLY show!'

Whatever Gerry decides to put his hand to, he will always suc-ceed. He has tenacity, talent, skills and intellect; and, most of all, as a person he makes an enduring colleague and friend.

Gloria Hunniford
June 2008

OUR DAD

Gerry Kelly has been a household name for over twenty years throughout the island of Ireland. He has come in to our living-rooms every Friday night, and with his honest and approachable nature has endeared himself in the hearts of young and old alike.

Those who know him see no difference between Gerry in 'real life' and 'Gerry on the telly'. Those who don't know him, meet him on the street and say, 'God, Gerry, you are much bigger in real life!'

Reading the book made us see him in a different light. Not so different that we didn't know who it was referring to, but different enough to see Gerry as a man, an entertainer, a friend and a professional—rather than just Our Dad.

Growing up with Gerry Kelly as your father had its advantages and disadvantages. My sister and I often got free concert tickets when we asked nicely, and got to meet the odd famous person from time to time! Dad would have summers off work, so we were able to go on great family holidays and spend time together. On the other hand, people would stare at us as we walked down the street, and made it difficult for us as teenagers to blend in with the crowd, as teenagers tend to want to do.

As we grew older, I suppose we came to realise just how successful our dad was. Embarrassment turned into respect and denial changed to pride.

He is a big family man. Behind all his success and his public image is a very supportive family. Dad includes us in all his decisions and in return we include him in ours. When his two 'babies' moved to Dublin, his heart was broken but he never stood in our way. However we have noticed that he does tend to play a lot more golf in Dublin than he used to!

Love ya, Gerardy,

xx

Sarah and Claire Kelly
June 2008

Chapter 1 ～

| THE DAY THE MUSIC DIED

'What I'm really trying to tell you, Gerry, is that *KELLY* will be coming off the air for ever at the end of the year'—the words of UTV's programme controller Alan Bremner heralding the demise of the station's longest running programme.

It was 16 August 2005, a day I'm unlikely to forget. It took a while for his words to sink in.

I knew the company was having problems convincing the ITV network to continue to take the prime time 9 o'clock slot on a Friday to show a regional programme. I knew they were coming under increasing pressure to comply with the wishes of their network masters and feature what the rest of the UK was watching at that time—*Morse* or *Frost* or *Taggart* or whatever.

But surely UTV could insist that Northern Ireland did not conform to conventional British viewing patterns and that we here still enjoy our talk shows. After all *KELLY* had been going for seventeen years and enjoyed some of the highest ratings UTV ever achieved in its fifty-year history.

The programme competed at an all-Ireland level, often successfully taking on RTÉ's legendary *Late Late Show* and more times than not beating the viewing figures of such national icons as Parkinson and Jonathon Ross.

We had a proven track record. *KELLY* had won numerous awards over the years for its entertainment quality and even in an age of multi-channel viewing still attracted a loyal following. So why shouldn't UTV continue to broadcast, at a time of its own choosing, what was often described as its flagship programme?

There had been some discussion months previously about moving KELLY to another night and perhaps broadcasting at a later time—11 o'clock had been mentioned. But why should we be pushed to the extremities of the schedule when only insomniacs and those returning from the pub would be our potential viewers?

Even though my brain was crowded with all these thoughts as I sat in the controller's office that August afternoon and listened to what he was saying, no words came from my lips. I felt the sting of tears at the back of my eyes. It was all so sudden. There was no time to rehearse my argument, no time to defend our seventeen-year record. It was all so final.

Throughout the history of KELLY, Alan Bremner had been one of the programme's greatest supporters. Programme controller and my boss he may have been, but I always considered him a friend and a confidant. He bolstered us when we were down and he rejoiced in our successes. So it wasn't easy for him to break the news to us, I know. It was well known that Alan was due to retire at the end of the year and I've often wondered if the two events were linked in some way. Try as I may over the following weeks and months, I never did get a satisfactory answer as to why exactly it was decided to take KELLY off the air. Alan has since admitted to me it was his call and his call only, but somehow I don't believe that's the full story.

Still reeling from the shock, I left Alan's office with my producer Patricia Moore. We went off for a coffee, seeking a quiet corner to try and make sense of what had just happened. After thirty minutes we parted, unable to fully comprehend the impact of Alan's decision. All we knew was that we still had fourteen programmes to make before the 16 December cut-off and our immediate worry now was how to tell the rest of the team and how to motivate them to work on a programme that was already on death row. If all this sounds like a bereavement, it's because that is exactly how it felt.

For seventeen years I ate, slept and drank KELLY. I was never off duty. Reading a magazine, listening to music, going to the theatre, reading the papers, talking to friends, going on holiday—all were opportunities to uncover a story for the show. It took over my life and I enjoyed every minute of it!

———

GK: You've got two grandchildren.

Marianne Faithfull: Two.

GK: I can't believe Marianne Faithfull is a granny.

MF: Kinda cool, isn't it? Great for my grandchildren. Imagine being able to say, 'My Granny is Marianne Faithfull.'

———

The weeks that followed that fateful meeting are still something of a blur. I somehow felt I had failed and was embarrassed to tell my friends. Even telling Helena was difficult. I think she thought from my tone that someone had died as I sat her down to explain what had been decided. As usual, she helped me get things in perspective.

I needed to get away for a while. Unusually, our two grown-up daughters Sarah and Claire agreed to come on holiday with us and so we headed off on a cruise around the Mediterranean, ending up in Venice. It was just what I needed, time to unwind and to concentrate on the really important things in life, like family. We had a ball on that holiday with the added bonus of the company of our two girls. It had been quite a while since they had last come on vacation with us and it reminded us of some of our happiest times as a family on holiday in Florida.

Back home after two weeks and I had reconciled myself with the decision to drop the show from the UTV schedule. It was now time to look forward. There was a fourteen-week season of the programme still to plan and then further discussions with Alan Bremner about its replacement in 2006.

How would we break the news to the press? I certainly didn't want, and UTV didn't want, the phrase 'Kelly Axed' to appear in the tabloid newspapers. Feelings of failure may have crossed my mind, but there was no way I was going to have newspapers infer that seventeen years of my life had ended in failure. That just wasn't the case. Nor was it UTV's reasoning to kick-start the 2006 season with something new.

At a further meeting with Alan, UTV's MD John McCann and our press department, I asked to be allowed to suggest the wording for the press release. It was now September 2005 and UTV had organised two press days, one in Belfast and one in Dublin, to announce its programme plans for the autumn. It was felt that this would be an opportune time to release the fact that KELLY would not be returning in 2006.

I agonised long and hard about how I wanted the story to break. Over the years the press had not been very kind to the programme. Some critics accused us of being fixated with soap stars, delivering only Z-list guests, and to top it all, at one stage someone even accused us of not welcoming Protestants on to the show. I have to say that made us laugh at the time, but when this particular suggestion was further championed by no less a person than the MP John Taylor in an article in the *Belfast Telegraph*, my laughter turned to anger. What bullshit! If Mr Taylor or his like believed for one minute that in a hectic KELLY office, working to the strictest of deadlines week in week out, our researchers had the time or the interest to ask the religion of our guests before inviting them on to the show, he was living in cloud cuckoo land. Researchers are constantly under pressure to come up with programme ideas and guests. They are generally young; all of them are bright and with a commitment and a passion for their work. Someone's religion is the least of their worries. To be so trite or so mischievous as to suggest that people were chosen because of where they lay their hat on a Sunday morning was at best disingenuous.

So for all those reasons it was important to me that whatever wording we came up with as to why KELLY was not coming back, it could not be used as another tabloid stick to beat the backs of some of the most dedicated and talented people it has been my privilege to work with.

KELLY was not just about me. Of course my name was the one in lights, but if any television presenter ever tells you that the success of a show is down to him or her, take it with a very large pinch of salt. Without the expertise of producers, researchers, directors, camera operators, sound engineers, production assistants, lighting engineers, floor managers and a multitude of other people even further behind the scenes, a television host can look very silly indeed. Over the KELLY years in UTV we had built up quite a team. Outside of RTÉ, I know of no other television company that is confident enough or capable enough to produce a complex light entertainment show live every week for two-thirds of the year. I was proud of those I worked with and I was proud of what we had achieved together. But how to end it?

I decided to say that it was entirely my decision to leave the show. Seventeen years had been a long run. It was time for change. I wanted to spread my wings, try something new and UTV had agreed to help me develop a brand new show for 2006. I wanted to leave KELLY while it was still performing well. That's what I said both in Belfast and Dublin. I was interviewed by the Southern press, was invited on to several radio shows, and my decision to quit was equally well covered here in the Northern Ireland papers and on radio and television.

The next day I opened the *Mirror*. Actually I didn't have to open it; it was on the front page. What did it say? 'Kelly Axed.' You just can't win, can you?

At no stage though was there ever any question of me leaving UTV. I am a freelance journalist with my own production company; I work on contracts. It just so happens that UTV and I were happy to renew my contract every two to three years for the past twenty years. It suited me and it obviously suited them. Alan Bremner and John McCann were at pains to stress that they still wanted me to play a pivotal role in UTV's programme output, and so I signed up for a further twelve months.

But before all that and before we could even begin to think of how we would replace KELLY in 2006, there was the little matter of planning for a further thirteen shows and one final farewell blast. The last show was scheduled for Friday, 16 December 2005. Alan Bremner said, 'Do whatever you want. Take two hours if you want. Don't worry about the budget. We want the final KELLY to be something special.'

Producer Patricia Moore took him at his word and began planning for something very special indeed, something I had very little control over, but something that I think was a fitting tribute to a programme that had become so much part of the lives of many people in Northern Ireland and further afield over the previous seventeen years.

———

Graham Norton:

There was a lot of wetting the bed and cross-dressing in the early years which was a very unhappy combination really. I mean, the dry cleaning bills alone …

———

| HELLO AND WELCOME

Have you ever noticed something about television programmes like KELLY? They never begin quite at the beginning. I'll give you an example. You are sitting comfortably, the programme titles roll, the camera zooms in on me and I say something like, 'Good evening and welcome to KELLY. Tonight on the programme we have an exclusive interview with Lord Lucan. I'll be talking to the captain of the *Marie Celeste* and we hear from a local man who has tamed a Yeti. But first Elvis the king, who's come out of hiding just for us.'

Note that the first item on the show is the last thing you hear announced. It's just a funny wee habit chat show people have. For once therefore I'm not going to do that to you and I'll start with the proper beginning, which is 20 September 1948, the day I was thrust upon the world. I was born the youngest of five, three sisters and one brother, to Isaac and Kathleen Kelly. Those who appeared before me were Patricia, the eldest, then Kathleen and Stella; after that it was Danny and then myself. There was a two-year gap between us all except between Danny and me, where the gap was four years. So I was ten years younger than my oldest sister Patricia. I'm told that all my sisters spoilt me rotten. They cooed and aahed over me for years and even at my present ripe old age, I'm often still treated as the baby of the house. I hesitate to remind them all of just how old I am as it might only serve as a reminder of their own mortality.

I was born in Thomas Street in Ballymena, Co. Antrim, of which I have little memory. When I was 3 years old the family left to live in Downpatrick, Co. Down, the area which I now consider my home territory. My parents originally came from Derry, where my father was working in the then thriving shirt industry in the city. Promotion took him to Ballymena and then on to Downpatrick, where he took up a position as manager of the now defunct Talmac shirt factory. We arrived in the County Down town in the early 1950s to occupy a house in the newly built housing estate of Ardmeen Green on the Ardglass Road. It was a four-bedroomed house on the edge of the town, brand new and a good place to live. I had in many ways an idyllic early childhood. There was a large expanse of grass just outside the house, a green. There were two of those greens surrounded by 104 houses and I could have named the families living in each and every one of those homes when I lived there. I can still name many of the original families, and our house, No. 45, is of course still there.

So there in the 1950s and 60s I grew up in a totally mixed Catholic and Protestant community and played interminably on that green. During the football season it was Wembley or Croke Park; it was Lord's during the summer, and in an Olympic year a magnificent stadium. It was the old-fashioned and rather healthy way of growing up, spending all our time outside playing. There was nobody to tell us to get off the grass because that was what the grass was for. Occasionally people did get a bit miffed when their carefully tended gardens were battered by our footballs, which were sometimes confiscated out of exasperation more than anything else. But in those days young people were expected to be playing boisterously and constantly.

I remember during one of the Olympics, probably Rome 1960, we held our own version on the green, with lots of races, high jumping, long jumping, shot putting and hammer throwing—anything from the big games we could emulate. Eight times round the green was a mile and from Bradley's lamp-post to Cunningham's was the 100 yard dash. But we needed medals for all the winners— all Olympic winners get medals, don't they? Now money was scarce, practically non-existent in fact, so the notion of buying medals from Magee's sports shop was a non-starter. Suddenly, young Gerry had a brainwave.

My sister Kathleen was an accomplished Irish dancer and was the winner of many medals, which conveniently came in gold, silver and bronze. Absolutely perfect! So, having sneaked into her bedroom and found her hard-earned stash of medals, I proceeded to hand them out to the deserving mini-Olympic winners. To this day Kathleen does not have a single medal to denote her triumphs. And, if they have retained them, an amazing number of Protestants from that estate have Irish dancing medals. Thankfully, Kathleen didn't miss them at the time and years later she thought they had simply been mislaid when moving house. Unfortunately I have not had the right opportunity since to tell her what actually happened. Now she knows.

———

Gary Lineker:

George was bullying his brothers one day. So I said, 'George, behave yourself.' And he turned to me, looked at me and said, 'You know the trouble with you? You think you are so good at football …'

———

It was a compact life in those days. My local primary school, St Patrick's, run by the De la Salle Brothers, was a leisurely walk of 500 yards from my home. Today of course that same religious order comes in for a lot of criticism, but I have every reason to be grateful to those Brothers whose efforts in the field of education are in danger of being disproportionately overshadowed these days. During the fifties and sixties the institute enjoyed its greatest numbers of any period within its 300 years of history, but after the sixties a rapid decline occurred when a significant number of members, for various reasons, decided to leave it. Nevertheless, today the De la Salle Brothers, alongside over 73,000 lay colleagues, see to the educational needs of almost a million students in eighty countries. That is a record of achievement the Brothers can be proud of.

Much of my early childhood was overshadowed by the fact that my father had a major alcohol problem. I wasn't aware in any great detail of his over-indulgence, but I sensed that all at home wasn't quite what it should have been. Being the youngest, the rest of the family tried to protect me from the reality of what was happening. I was too young to ask any questions and even if I did, I doubt if I would have been told the truth anyway. Children at that time were to be seen and not heard. So, oblivious to the adult unhappiness around me, my early years were as they should be, carefree and happy.

But life in the Kelly household was soon to be turned on its head when, in the early sixties, my father left the family home on the pretext of going to Scotland to work. Whether he did find employment or not, no one knows, because we never heard from him again. He literally abandoned his wife and five children without a single thought as to how we would survive. I'm sure my mother was distraught, but I didn't know, nor was I allowed to see, the despair his departure must have caused. When it finally dawned on us that he would not be coming back, I think we simply stopped talking about him. He had left our lives and that was that. I never asked when he was coming back. I think that instinctively I knew he would never return. I was not unhappy about that because I had experienced the rows between my parents and wanted an end to them. He was a highly intelligent man with a very good job but he was an alcoholic which so often has a devastating effect on families. Our situation was no different from many others. So I don't remember my father with any degree of fondness. In fact for many years, until fairly recently actually, I resented and hated him for what he did to our family. I've mellowed only slightly over the years, but my blood still boils when I recall those nights I lay in my bed in Ardmeen Green as a child listening to arguments and raised voices from downstairs.

One day in particular I do remember. My father took me with him in the family car, an Austin A30, to Derry to visit my paternal grandparents. He stopped frequently at pubs along the way, leaving me in the car with money to buy sweets and comics like the Beano and the Dandy. I thought he was just in visiting some-body. At some point he decided to divert to Barry's Amusements in Portrush, a treat for me. But by this time, he must have been quite drunk and on entering Portrush he emerged from a minor road without stopping. I remember looking to my left and saw an Inglis bread van bearing down on us. It hit our car side on, overturning it. Our injuries were limited to cuts and bruises, thank goodness, but that in no way mollified my mother, who went ballistic with anger. After that episode I was never ever allowed in the car with him again.

Although I am now aware of the nature of alcoholism, I can never forgive him for leaving the family. I know I missed an important element in my life by not having a father, and in later life the sad experience made me determined that if ever I became a father myself, I would try to be the best father possible. I love being a father and I love my family. I simply cannot put myself into the shoes of any man who could walk out on his children and his family for whatever reason. Though I acknowledge the addictive nature of alcoholism, I cannot have sympathy for him. He forsook his family of five, the youngest being myself, a mere 10 years of age. He abandoned his wife, who had left school at the age of 14 with no qualifications, so had nothing to fall back on to earn money to feed us. At the time Mum was in her mid-forties with only her grit and determination to get on with life and look after those now left in her sole charge. A father who could do such a thing remains beyond my comprehension and I've never had any inclination to find out where he went. As far as I was concerned my father died when I was 10 years old.

How my mother coped is beyond me. Obviously she needed a job. The only work available locally was in the Downshire Hospital, where she became a cleaner. In the beginning it was a case of doing anything she could to make a living, but she was not the kind of person to fatalistically accept what had happened and wallow immobile in self-pity. She had the drive, self-belief and ambition to use her abilities to the full. She set her sights on becoming a state enrolled nurse.

State enrolled nurses (SENs) are no longer trained. They used to follow the first year of the training for state registered nurses and then had another year of training before sitting SEN exams and becoming registered. Formerly there was a large segregation between 'green' SENs and 'blue' SRNs (the colours referring to the colour of nurse's uniform they each wore). SENs were very much complementary to the nursing team, remaining at the bottom of the nursing structure and concentrating on bedside nursing and patient care, but they were ineligible for promotion to positions such as senior staff nurse or ward sister. However, qualified SENs were eligible to enter for SRN exams.

For my mother who had never taken an examination in her life, this was an entirely new and unfamiliar experience, an added pressure on top of being the only bread-winner in the family. I remember her, tired after a day's work, struggling with medical books far into the night. I remember trying to help her, but I was unable to understand what she was studying. I knew about passing exams, but that was not in itself much help. But she not only passed her SEN exams, but went on to pass the SRN examinations and worked happily as a state registered nurse to her retirement. I have nothing but love, respect and admiration for what she achieved.

Recently I was asked by the South Eastern Education and Library Board to talk to people with poor educational achievement who were trying to better themselves. I decided to recount the story of my mother. Recalling the detail brought tears to my eyes. She kept the family together with the help of her own mother Nana, as we called her. Nana lived with us and in an odd way it was she who raised me while my mother stepped into the shoes vacated by my father.

There was never much money about, but I don't recall that. I do remember there always being something in the house for us, always a welcoming presence in the home. It was a real home. Those two women, working together, did an immense amount for all of us and I will be grateful to the end of my days. The two of them minimised the damage inflicted by the departure of my father as much as anyone could. Having said that, I think being abandoned by him hurt me more than my older siblings, maybe because I was so young, but old enough to know that he had walked away from all of us.

As for the rest of the family, Patricia, the eldest, used to work as a secretary with my father in the shirt factory in Downpatrick; Kathleen went off to work in Belfast; Stella got married at a young age and left the family home to live in Scotland; Danny shuffled about the place and didn't seem to do very much. He too went into the shirt business in Belfast. But his saviour was Gaelic football, at which he excelled, and he was a member of the Down team which won the All-Ireland in 1968. He also went to Scotland to work where he eventually married and settled down in Peterhead. We remain a close-knit family, though I'm probably the worst at keeping in touch. The rest complain to me about that from time to time. 'Gerard, why don't you come and see us more often? Do you not know how to use a telephone?' Patricia will say. Incidentally, the family all call me Gerard. If any of them called out 'Gerry' I probably wouldn't turn round, thinking they were calling someone else. Still, family is family, and at a time of crisis we're as thick as thieves.

When all had flown the nest, I was the only one left with my mother and Nana and that meant I was very much on my own in my teenage years. My mother died in 1982 which meant she just about saw me started on my television career. She loved going down to the local Owenbeg Bowling Club in Downpatrick. She once told me that an Irish bowling champion was visiting the club when I had begun working on *Good Evening Ulster* with Gloria Hunniford. 'Nobody spoke to the lady champion,' she told me, 'because they heard I was your mother, so they all wanted to talk to me rather than to the important visitor.' She was very proud that her youngest son was on television. And I used to say, 'Mammy, don't be saying things like that!' Now I wish she was still around so that she could say such things. Considering the life she had, the joy she derived from seeing me on television was immense. In an age when hundreds of TV stations are available, it can be difficult to appreciate just how special appearing on television was. A TV appearance retained an aura of novelty and conferred an element of greatness upon those who appeared. It was the beginning of celebrity, I suppose. Important people appeared on television; not the likes of us.

From St Patrick's Primary I went to St Patrick's High School, or the Red High as it is known hereabouts. Paradoxically, the Red High is the Catholic school and the Green High is the Protestant school; they were nicknamed after their uniform colours. Of course the Green High was mixed boys and girls while ours was for boys only.

Schooldays were good. I was very successful in the GCE examinations, which were the leaving certificate qualification around the mid-sixties. And of course as a child of the sixties I discovered the Beatles and pop music and like so many of that time, I joined a band. It consisted of Anthony Blaney, the lead singer; Michael Edgecombe, lead guitar; Peter Mahon, drums; André Wilding, base guitar; and myself on keyboards. André's father was with the RAF stationed at Bishopscourt, which was a fully functioning defence establishment outside Downpatrick, so his somewhat exotic name with the accented 'e' was his real name, not a stage name. All the rest were local Downpatrick lads and we performed under the name of the Outer Limitts. At the time there was a science fiction TV series called the *Outer Limits*, from which we took the name, but we thought that the TV producers might claim copyright for the name so we put two 't's in Limitts. In retrospect, of course, the likelihood of TV moguls of the giant entertainment industry of the United States of America feeling sufficiently threatened by a five-piece combo from downtown Downpatrick to prompt legal or other copyright action is laughable. However, we were taking ourselves seriously. In the event, no matter how we stressed to promoters that there were two 't's in our name, nobody except ourselves ever spelt it that perverse way.

It was the wonderful and exuberant time of flower power just as the era of the Irish showbands was ending. I found some flowery curtain material and asked a girl in Downpatrick to make up costume trousers for the band, with flares of course, the must-have fashion. It may be interesting to note that the width of the trouser flares was wider than our waists, which were between 26 and 28 inches in those days. The flares were between 30 and 32 inches. And of course our hair was long. Our repertoire consisted of all the hits of the day. My party piece was a cover of Procul Harem's 'Whiter Shade of Pale', with the significant proviso that while I had a great love of music, I really couldn't play the organ. I could play chords with my right hand but could not read music. While I bluffed my way, the rest of the guys were quite talented. I was clearly the weakest link. Peter Mahon began the band with the name the Beez Neez and in the beginning I sang. The big step forward was finding André, the base player. We bought our instruments on hire purchase from Crymble's of Wellington Place in Belfast, a Mecca for musicians. Looking back, it was generous if not downright foolish of the company to allow us credit. A reasonable guitar or amplifier was about £100 at the time and we were getting £5 a gig (not a fiver each—the total payment to the band was £5), out of which the instruments were financed.

We played our first gig in Saul and a second gig the same night in the Downshire Hospital a few miles away in Downpatrick. I would like to say that the Outer Limitts put the village of Saul on the map, but the patron saint of the island had already done that by living in Saul and dying there in the 432. I remember thinking as we furiously rigged and de-rigged our equipment for two venues on the one night: 'This is it, the life of a rock star. It's all about to happen for me.' We even had our own rehearsal rooms, rented from Barney Morgan, the local Calor Gas supplier in St Patrick's Avenue in Downpatrick. Today the health and safety people would have thrown a fit at the mere thought of our electric equipment going full blast among all those gas cylinders.

All this was taking place during my crucial A level years and inevitably schoolwork came a bad second to playing in the band. In fact I did no schoolwork whatsoever. However, we had a De la Salle teacher, a Dundalk man, Brother Damian Kirk, who became one of the most influential men ever to teach me. He instilled in me my love of English literature. Even in that barren A level year I remember him as an inspiration. He treated his students as adults and knew the value of talking to us in tangents. He would allow us to explore highways and byways ostensibly departing from the track of a particular lesson. He did not constantly harp upon the necessity to get the course work under way, important though it was. He encouraged us to debate and discuss matters of the moment and what was of concern to us. Even today, almost half a century later, alumni of his class will remember Brother Damian as one of our best teachers.

I got through my A levels in English, French and Irish, but not with the grades expected of me, although they were good enough to qualify for Queen's University in Belfast. But that was not where I wanted to go. I had my heart set on being a teacher, so off I went to Hopwood Hall, a De La Salle Teacher Training College in Manchester, where I took English as my main subject.

———

Frank Bruno: I would like her to go into boxing because women are nice creatures. They are beautiful creatures. They have nice samanthas …

GK: Nice what?

FB: Samanthas … Boobies.

———

Of necessity I had to leave the Outer Limitts who went on to a more professional level, changed their name to the Clouds and went off to play in Hamburg. I was tempted to join them. After all, they were following in the footsteps of the Beatles and they hadn't done too badly. But I knew instinctively that third level education was a better bet and that rock stardom would have to be put on hold.

Hopwood Hall was almost a home from home because in my year about 40 per cent of the intake was Irish. Very soon I became involved in student politics and was elected as first year representative on the students' union, looking after the interests of first year students. I loved student life in Manchester. It was my first time away from home and I revelled in my new-found independence. Nevertheless, during that first term I was a little homesick and couldn't wait for Christmas to get home again. But by December 1967 the UK was in the midst of a huge foot and mouth scare and there were rumours that all flights and sailings to Northern Ireland would have to be cancelled; no one would be allowed to travel out of England. The thought of spending Christmas on my own away from family in a grotty hostel outside Heywood in Lancashire filled me with dread. Thankfully though, restrictions did not have to be enforced and so we all made it home.

In my third and final year, 1969–70, I had become so interested in student politics that I stood for and was elected president of the Student's Union Council. It was a hectic year having to combine my studies with my duties as president. There was no such thing in those days as taking a sabbatical year when I could have deferred my studies for twelve months to concentrate solely on student affairs. It's the norm in most universities today, but in 1969 it would have been regarded as rather adventurous for Hopwood Hall. That aside, it was a landmark year for me. Looking back on it now, I realise that whatever skills in leadership or communication I possess today were first developed in my year of the presidency. Dealing with the university authorities when representing the views and feelings of the student body was an onerous and daunting task. Whatever contribution I made to improving student life has passed unrecorded, but I do know that my personal growth was immense. I began to develop a self-belief and a confidence in myself that no formal education could provide. As a student leader I was invited to speak at protest rallies around the country, attend dinners, articulate the thoughts of a generation of students and at the same time make sure I passed my final exams. It was tough but I loved every single minute of it.

I remember that at one protest rally in London I shared a platform with Jack Straw, who was to rise to some of the highest political offices in the land, becoming both Home Secretary and later Foreign Secretary. Jack Straw had been president of Leeds University Students' Union from 1967 to 1968 and of the National Union of Students from 1969 to 1971. Our paths had another similarity in that he has also worked in the television business, for Granada Television's *World in Action* programme as a researcher from 1977 to 1979. Just think I could have been . . . Nah, forget it.

My years at college were an exciting time. There was student unrest all over Europe and back home there were the first stirrings of the troubles. I remember a group of us parading round St Peter's Square in Manchester chanting 'One man. One vote.' However, notwithstanding my involvement in student politics, I was not very political in terms of what was happening in Northern Ireland. I was aware of some differences between the communities, of course, but while I was growing up they didn't seem to matter very much. As children in Downpatrick we played with each other, meeting up after the final school bell. We went to different schools but that was the height of it. It didn't mean a thing to us in those far-off innocent days.

My earliest instruction came from my grandmother. We called her Nana but her real name was Mary McLaughlin. The tragedy of Nana's life was that her husband had died shortly after their marriage, not long after my mother was born. Soon after my mother married, Nana came to live with her and her new husband. Nana was from the old brigade of Derry people who knew all about gerrymandering, which was rife in that city. She explained it to me but it was not until I was in Manchester that I began to become aware that 'one man, one vote' was an important issue and that it would be an ingredient within the basket of grievances which would destabilise the situation back home.

Nana was the most important person in my early life. My mother would have been out at work while Nana was the constant presence in our home. When all the other siblings of the family had gone, I was the last one left, the one who would be there with her. I adored that woman. I had always told her that I would get a teaching job in my local primary school and that I would be able to return home each day and have lunch with her. But in the summer of 1970, just after I qualified from college and before I took up my teaching appointment in St Patrick's Primary School, Nana died. Over thirty-five years later it still brings a lump to my throat as I recall that I never actually did get to have that midday meal with her.

———

GK: Does it upset you when people call you arrogant?

Michael Winner: No they don't.

GK: Yes they do.

MW: Nobody has ever called me arrogant.

GK: You are arrogant, Michael.

MW: Ah yes, you did.

———

Chapter 3

GRAND PLANS

Helena, my wife of thirty-one years, is an Ardglass girl born and bred. She was a hairdresser in Anne Ross's salon in the village by day, but in the evenings she shared my love of performing music. While we boys were playing our hearts out in the Outer Limitts Helena was singing in a folk group called the Islanders with two other lads from the area, Dick Killen and Gerry Curran. The group's name was derived from two local landmarks, Gunn's Island in Ballyhornan and Coney Island outside Ardglass. Even before I met Helena, I had known of her reputation as a really fine singer in a group which was garnering quite a name for itself in the Northern Ireland folk scene. They had even appeared on television, an accolade in itself in those days, and had toured with the iconic Jimmy Young. So I was very much aware of who Helena Fleming was. Even though I was living in Downpatrick and she, just six miles away in Ardglass, our paths didn't cross until one memorable night at a dance sixty odd miles away in County Louth.

In 1970, my first year teaching, we lads would go anywhere for a dance. On a Friday night it would usually be St John's Hall in Ballyhornan, or on a Saturday the Central Ballroom in Newcastle and on a Sunday the Canon's Hall in Downpatrick. Those were all local dance venues, all the more important then when cars were not as easily obtained as now. If we did manage to lay our hands on some wheels, then it would be Belfast and Caproni's or the Orpheus.

By 1971 I was in my second year of teaching with the princely salary of £56 a month, one of the fortunate few able to afford a car—a second-hand, two-toned green Ford Anglia if you must know! So almost every Saturday night myself and a few of the lads would kitty up two or three pounds' worth of petrol and off we'd head to the dance in the Ballymascanlon Hotel just north of Dundalk, a round trip of 120 miles. The hotel is based on a big Victorian house some 150 years old, surrounded by mountains and forests, which gives the place a bit of character. The estate also encompasses the 5,000-year-old Proleek Stone, a cairn consisting of a thirty-ton capstone on two stone supports. It is regarded as one of the finest examples of a neolithic portal tomb on the island. So the place is steeped in history, not that I was particularly interested in all that then, it has to be said. It was a Saturday night, time for some dancing, for checking out the bands and perhaps a chance to chat up a few girls.

Helena too used to go down to the hotel on a Saturday with a bunch of her girlfriends, just as I did with my friends. That's the way it was then, girls on the left, boys on the right, so to speak. Things began slowly with the two groups meeting together and simply enjoying the occasion, but my interest was rapidly being drawn to this beautiful girl who stood out from the rest. She didn't drink (and still doesn't), had a quiet, reserved manner and was wonderful company. Even though we joke about it today, I fancied her a lot more than she fancied me, but I was determined to work at it! Finally I won her heart and five years after we first met, we married on 3 November 1976. It was the best decision I ever made.

Working in television can be a very selfish existence and our first years of marriage were not the easiest. In the television business of those days there was an ethos of drinking. Every office in UTV had a drinks cabinet stuffed to the gills with alcohol—whatever you wanted, vodka, gin, whiskey. Out at press conferences also, a daily occurrence, the drink flowed freely. There were also the long leisurely lunches where the drinks bill would often cost three and four times as much as the meal itself. This was the television lifestyle of the late 1970s and early 80s. So why not drink? Sure we weren't paying for it. Even if we were, we could always claim it (and a little bit more) back on expenses. I stop short of saying that you were almost expected to drink, but you would have been the exception if you didn't.

All my early life I had fought against my father's alcoholism. Throughout university I vowed I would never drink; I would not become like him. I was 22, in my first year of teaching, before I took my first alcoholic drink. I didn't particularly like the taste. The only drink that was in any way palatable to me then was white wine. So that's what I stuck to.

By the time I arrived at UTV I still had little experience of alcohol, but I suppose like many others before me I got caught up in the glamour and glitz of television networking and socialising. Drink was very much part and parcel of the business. It was easy to justify late boozy nights as part of the job. I needed to get my name out there, make as many contacts as possible, and if a pub or a hotel bar were the places where such business was done, then I should be there.

I admit now there was a time when I did drink too much. It was the only major issue that Helena and I ever quarrelled about. Even though I argued with her that I was only aiding my career, social-ising with workmates and meeting other media people, I also knew in my heart of hearts that she was right and that I was only fooling myself. It took a few years before the penny dropped.

Without any shadow of doubt, it has been Helena who has kept the family on an even keel and I could not have had any success in my career without her love and support over the years. She has never been one to push herself forward and never got involved in the television world, but I know she is the real star in the family. Only rarely would she come to a function where I was featuring. She didn't like being with people she didn't know, making small talk while I performed on some stage or other. She would always prefer to be at home with our children. In fact in the seventeen-year history of KELLY I think she was only present in the studio on a handful of occasions. Not that she wasn't interested. On the contrary, she would sit glued at home to every single performance of KELLY and ultimately became its finest critic. First thing after the show on a Friday, I would phone home knowing I would get an honest and accurate assessment as to how the programme went down. She was never far wrong.

We have two wonderful daughters, Sarah, born in 1979, and Claire in 1981. For Helena and myself, it has to be said, we love being parents. But there was a time when it seemed the joys of parenthood were not to be ours. Shortly after our marriage Helena suffered three miscarriages and so devastated was she that I just didn't want to put her through that physical and emotional trauma for a fourth time. But we were so much in love and so much wanting a family of our own that the inevitable happened again. Helena was pregnant. This time we took no chances. We scrimped and saved to send her privately to a wonderfully under-standing local gynaecologist, Mr Thompson, who immediately set Helena's mind at ease. It was a long nine months with a few minor scares along the way, but on 29 June 1979 all our hopes and dreams became reality.

In those days not only was it not expected of the father to be in attendance at the birth, but a maternity ward wasn't a very welcoming place for him to be. How times have changed! So I conformed to the custom of the time and waited by the phone at home for the news. When the call eventually did come through I was at Helena's bedside in less than ten minutes. Looking tired but deliriously happy, Helena handed me our first born. She already came with her name, Sarah, after Helena's maternal grandmother. It was the proudest moment of our lives.

Back home the three of us settled down as a family and very soon Helena became pregnant again. The excitement of having a brother or sister for Sarah was immense. But once again our hopes were dashed when Helena lost the baby after three months. This time we consoled ourselves in the knowledge that at least we had Sarah and we should be thankful for that. But I knew Helena was heartbroken. Mr Thompson told us that there was no medical reason why we couldn't have another baby and encour-aged us to try again. Neither of us wanted Sarah to be an only child and so we thought we'd risk it one final time. And in answer to our prayers, Helena did become pregnant again, carried the baby for the full term and on 7 October 1981 Claire was born.

At that point we decided our family was complete, not wanting to tempt fate again. So in many ways we feel we have six children, the two we can see and the four we believe are embodied in the very hearts and souls of Sarah and Claire.

I qualified as a teacher in June 1970 and set about getting a job. It was a lot easier then to secure a teaching post than it is today. I simply phoned up the headmaster of my old primary school in Downpatrick and told him I was qualified and available. He had a vacancy and I started that September in the primary school I had gone to myself. That was the way it was then. Schools were continually on the look-out for teachers.

So from September 1970 to January 1972 I was on the staff of St Patrick's Boys Primary School, Downpatrick, teaching Primary 4 with forty-six pupils in the class. Forty-six 8-year olds in a class made teaching horrendously difficult. For example, if you spent two or three minutes with each child individually, listening to them read, say, three-quarters of the teaching day was gone. Teaching was therefore minimal with a class that size. But I loved that job and I loved the age group I was teaching.

At 8 years old everything in the world is new and exciting. At least that's how I tried to present each day to them. I would dream up new and innovative ways of presenting the curriculum. I can remember devising what I termed Bingo maths, a way of revising what had been learned. In art class I would get the children to make Bingo cards. Then in maths we would play the game. For example, instead of calling out 2 and 4, 24, I would say 4 multiplied by 6 or 30 minus 6.The pupils then had to work out the answer and cross the correct number off their cards if they calculated correctly. It was a way of stimulating and grabbing their attention and at the same time there was great educational value in it.

The degree of difficulty in working out the answers could also be varied, so I could stream the kids according to their ability. For the brighter pupils, the question could have been as difficult as

8 multiplied by 7, minus 6, and for others it might have been as simple as 8 plus 4.

I was always a great believer in children performing to the best of their ability. Regardless of the level of intelligence, which varied massively in a class of forty-six, I always encouraged and rewarded each child who did the best they possibly could. You can't ask for more than that. Incidentally, three months after my brilliant creation, Bingo maths, Johnny Ball came up with a similar idea for his televised schools programmes. Bummer!

Other memories from those early teaching days include bringing out the guitar at every available opportunity. Even if I couldn't work a song into one of the subjects, we would always finish the day with a verse or two of something. My whole teaching philosophy centred round learning through enjoyment. I wanted the children to look forward to their days at school, not some place they dreaded going to. About a year ago a former pupil of mine, who is now 46 years old, told me he still remembers all the words of 'Old Stewball was a Race Horse'.

——

George Galloway MP: *There are lots of evil men responsible for hundreds of thousands of deaths.*

GK: But what do you expect George Bush and Tony Blair to do?

GG: Well I think George Bush is an evil man responsible for hundreds of thousands of deaths. These people prop up all the other dictators in the world. They just fell out with that particular dictator.

——

Around this time I got involved with the old Down County Education Committee, now the South Eastern Education and

Library Board, who were keen on developing a more informal approach to education through their Youth Service department. A fellow teacher in the school, Pat McKinney, joined me in this interest and we met with the Education Committee's youth officer, the late Stanley Baird, who asked us to become peripatetic youth leaders. First I had to look up the meaning of 'peripatetic'! The job required us to go around the various youth clubs in the evenings, the overwhelming majority of which at the time were housed in schools. Our role was to talk to teachers and encourage them to relax the rules of the teacher-pupil relationship when operating youth clubs. At that time practically all youth workers were teachers. This was not particularly ideal, not least because teachers did not necessarily make the best youth leaders. For example, if a kid had fallen foul of a teacher by day in school, say by not doing their homework, that child was hardly going to turn up that night at a youth club led by that teacher in the role of youth leader.

As part of a solution, therefore, we tried to get teachers to slip into the role of a more relaxed youth leader, but it couldn't always work. Nevertheless, this whole area of informal education intrigued me because I realised that youth work has a valuable educational role. Youth clubs should not simply be about playing indoor football or table tennis in the evening with young people though at the time, with the troubles looming ever larger, we were trying to keep youths off the streets. A youth club was at least a safe haven away from the street riots. But first and foremost it had to be a friendly, welcoming environment for young people, not something reminiscent of school, even though the surroundings might necessarily have been a classroom. It was a difficult task to be a teacher by day and a youth leader by night, and only those with a deep understanding of education in the fullest sense were successful.

At the end of 1971, a full-time position as a divisional youth officer with the board came up. I had enjoyed the work I was doing in the evenings with them so I decided to apply for the vacancy and leave my teaching job in St Patrick's. I was successful and started in my new position in January 1972. At the time, probably because of what was happening on the streets, a lot of government money became available for projects channelled through the then Community Relations Commission. The commission itself was a child of the troubles in that it was established by the government at Westminster to improve relationships between the two communities as the rupture became more serious. The commission had concluded right from the beginning that there was a lack of local community leadership to provide stability. One of its strategies was to create a pool of community activists who would, it was hoped, eventually connect across the divide.

So it was a good time to make the move out of teaching because there was a flowering of local community activity. Community action was a less destructive way in which to work for social change. It was interesting that when powers were returned briefly to the Northern Ireland Assembly in 1974 (the old Stormont parliament had been prorogued amid rising disorder in 1972), one of its first steps the following year was to close down the commission, arguing that it was no longer necessary since there was a new representative assembly. However, the seeds had been sown and community activity in working-class districts expanded.

The academic world was beginning to see the relevance of youth and community work as well, so short six-week courses were introduced for all entrants at Stranmillis, St Joseph's and St Mary's Teacher Training Colleges in Belfast. St Mary's College was originally founded by the Dominican Sisters on Belfast's Falls Road in 1900 for the training of teachers with a Roman Catholic ethos. Through its connection with Queen's University it offered Bachelor of Education degrees. Now it introduced youth and community work as part of the training and advertised for lecturers to take the courses. I decided to apply. Again I was successful and I re-entered the world of education in time for the start of the new academic term of September 1973.

Initially, all students in the college were to take this six-week course. It was a great success and eventually youth and community work expanded to become a subject in its own right. So now students could go through the training college with youth and community studies as their main subject. However, this changed the nature of the course. Of necessity it became much more academic rather than practical and I didn't particularly like this development. What's more, I was really too young for the position I found myself in. I was only 25 years old—not much older than the students I was trying to teach. Remember it was an all-girls college and, if truth be told, I fancied half of them. I became increasingly unhappy with the job and found myself on numerous occasions completely out of my depth. For example, I could be lecturing to mature students, perhaps 50-year-old women who had raised a family and had re-entered the world of education. Now what could a young guy like me possibly teach such a person about dealing with young people? It just didn't sit easily with me, so I decided to leave. Normally it's not a clever decision to leave one job before having another to go to. And it's certainly not too bright to plan your wedding while being unemployed. But Helena and I had set the date, 3 November 1976, and it was now June 1976. I was too proud to postpone the wedding and in spite of Helena's suggestion that we delay for a few months, we finally decided to stick with our plans.

In those circumstances, Mr and Mrs Fleming, Helena's parents, may have had their doubts about their daughter's prospects, but they never voiced them. Instead I was made welcome into their house from day one. But in those days, unlike today, you could have confidence in getting a job. I did have qualifications and I was in no doubt that I was between jobs, not chronically unemployable. I would be back in employment somewhere before the wedding. No problem. However, September and October passed and I still had no job.

The wedding itself had been a small affair which Helena's parents, Eddie and Mary, paid for. We managed a honeymoon of sorts, going to the South of Ireland, spending our first night for sentimental reasons at the Ballymascanlon Hotel. After that we toured in my old Renault 11 down to Limerick, staying in bed-

and-breakfasts because we could not afford any more hotels. In fact we really couldn't afford the honeymoon. We had planned to stay a week, but we returned early because we ran out of money.

Two weeks after our return, a letter from Belfast City Council dropped through the letterbox of our rented accommodation. It was an interview for a job which I had forgotten I had applied for, with the new Leisure Services Department in Belfast City Council.

Back in the 1970s the concept of leisure centres was in its infancy. Maysfield Leisure Centre in east Belfast was to be the first of these new facilities, followed closely by four others to provide for the whole of Belfast.

I had applied for the position of Development Officer and the role was to prepare local communities for these centres and explain how they could be utilised to enhance people's leisure time. That might seem odd or even ridiculous today, but remember there had been no leisure centres at all in Northern Ireland, so nobody knew what they were and the concept behind them.

I wasn't convinced I actually wanted the job, but the prospect of continuing married life without money soon changed my mind. I rationalised that I could always leave if I didn't like it. After all it's always easier to get another job when you've actually got one.

The interview went well. I had done my homework and appeared reasonably knowledgeable when questioned. But now the wait. For my own confidence, for my own sense of purpose, I wanted that job so badly. I needed it. Within days the letter arrived. I remember not opening it until Helena had left for work. If I hadn't been successful, I would need time to hide my disappointment before telling her. To my relief the city fathers in their infinite wisdom decided to appoint me and I was to take up my position on 2 January 1977. There was a Santa after all.

My role was to organise communities, explain to them what these new-fangled buildings were and how they could be utilised. In my down time I was also expected to organise the Belfast Festival, a City Council responsibility at that time. But the main job was to prepare communities for the leisure centres. After Maysfield came Andersonstown then the Shankill Road, Beechmount on the Falls Road and Avoniel over in east Belfast. These were the five original centres for Belfast. I was saddened recently to see that the Maysfield Centre, a valuable resource for the local people, had closed after a quarter of a century.

I remember one winter's evening going up to the Shankill Road to talk to the locals about what a leisure centre would mean to the residents there. Local politician Hugh Smith was there in his official capacity. The Shankill Road centre was to be a little different to the others. They were to have a leisure pool which was a 'splodge' shaped design and it also had a wave-making machine which sent waves lapping to the edge. So there I was excitedly explaining all this in a detailed and perhaps apprehensive presentation when Hugh got to his feet. 'Mr Kelly,' he said, 'what are we supposed to do in the Shankill Road with a leisure pool?'

I really had no idea, so I ventured, 'Well . . . eh . . . you could have Caribbean evenings.'

He stared at me wide-eyed for some seconds and then exploded. 'That's all we effing well need on the Shankill Road, effing Caribbean evenings!'

I was just a young fella and I had no idea how to treat Hugh. I was halted in my tracks, too young and inexperienced to be aware of how daft my words sounded. I blundered on. Hugh just sat there shaking his head. But this did not affect the prospects of the Shankill Leisure Centre, which went on to be a huge success. Hugh and I later became great friends. He went on to become Lord Mayor of Belfast and continues in public life as the Progressive Unionist Party councillor for Court area of Belfast, which encompasses the Crumlin, Glencairn, Highfield, Shankill and Woodvale districts. He knew that the last thing the impoverished Shankill needed was a make-believe Caribbean beach. In spite of my efforts the leisure centres came into being, but I'm proud of the small part I played in preparing the customers for these new facilities—none of which I believe ever sported plastic palm trees.

So how did I get from leisure centres to broadcasting? Like so much in life, it was by accident. I happened to be in the right place at the right time, and that place was my own doorstep.

My brother Danny played for the Down Gaelic football team in 1968. Indeed he was the goalkeeper when they won the All-Ireland championship that year. In the mid-1970s the late Dan McAreevey, who was then the chairman of the SDLP, was doing a little GAA reporting for UTV. Dan began to feel that GAA reporting and politics didn't mix well, so he resigned. Leslie Dawes, who was UTV's sports editor, then began scouting around for a new GAA correspondent. Leslie lived in Downpatrick not very far from the Kelly household. I wasn't married at the time, so I was still living at home with my mother, as was my brother Danny, who looked somewhat like myself with curly hair and a beard.

When Leslie came up to our house in Ardmeen Green, I assumed he was looking for Danny when I answered the door. I'm not sure he knew the difference between us. So Leslie opens up with, 'Would you be interested in doing a bit of part-time presentation on GAA? Would you come to UTV for an audition?

'Certainly, Leslie,' said I. And that was that.

Only when I had closed the door after Leslie departed did it dawn on me what had happened. I had been offered an opening as a GAA reporter on television. This was a bombshell since I knew very little about the game, certainly not enough to embark upon insightful professional commentary and analysis in front of a large knowledgeable audience. My initial reaction once that door had closed was slight panic. And then I realised—he thought I was Danny! But the more I thought about it, the more I became convinced that Leslie Dawes would not make a mistake like that. No, it wasn't possible. Still I kept my thoughts to myself and never mentioned the visit to Danny. The following day I raced off and bought every book I could find on the GAA and began a crash course. What I desperately needed was something entitled GAA *for Dummies*.

The following week I travelled to Belfast for the audition fully expecting Leslie to tell me it had all been a huge mistake and it was really Danny he had been looking for all along. But nothing was mentioned. I did my little bit in the studio, read a few scripts to camera and did a mock interview with one of the researchers. I didn't find it too daunting, a little nerve racking perhaps, but then I thought what the hell. I had nothing to lose and sure if I wasn't good enough I could always recommend my older brother who after all was on an all-Ireland winning side. To my surprise and delight, within minutes of leaving the studio Leslie offered me the job. I was to be working with him and Jackie Fullerton on UTV's Friday sports programme *Sportscast*. Well, you could have knocked me over with a feather. I floated back to Downpatrick, my head full of visions of myself on TV. Me! It wasn't a full-time job, I know, but it was a start, a new beginning, a new opportunity. I was still working for Belfast City Council and in those first heady days of television work, little did I realise that my council job would be responsible for cutting short my television career almost before it had started. The episode drove me almost to despair.

In those days the trade unions had real power and in many workplaces you needed to be a member of the union for that job, otherwise you couldn't be employed. It was called the 'closed shop' and this system bedevilled the workplace. In UTV and else-where the closed shop meant that a union could prevent anyone working merely by denying them union membership. The union affecting me was the National Union of Journalists (NUJ). To get a union card you had to be able to show that two-thirds of your income was derived from journalism. Since Belfast City Council was the main source of my income, I was denied NUJ membership. But to work in television as a reporter, you had to be a member of the NUJ. Catch 22. I couldn't do the job unless I had the card and I couldn't get the card unless I had a job. The net result was that after about six months at UTV, I was blacklisted by the NUJ and their members at the TV station were ordered not to work with me. So UTV management were forced to take me off the screen and I was back where I started. Served me right for not telling my brother Danny the truth in the first place. But I was furious. I thought this was a highly restrictive practice and very unjust, but there was nothing I could do about it except try to find a way round the difficulty.

During those six months I had developed a taste for television. I liked it. A lot. I felt at home. I reckoned that with more experience I could be relatively good at it. I had been working with Jackie Fullerton with whom I was getting on well and who was to become a lifelong friend. I tried every way possible to get an NUJ card, including going through the Dublin branch but came up against a brick wall every time. There was nothing for it. I was forced to leave UTV, but I had a plan to get back in—a drastic plan that would take time, a lot of soul searching and a large sprinkling of luck. But I was determined to go for it.

And so for the second time in two years I made plans to give up yet another good pensionable job and venture out into the unknown. If only I could get an NUJ card I felt sure that I could find work in television. But to get the card I needed to leave my employment with Belfast City Council and hope that someone, somewhere in the journalistic world would give me a job. If so, the NUJ card would follow automatically.

But I had little or no experience, no qualifications for such a world. In addition, I was now a married man with responsibilities. Was I about to make the biggest mistake of my life? Why was I not content to stay on in my present job or even go back to teaching, to the world for which I was qualified? With my experience at St Mary's I could apply for a headmaster's job in a small primary school or deputy head at least. My future would be secured. Who did I think I was? Me and my big ideas. Television indeed! And even if I did wangle an NUJ card somewhere, there was no guarantee I would ever get a job back in television.

Helena and I struggled for weeks over what I should do. But the more we spoke, the more we became convinced that if I didn't follow the dream now, it would be too late in three or four years' time. If I was ever to make the leap, it had to be now. Helena was still working as a hairdresser, we had no children, no mortgage, just a weekly rent. We reckoned we could survive even if it all went pear shaped. With the decision made, I handed in my resignation to Belfast City Council and prepared the ground for hunting down that elusive NUJ card.

———

Kathy Lett: The sucking, the tucking and the plucking. It's all completely mad. Basically all they do with face lifts is drag everything up. The ankle becomes the knee, the knee becomes the navel, the clitoris becomes the chin. And that's how you know the recipient of plastic surgery. It's a woman who is rubbing her chin too vigorously. Is that too rude? Australians—you can't take us anywhere. (extending her hand over the desk towards Gerry) If I get too rude, you have to slap me.

Gerry playfully slaps her, spilling a glass of water. The audience is delighted.

———

And so it was that in early 1978 I made an appointment to see Colin Creighton, the owner of the *Down Recorder*, my local newspaper in Downpatrick, and explained to him the situation. I needed to get a job—any job—in journalism. As a relatively small local paper, I knew it would not have the capacity to take on someone superfluous. But I wasn't asking for full-time employment. I wasn't even asking to be paid. I told Colin I was prepared to work for nothing. I would do whatever work was demanded of me. In return, all I asked for was some journalistic training and the paper's agreement to support me in obtaining a union card.

Colin was somewhat taken aback. It wasn't the usual kind of pitch to make for a job. Nevertheless he agreed, even throwing in £10 a week which he described as petrol expenses. In the circumstances, it was a very generous offer, but alas not sufficient for the running costs of my beloved Ford Cortina Mk 2 which I eventually had to sell.

But I was in. I could now write on my NUJ application form that I was a full-time working journalist which would by right entitle me to a union card. Within four weeks my application was accepted and I became a fully paid up member of the NUJ and the proud possessor of an NUJ card. Part one of my grand plan had been successful.

Working in the *Recorder* was both an eye-opener and a delight. The editor, Joe McCoubrey, was kindness personified and taught me a great deal about the profession I had entered. He had me subbing sports reports to start. He then sent me out to find a few local stories for myself and write them up. All the time he kept a watchful eye, gently suggesting changes here and there to the articles. Bring that paragraph up to the top. Drop that sentence. Always remember who, why, where and what. Finally, he trusted me to attend the courts in Downpatrick and Newcastle and to write up the weekly list of traffic offences, burglaries, drunkenness, hooliganism, theft, TV licence dodging—the bread and butter of any local newspaper.

I loved the work and will be forever grateful to the *Down Recorder*, but for three months I hadn't earned a penny and any little savings—£500 from the sale of the Cortina—was fast running out. I needed money and I needed to get out of the *Down Recorder*.

Then towards the end of 1978 something happened that would change my circumstances and push open the door to the world I had been seeking, television. During the mid-seventies, Gloria Hunniford was presenting a two-hour programme on Radio Ulster. It was probably the most popular radio programme in Northern Ireland and clearly Gloria was making her mark as a broadcaster to keep an eye on. UTV had one of those eyes. In 1978 they pounced and brought Gloria from the BBC to start a new television programme called *Good Evening Ulster*.

It was Brum Henderson who was instrumental in this move. Brum (short for Brumwell) Henderson was the first managing director of Ulster Television, from 1959 to 1983, then its chairman until 1990. He was a young man of 29 when Ulster Television first won the franchise to broadcast commercial television to Northern Ireland in 1958. At that time he would have expected to be running a station majoring in light entertainment. However, the events of 5 October 1968 in Derry/Londonderry changed the scene. Television pictures on UTV and BBC of policemen batoning demonstrators created an international sensation and Ulster Television changed rapidly from a being popular entertainment station to a current affairs centre with some entertainment.

Good Evening Ulster was to be a new style six o'clock programme, ground breaking because it was the first time any of the fifteen stations making up the ITV network tried an hour-long magazine programme at teatime. It was heavily criticised at the time, but then people who break new ground must expect that. In 1979 the troubles were at their height and the Northern Ireland public was being fed an unrelenting diet of bombs and bullets on the early evening television screens. The conventional wisdom was that this had to be covered and it necessarily took up much of a half-hour news and magazine slot at teatime. But some people in UTV began to think differently. The rationale for the new programme was that while the troubles were important, there was still a large segment of people's lives that was not related to the troubles and this was being neglected. So inside UTV they said, let's give the news what it's worth. If on the day there are ten minutes of hard news, then we'll give it ten minutes. If it's worth thirty-five minutes then thirty-five it will be. But let's be flexible enough to do that. There is still a normality in the lives of very many in our audience, so let's start reflecting that.

With Gloria now firmly in the UTV stable and this new programme to be built around her, I knew there would be vacancies for reporters and so I applied for a job. With my NUJ card firmly secured, I felt confident that my application would be treated seriously. As it turned out, I was called for an interview which lasted about thirty minutes during which time I hardly opened my mouth. I met with the producer, a brilliant young Englishman called Alan Wright, who then proceeded to tell me in great detail his plans for the programme. Still a little wet behind the ears and not understanding fully what he was talking about, I nodded knowingly and assured him I was the right man for the job. For some inexplicable reason he agreed and I was offered the position there and then, starting in January 1979. To say I was thrilled was something of an understatement. As I drove home to tell Helena the news, I felt totally vindicated for giving up my good, pensionable jobs first with St Mary's, then with Belfast City Council and risk all in the hunt for an NUJ card. The grand plan was coming together sooner than I thought.

———

A young Charlotte Church:

… and the Queen said, 'Do you sing often?' and I said, 'eeer…' then Prince Philip said, 'Elizabeth, don't you know who this young girl is? She has a CD out and is always on Classic FM.' And Queen Elizabeth said, 'Oh yes, I seem to remember that.' She's really nice though. They both are. The first time she shook the ends of my fingers but really softly. And then the second time when I met her at the Royal Variety Performance she nearly took the ends of my fingers off, gripping them really hard.

GK: So the more she knows you, the higher up your arm she grips?

CC (laughing): Probably.

———

Good Evening Ulster fashioned a new beginning in television for me. I was appointed as one of the general reporters alongside Jeannie Johnston, Gary Gillespie and Jackie Fullerton on sport.

We were the original on-screen team backing up Gloria who was the big star. Our role was to scour the country looking for stories. I was on the road every day with a film crew looking for characters and stories that would make the programme that night.

Television captured the pictures on old-fashioned film in those days and you had to be back at Havelock House at 3.30, 4 at the latest, to allow enough time for the film to be developed and edited for 6 o'clock. The reporter was responsible for getting his or her own stories ready. It was a huge responsibility and it brought a lot of pressure five days a week. But what a learning curve. I learnt nearly as much in that first year about the art of television as I did during the rest of my career. Gloria still says it was the most innovative television she has ever been involved in. It blazed a trail.

Good Evening Ulster was so successful that we were disappointed if we didn't get the programme, all five editions, into the top ten most watched programmes of the week. And for a local programme, as distinct from one from the network such as *Coronation Street*, this was extraordinary. As I look at television schedules today, I think they are losing their sense of local identity, with the networks making fewer and fewer time slots available for inserting local programmes. And the simple reason is that the big city stations across the water, which effectively drive the central ITV network, find it difficult themselves to attract good audiences for their local programmes. Those big city audiences prefer network programmes, but in Ireland, Scotland and in rural parts of England and Wales, there remains a strong appetite for well-made, well-resourced local programming.

In my view, as we move more and more into a multi-channel world, with television programmes from national and international networks, it is the local voice which will be unique and which will attract sizeable local audiences. Regionality and locality will be a strength. Look at the way UTV has begun heavily branding all its programmes as UTV programmes, even though most are from the ITV network and therefore from outside Northern Ireland. Local identity is seen as important. The ITV network probably doesn't like this very much, but it is clever footwork by UTV and there is not much the ITV network can do about it.

But back to 1979. Alan Wright was the young producer brought in to set up the *Good Evening Ulster* programme. He was the new kid on the block, young, go-ahead, a whiz kid with television ideas I didn't even know existed. I had never met anyone quite like him. Gloria too was unique, a true professional whose personal charm and charisma endeared her to all. Both had a huge influence on my career. From them I learned that success comes only through hard work. Good presenters make television look easy and few were as good as Gloria Hunniford. She taught me the importance of preparation, of meeting deadlines, of doing your homework, of really learning your craft. By the time you went into the studio to present a live programme, every base should be covered, every eventuality catered for, every potential pitfall identified. Then and only then can you concentrate on your performance. Then and only then can you call yourself a television presenter. But if all you want to do is sit and look pretty on the box and become a 'television celebrity', forget it. People like that are two a penny. They may get their fifteen minutes of fame—and God knows many have—but that's not what Gloria was about. Nor was it what I wanted to be about.

This was going to be my life's work. This was how I hoped to earn enough money to raise a family, perhaps afford a mortgage and certainly I hoped to be doing this for a long time to come. I was in it for the long haul. So in those early days I vowed to keep my head down and learn as much as I possibly could from those around me about the art of making television programmes.

But after only nine months in the job, I found myself back out on the street. Union trouble again. I was beginning to think the trade union movement was carrying out a personal vendetta against me. However, this time they were about to flex their muscles big time. The Association of Cinematographic, Television and Allied Technicians (ACTT) and the Electricians Trade Union (ETU) called for industrial action throughout the network over pay and consequently every one of their members walked out. ITV was on strike. Press button 3 on your television sets during the late summer of 1979 and all viewers saw was a caption apologising for the loss of service.

Technicians from UTV were among the first to begin strike action on 9 August 1979. With *Good Evening Ulster* not due back until September, there seemed plenty of time for the issues to be resolved. Little did we know that it would take almost three months before the dispute would be finally settled.

The NUJ was not on strike, but what good were journalists and presenters when every cameraman, sound engineer and electrician was taking industrial action. We had no option but to show our solidarity with the other unions and soon we too walked out.

The ITV strike of August–October 1979 was a landmark piece of industrial action in the industry. The only other time I had been involved in anything like it was at college when we, as trainee teachers, joined with working teachers in a one-day stoppage, again over pay and conditions. But this was different, more real, more frustrating, and with no pay for ten weeks it was financially draining. Our daughter Sarah had been born just two months earlier in June and, as you know, a baby can be a very expensive commodity.

I remember going to the local 'brew' office wanting to sign on. They told me I couldn't as I was involved in industrial action, but if I was suffering hardship in providing for my daughter, I would be eligible for free milk for her. I nearly exploded. I told them where they could stick their bloody free milk! In the end I borrowed £250 from the NUJ strike fund with a promise to repay it when the dispute ended.

During this time BBC Television had the field to itself. There were two massive stories during the strike. One was the killing of Lord Louis Mountbatten, the other the visit of Pope John Paul II to Ireland.

Seventy-nine-year-old Mountbatten was the Queen's cousin and a great-grandson of Queen Victoria. He was killed in his boat, the Shadow V, by an IRA bomb, along with two teenagers and an 83-year-old female family member. Despite security advice and warnings from the Garda Síochána, on 27 August 1979 Mountbatten decided to go sailing in his thirty-foot cruiser which was moored in the small harbour at Mullaghmore in County Sligo. The Provisional IRA had earlier fitted a 50 lb radio-controlled bomb which they detonated before the boat reached Donegal Bay. Mountbatten's funeral on BBC was seen by 17 million people, a huge audience drawn by the stark tragedy of the event, but also because there was little else to watch.

Then, eleven months after being elected Pope, John Paul II paid a visit to Ireland. When his plane touched down at Dublin Airport on 29 September 1979, it was the first time a reigning Pope had ever visited the country. With open-air masses in Drogheda, the Phoenix Park, Galway and Knock, his every word was covered by television stations from all over the world. But, alas, not by UTV. For different reasons, two tremendous stories I would love to have worked on had been frustrated by the strike. The dispute finally ended on 24 October 1979 and ITV returned with the Mike Sammes Singers and the ITN News with Leonard Parkin. I couldn't wait to get back to work.

———

Anne Diamond:

Because I've been on both the female sides of the eternal triangle I wanted to show that it's not always as you read in the press, 'Scarlet Woman', and suddenly she is a terrible person. A lot of scarlet women are actually human beings and they hurt a lot.

———

One of the most vivid and exciting memories of my time in GEU, as it became known, was St Patrick's Day 1980. It had been decided to take the programme lock, stock and barrel out of the studio and to present it live from the St Patrick's Day parade in New

York. Almost thirty years ago I can't begin to tell you how big a deal that was for UTV.

To do the show live meant hiring a satellite to beam the pictures back home. A satellite! Only eleven years previously a man had walked on the moon for the first time, and now we were talking about using a satellite to make a television programme! Of course it was tried and tested technology, but only for the big boys like Granada TV, Yorkshire TV, LWT and so on. But it was still new and very, very expensive, and here we were proposing to book a satellite for an hour-long programme in Belfast. Mind you, such was the success of GEU that if Gloria said she wanted to do a programme from the moon itself, she would have been allowed to do so. Anyway, I was delighted when I was asked to head out to the Big Apple to do the programme with Gloria.

The programme editor, Ian Sanderson, had gone out a week before our arrival to set up some stories. By the time we arrived though, he hadn't had much luck getting big celebrity names to come to UTV's appointed location which was to be halfway up 5th Avenue. On hearing this, Gloria was a bit miffed. She delved into her handbag, brought out a little address book and began tapping in numbers on the nearest telephone. 'Hello, Mia?' enquired Gloria. 'This is Gloria Hunniford from UTV in Belfast. We met in London a few weeks ago. Listen, we are in New York for the St Patrick's Day parade. We're televising it. Would it be possible for you to come along for an interview? You will? Great. I'll get someone to contact you later about times and location and so on. See you then. Bye.' Setting the phone back down, she turned to Ian and said, 'Mia Farrow will be there.'

Boy, was I impressed! Ian, however, was feeling just a little inadequate. He had been there all week and hadn't got anyone, while Gloria wasn't in New York five minutes and had managed to book Mia Farrow!

On St Patrick's Day itself we were at our outside broadcast location on 5th Avenue from first light. A lot needed to be done. The OB trucks, cameras and satellite dish all had to be in place before the crowds began to gather in their thousands. We were going live to air at 6 pm GMT, which meant it was noon in New York. As the bells in the nearby St Patrick's Cathedral pealed out 12 midday, the *Good Evening Ulster* opening titles rolled. Cue Gloria.

'Good evening and welcome live to New York where in just a few minutes the biggest St Patrick's Day parade in the world will get under way. But first we go back to Belfast for today's news. Join us again in ten minutes live here in the Big Apple.' We were up and running. The satellite was working and it was all looking good. We now had ten minutes to organise ourselves while Brian Baird was reading the news in Belfast.

On returning to us, the first item was to be Gloria explaining the intricacies of this modern satellite system, how the pictures were beamed twenty-two miles into space, bounced off a satellite, returned to a land dish somewhere in the south of England then up to Carlisle and finally to the transmitter on the Cave Hill and the homes of Northern Ireland.

To relate this, she positioned herself just at the edge of the pavement with the cameraman in front of her, two or three feet on to the road itself. Bad mistake. For security reasons no one, but no one, was allowed to encroach beyond the barriers that were positioned along the edge of the pavement the whole length of the parade route. And to ensure there were no breaches of security, horse-mounted members of the NYPD patrolled the edges of the road, at quite a gallop it has to be said, and stopped for nobody.

Just as Gloria was doing her straight to camera, explaining the space technology—I think she got to the bit where the signal was beaming off the satellite back to earth—disaster struck. An over-eager cop on horseback either didn't see or chose to ignore the presence of our American cameraman standing on the road. The horse hit the guy with such a thump that his camera flew ten feet into the air whilst he was knocked six feet forward and landed in a heap on the road, blood pouring from his head and hands.

Viewers at home must have wondered what on earth was going on. One minute they were looking at Gloria, then the sky, followed by a pretty close-up of the green line painted all down 5th Avenue. The director cut to a shot of the parade from another camera while Gloria tried to explain what had just happened. Meanwhile two burly American prop guys working with us lifted the stricken cameraman to his feet, pushed the camera back into his hands and held him upright by his armpits while he attempted to continue filming.

In fact that was how he had to remain for the rest of the programme. We couldn't let him go. He was the main cameraman and there was no substitute. We couldn't even find a medic to administer some first aid. But you'll be glad to know that we were able to wipe the blood away from his eyes! Well, it was either that or waste all that money on a satellite!

Twenty minutes later and the parade was grinding to a halt. There was a bit of a hold-up at the front that snaked its way back causing a standstill in the middle. At that point Gloria had been describing and explaining the various groupings passing by, but with nothing happening in front of her, having to keep talking was becoming increasingly difficult—even for Gloria Hunniford. We decided to go to a commercial break in the hope that when we returned in a few minutes the parade would be on the move once again.

It was during the break that Gloria recognised a face just yards from where we were in the parade that was by now static. It was Rosalynn Carter, wife of the President, Jimmy Carter.

'Gerry, take a cameraman with you and go and doorstep the President's wife. She's there in front of you,' screamed Gloria.

Now to 'doorstep' someone in television terms means to go up to them univited and start asking questions. I may have been a rookie reporter, but even I knew that a president's wife would have bodyguards. Even I knew that if you walked unannounced anywhere in the direction of the wife of the President of the United States, you would at best be tackled to the ground by huge men in trench coats and incarcerated in Alcatraz or at worst shot dead where you stood. After all, look what happened to our cameraman and he was only standing on the road!

Thankfully, before I was about to communicate my mutinous thoughts to Gloria, the parade moved off and Mrs Carter was lost in a sea of green. I just shrugged my shoulders to Gloria, an action which hopefully indicated my willingness and at the same time expressed my disappointment that the parade had moved off just as I was about to approach Mrs Carter. I think Gloria fell for it.

Despite all that, the show was a huge success and a ratings winner. But there was no time to rest on our laurels. That night we had a small celebratory meal and then off to bed. Tomorrow was an early start. It was Tuesday morning. We had a plane to catch. Gloria still had four more nightly shows to do that week in Belfast.

Such were the rigours of *Good Evening Ulster* that on only two occasions can I recall Gloria missing a programme. The first I remember well. It was during the second season of the show. As the full-time reporter privy to all decisions concerning the programme, I was fully expecting to be asked to step temporarily into her shoes. That morning, however, I discovered that I wasn't the first choice to replace her. Programme controller Brian Waddell had already asked sports reporter Jackie Fullerton to fill in. I was totally deflated. Jackie and I had become good friends so I wasn't angry at him. He hadn't pushed himself forward, but I was angry at the fact that I had been overlooked. After all, Jackie was only involved in the sports section of the programme. He didn't sit in on production meetings every day; he wasn't out on the road with a film crew Monday to Friday desperately trying to come up with new and novel ideas for the programme. I felt I had served my apprenticeship and if anyone was going to stand in for Gloria, it should have been me. I approached Jackie with my concerns.

'I didn't ask for the job,' Jackie replied. 'I was told to do it.'

'I know,' I replied. 'It's not against you, Jackie, but I'm going to see if I can get this changed because I think I should be doing the anchor job.'

'Away you go,' said Jackie. 'This is not my doing and I don't have any problem with you trying to change things.'

I took my courage in my hands and went to Brian Waddell's office and entered reverentially.

'What can I do for you?' he said.

'Gloria's off,' I said.

'I'm aware of that,' said Brian.

'Well, I thought I might have been given the presenting job while she's away.'

'Did you? Well, there's a good reason why that didn't happen.'

'Which was?'

'You're not good enough yet.'

Talk about a kick in the nether regions. I blushed with embarrassment. I couldn't even find the words to argue, so I excused myself and exited as quickly as I could. No small talk, no appeasement, no breaking it gently—just, you're not good enough yet. It was certainly a blow to my self-confidence and a sharp reminder that I still had a lot to learn. The next time Gloria was missing, I didn't even ask.

Good Evening Ulster enjoyed huge success over the two years it was on the air. Gloria of course was the star; the rest of us were only bit players. But everyone who worked on the show would agree that it was the most challenging and rewarding experience we could have had.

During the summer break of 1980, Gloria's name and fame had spread to England. Radio 2 had heard about her and asked if she would like to stand in for Jimmy Young on his daily show while he was on holiday. It was only a two or three-week stint, but she jumped at the chance.

Gloria returned to present *Good Evening Ulster* that September and the team reassembled to prepare for another year. Little did we know then, however, that GEU's days were numbered. Gloria had so impressed the Radio 2 bosses during the summer that they offered her her own daily radio show based in Broadcasting House in London. It was obviously the break Gloria had been waiting for and even though it was radio she was going to and not television, it was too good an opportunity to pass on. She announced that she would be leaving UTV at the end of 1980.

With such short notice, UTV bosses now had a dilemma on their hands. What would replace *Good Evening Ulster*, and more importantly as far as I was concerned, who would replace Gloria?

I had hoped it might be me, even though Brian Waddell's comments the previous year still echoed in my head.

As it turned out, the programme name was to be retained and by way of contrast to what had gone before, it was decided to have a double-headed presentation with Gary Gillespie and me. Obviously it was thought no one single person could replace Gloria. Even so, I was thrilled. Three years after walking out on my job in Belfast City Council and after only two years in television, I was chosen to present UTV's evening show—well, half-present it anyway. Still, I felt I had arrived.

My excitement though was short lived when I discovered the format the new show was to take. The programme would now start at 5.30 pm, break for the ITN News at 5.45 pm from London and return to us at 6 until 6.30. It was an awkward programme both to make and watch.

Let's take a typical day. Gary and I would start at 5.30 with the local news, recapping the local news headlines at 5.45 as we left UTV to go over to ITN in London. If, as often happened during the troubles, the main national news of the day was some horrendous story relating to Northern Ireland, then ITN would begin with that same story. They too would end their bulletin at 6 pm with a recap of the main points, which again would be the lead Northern Ireland story, meaning we would come back to *Good Evening Ulster* at 6.00 with the self same top story. Are you still with me? So viewers here would have heard the same news story on six occasions between 5.30 and 6.30. Northern Ireland news was depressing enough in those days, but to hear about the latest atrocity six times in an hour served no purpose whatsoever.

UTV could scarcely have planned a worse teatime news output. This revamped *Good Evening Ulster* was a truly awful programme which just didn't work. Through no fault of ours, Gary and I bore the brunt of the programme's non-performance and our contracts as the main presenters were not renewed. I was gutted. The programme was taken off the air that summer and frantic meetings were held immediately to put things right before returning in the autumn. I knew in my heart that I would not be playing any part in a new revamped programme. My rise had been brief; my fall was to last much longer.

The brand name *Good Evening Ulster* was again retained, the show would revert to its usual start time of 6 pm and a new presenter was brought in. UTV wanted to groom a successor to Gloria Hunniford who could show something of the star quality she possessed. They chose a young 22-year old who had been working part time on UTV's Farming programme. His name was Eamonn Holmes.

———

Guest: I prefer to call him that hypocritical sanctimonious little prig.

GK: Watch it, girl. Libel. Watch it.

Guest: No, no. That's just vulgar abuse. That's OK.

———

So, from being front of camera five days a week I was now shunted off to a single half-hour a week programme called *Lifestyle*, which dealt with social issues and very soft magazine items. Anne Hailes co-hosted it. It was not a good programme and I hated working on it. It was badly constructed and it did not have the resources it needed.

As one TV critic at the time wrote: 'I watched *Lifestyle* last night. It had neither life nor style.' I agreed with him.

And so began the darkest period of my life in television which was to last for over four years. I was stuck in a programme I didn't like and I was working under a new acting programme controller, the late Derek Murray, who didn't particularly like me.

Lifestyle was recorded on a Monday afternoon and, to be honest, it didn't take very long to prepare. I could do in a day what I was given a week to do. I was bored, demotivated and intellectually unchallenged. To relieve the boredom I found myself going over to a nearby bar each afternoon where I knew other off-duty UTV people would be. Of course, all too often when I did, Derek would be deliberately looking for me. He knew where I was but he would not call me back. He would wait until the next day, call me in and say, 'I was looking for you at about 4 o'clock yesterday afternoon. Where were you?' knowing full well where I was.

'I was across the road in the bar, Derek. I had nothing to do.'

'The bar is no place for you to be seen,' he would reply.

Listening to him, reading his tone and body language, I really believed I was on the way out. It was very evident that Derek was not going to create a programme vehicle for me. If he couldn't see any future for me, then what was the point of hanging about UTV. It was becoming increasingly evident that I had arrived at a cross-roads. Either my television dream had come to an end and I would have to go back to teaching, or I could try and move on. Moving on, of course, would mean leaving UTV and trying my luck with other broadcasters, the BBC or perhaps RTÉ. Something had to happen and quick.

Chapter 4 ~

| HIS MASTER'S VOICE

I had always harboured ambitions to host my own chat show, but from my lowly position in UTV in the mid-1980s such a dream was a million miles away. In any case, UTV was still very much a news-based television station and had never seriously thought of entering the light entertainment field.

In a last ditch effort to salvage my career, I confided in two men, Andy Crockart who was a programme director with the station and John McCann who was then UTV's financial controller, now group managing director. To my surprise they both expressed faith in me and told me to stop thinking of leaving, assuring me that somehow there were opportunities around the corner.

This was exactly what I needed to hear and was delighted that I had the support of two of the company's top people in whom I could confide and consult. John's involvement though was rather strange. I could understand Andy's backing since he was a friend and a programme maker, a television director, but John was an accountant and to this day I'm not quite sure why he took an interest. Perhaps he saw something in me that I wasn't even aware of myself. John himself would tell you that he couldn't make a television programme to save a spreadsheet but that he does know a good television programme when he sees one. He regards himself as typical of UTV's audience and to this day, even in his exalted role of managing director of the group, he maintains that interest in broadcast output. Over the years his antennae about programmes and programme makers tended to be accurate and probably helped him on his way to the top of the tree.

Organisationally, he was quite a good antidote to programme makers who, let's be honest, can sometimes become very wrapped up in what they're doing, to the point of losing a wider perspective. Whatever their reasons for supporting me, I'll always be grateful for their encouragement and advice at a time when my morale was at an all time low.

The brand leader in Ireland in the type of television I was interested in was of course RTÉ's *Late Late Show* with Gay Byrne. It was a superb programme, brilliantly produced and presented, and it commanded huge audiences on a weekly basis. I had always thought that we in UTV could emulate the *Late Late* and put our own Northern Ireland twist to such a programme. To find out what made this show so special, Eamonn Holmes and I went down to Dublin and sneaked anonymously, as we thought, into the *Late Late* studio audience. We wanted to see Gay Byrne in action and discover how he went about handling a two-hour live chat show with star performances in front of a live audience.

What we saw was a revelation, a master class in television presentation. For over two hours we were mesmerised as Gaybo strolled through interview after interview. From a heartbreaking chat with the parents of a 5-year old killed in a farm accident, to joking with the latest trendy comedian; from a knowledgeable interview with a member of the Dáil, to talking with American film star Robin Williams—we sat with our mouths open. How does he do it? It all looked so seamless and effortless. No wonder Gay was the most accomplished chat show host in the business and no wonder the *Late Late Show* was the most watched television programme in Ireland. That night we saw what the future could be like, but as Eamonn and I made our way back to Belfast, we knew deep down that UTV, even if they had the will, was nowhere near capable of putting on such a show.

The station was still in the grip of the trade unions which created a highly restrictive environment, a system that actually got in the way of making television programmes. For example, any work carried out by UTV staff in the evenings was considered overtime. Working at the weekends was also deemed as overtime,

which was one of the reasons why UTV did not have camera crews
scheduled for duty on a Saturday or a Sunday. We used to joke
that if the Second Coming happens on a Saturday night, UTV's
audience won't know about it until Monday evening! In such an
environment it would have been impossible to produce a live
weekly chat show and in any case I was no way near capable of
presenting such a show, even if it was on offer. Having watched
Gay Byrne, both Eamonn and I realised we had still a lot to learn.

Undaunted, I continued to talk with John McCann and Andy
Crockart and very soon came up with an idea of a six-week series
called *Kelly's People*, six studio-based programmes dealing with a
particular theme. The series met with moderate success, although
in hindsight I think UTV management was more interested in
assessing my ability to host the show rather than looking for big
ratings. I obviously impressed to some degree because I was then
offered two further series, *Kelly's Eye* and *Kelly On Tour*. UTV had
just purchased a brand new multimillion pound outside broadcast unit which meant we could now go to any location in
Northern Ireland and make programmes live or recorded.

For *Kelly On Tour* we decided to visit Newry, Derry, Enniskillen
and Bangor and make two programmes in each town. We brought
celebrities to our locations. I remember George Best in Bangor, a
young, virtually unknown Daniel O'Donnell in Enniskillen,
Northern Ireland goalkeeper Pat Jennings in his home town of
Newry, and Tony 'Is This The Way To Amarillo' Christy in Derry.
Mixed in with the celebrities were chats with local people about
life and living in the various towns. To my great relief the shows
were an instant success.

But there was one other programme in the run that I will never
forget. Talk about being thrown in at the deep end. My producer
at the time thought it would be a good idea if we did a programme showing the differences between living in Northern
Ireland and living in the South of Ireland. We would look at
cultural and social differences, the cost of living on both sides of
the border, job opportunities and so on. What he also suggested
was—and this was the daunting part—that we should somehow

seek a link-up with the *Late Late Show* in Dublin, as both pro-grammes transmitted at roughly the same time. If the *Late Late* would play ball, we would be asking for a section of Gay's audience to be made up of Northerners living and working in the South and our audience in Belfast would include Southerners living and working in the North. At a given time, the two shows would link up live and the discussion could start. Gay would handle the debate from his end and I would do likewise from Belfast. Obviously there would be a lot of cross-talk from one studio to the other which should make for a lively and topical debate. We really only wanted a section of our programme to deal with these issues, about fifteen minutes or so, after which both shows would continue on alone.

It was a very good idea and indeed, when we approached Gaybo about it, he too was impressed with the proposal—so much so in fact that he invited me and my producer down to RTÉ to discuss the idea further. As we entered the inner sanctum of Gaybo's office, I felt just a little nervous and intimidated. Not that Gay made me feel that way—he himself was charming and wel-coming—it was just that I felt a bit of an impostor in his presence. Here was a man who was undoubtedly the greatest exponent of the chat show format Ireland has ever produced, a living legend in broadcasting terms, and here was I with no track record, no experi-ence, a bundle of nerves, and I was asking him if he would share the most watched television programme in the country with me.

But what happened next was just extraordinary. Gay not only liked the idea and was prepared to do the link-up with us, but he took the proposal one step further. 'I'll tell you what, Gerry,' he said. 'Why don't you do your entire *Kelly's Eye* programme from the *Late Late* studio here in RTÉ. I'll hand over the first forty-five minutes of my show to you. Your people will invite the Southerners in the North into the audience and we'll invite the Northerners in the South. You do your thing and I'll sit in the wings. What do you think?'

What did I think? Gay Byrne was offering me the opportunity to sit in his chair and present the first forty-five minutes of the

Late Late Show which would be shown simultaneously on RTÉ and UTV. An all-island link-up and he was asking me what I thought? Bloody hell! This was an opportunity of a lifetime, but sadly my overriding emotion was not one of euphoria, it was one of inadequacy. There was no way I was ready for such a gig. I didn't have the experience, the confidence or the ability to pull it off. I would have to pass on the idea—too much, too soon. My mind was made up. I would have to pull the plug on this now before it got out of hand. 'Great idea, Gay. Let's do it' I heard myself say.

If I hadn't recognised my own voice I would have sworn some-one else in the room said it. With that, Gay reached across, shook my hand and said he looked forward to working with me. After a few more pleasantries we left his office and as we made our way towards the car, my producer said, 'For a moment there, Gerry, I thought you were going to refuse to do it.'

'Not a chance,' said I, still in disbelief at my response. 'It never crossed my mind.'

Having committed ourselves to the programme, we now had to make it work. We spent many long hours on the phone trying to track down Southerners living and working in Northern Ireland. Believe me, back at the tail end of the 1980s that was a lot more difficult than you might expect. Only a handful had ventured across the border to seek a living and it took forever to hunt them down. Northern Ireland wasn't seen as a particularly warm house for Southerners at that time. In the end we found a dozen or so who were prepared to talk about their experiences in the 'wee six' and who were willing to join us in the audience at RTÉ.

On the other hand there was no difficulty at all tracking down Northerners who had gone south to seek fame and fortune. In fact we had an embarrassment of riches. From successful builders to high flying captains of industry, the South of Ireland seemed to be awash with Northern accents.

With our audience in place and a lively debate on the relative values of life north and south of the border guaranteed, we turned our attention to how we would start the programme. In the end we decided to give it a real Northern flavour by interviewing three well-known Northerners working in the Republic, Derek Davis, who was from Bangor in County Down and a major television presenter in RTÉ, George Hamilton from Belfast, the voice of RTÉ Sport, and Cathal McCabe, a Derry man and head of RTÉ Radio. After a chat with all three we would go to the first commercial break and return with the main half-hour debate in the audience with our invited guests. Everyone was happy with the running order and with the calibre of our guests.

But just before the *Late Late* opening titles rolled, Gay came to me and said, 'After I explain what we are going to do on the show tonight and then introduce you, where do you want me to go? Do you want me to disappear or stay in the studio and join in the conversation?'

My mind was screaming 'Disappear, Gay, disappear', but once again my own voice betrayed me. 'Whatever you prefer, Gay,' I heard myself say nonchalantly. 'I don't mind.'

'In that case,' he said, 'I'd like to stay if that's all right with you.'

So that's what it was all about! Gay wanted to sit in for the entire debate. Obviously he was going to upstage me and I would end up looking the complete rookie that I was. He'll take over the show when he sees I'm floundering, reaffirming his rightful place as king of the chat shows. I was about to be exposed for the fraud that I was.

Mulling over these thoughts as I stood in the wings waiting for Gay to introduce me, my pulse began to race, my heart thumped in my chest and sweat began to pour from my forehead. I cannot recall one word of Gaybo's introduction and only for a gentle shove from the floor manager, I would have remained backstage, rooted to the ground. As I made my way towards Gay's out-stretched hand of welcome, I thought, 'You traitor. How could you do this to me. How stupid I was not to cop on to your little plan. *Et tu*, Gaybo.'

'Thanks, Gay,' I said. 'Are you nipping off for a cup of tea now?'

'No,' he replied. 'I'll just sit quietly over there.'

'No problem,' says I.

Mustering all the strength and confidence I could, I introduced the first of my guests, Derek Davis. Happily, I knew Derek from old and the interview went well. No interruptions from Gaybo. After Derek came George Hamilton and still no interruptions. Finally, Cathal McCabe. Gay continued to be silent. That took us into the break. The pulse rate had slowed somewhat, but my shirt was now soaking with sweat. Keep going, I urged myself. Forget Gaybo.

Next came the big discussion. As I made my way over to the audience, I thought, surely Gay will make his move in this segment of the show. He was an expert in the art of conducting a debate involving many contributors whereas this was new territory for me. Here's where he'll jump in and take over, I thought.

It's at this point where recalling details of the debate is rather fuzzy, but I do remember what Gaybo did. Yes, he did get involved in the discussion, but in a manner that showed how completely childish and irrational I was to believe that he would even contemplate some form of ambush on me. Gay was fascinated with the subject of north/south relations. He genuinely wanted to be part of the debate and when he did contribute, his remarks were incisive and perceptive. He never once hogged the discussion and never once tried to usurp my position as presenter. In fact, he helped me enormously to look and sound good. He knew what he was doing and I thank him for that. It's little wonder he is universally regarded as the ultimate professional.

From my point of view, the show was a resounding success. UTV management had made the trip down and after the programme we were all invited to a drinks reception with the director general of RTÉ. Speeches were made and many nice things were said, but I will be forever grateful to Gay for his generosity and his help in giving a rookie Northern chat show host a leg-up.

With this renewed confidence I looked forward to the next piece of the jigsaw. I began to feel comfortable in my role and knew instinctively that this was the kind of television I wanted to do. This was exactly where I wanted to be. Whether anything would come from this series or not I wasn't sure. All I did know was that I had found my niche and that I could do the job. OK I had a lot to learn, but I was a willing and eager pupil. Thoughts of leaving television evaporated. I had a renewed belief in myself, my morale was boosted and I was ready for the next step. I had always dreamed of my own chat show and now I was within grasping distance of it. But would UTV agree? Had I convinced them that I was capable of taking on a live entertainment show every week? I waited three months for an answer to that question.

———

GK: How have you replaced that adrenaline rush of live television?

Gay Byrne: I'll tell you how. It has been a learning curve. Unlike the Late Late Show—*and many people here will have been at the* Late Late Show *and I'm talking about the real* Late Late Show, *of course (grinning as the audience bursts into prolonged laughter). Stop, stop, please. Stop … stop. It's very bad manners to mock the afflicted.*

———

It came in the summer of 1989 when UTV management called me to the boardroom to inform me that they had decided to take the plunge and go with a one-hour entertainment show at 10.30 on Friday nights to be known as *KELLY*. I was stunned into silence although I did manage an internal thank you to John McCann and Andy Crockart for believing in me and supporting me. Without them I would not have achieved my ultimate dream which was now about to come true in a matter of a few short months. *KELLY* was scheduled to start on 15 September 1989, one week before my 40th birthday.

In hindsight I was unaware, thank God, of just how much UTV was investing in me. It was a huge undertaking for one of the smallest television stations in the ITV network and had I analysed the huge leap of faith they placed in me, I might have had second thoughts.

The fact that the programme was to be named after me was also very flattering. Admittedly, there was a tradition of using 'Kelly' in the titles before, but this was somehow different. Even Gay Byrne didn't have his name in the *Late Late Show* titles!

————

GK: *Did someone suggest that you present the news perched on a desk?*

Kirsty Young: *There are quite a few ways. There is a serious perch, a casual perch.*

GK: *What's the difference?*

KY: *You really want to know?*

GK: *I do.*

KY (demonstrating): *A serious perch is two buttocks on (the desk). And a casual perch is like that (shifting to a single buttock perch).*

————

The first priority was to build a team around me capable of doing a live one-hour show every Friday. Key to the whole project was the appointment of a producer/director and when Belfast man David Donaghy was given the job, our problems eased tremendously. David was a young, ambitious producer with bags of talent. I had worked with him before on the *Kelly On Tour* series, so I knew not only would the job be done and done well, but we were also going to really enjoy the experience no matter how long it lasted. David's abilities in a television studio were only equalled by his sense of fun. He is one of the unsung heroes of the KELLY success, but I know, had it not been for his extraordinary talent, enthusiasm and commitment in those early days, the show could have floundered after two or three years.

The rest of the team was made up of Sarah Bell, a programme assistant cum researcher, John Daly who was then working with Downtown Radio who also did some part-time research and Michael 'Hendi' Henderson looked after booking the music. Altogether there were only four, sometimes five of us. Small but beautiful as they say.

We had no blueprint for success. There was no one to tell us what to do or how to do it. Not only had we to make a weekly mass audience chat and entertainment show, we also had to train ourselves for the task as we went along. There was little formal structure in the background. We did know however that there were four important ingredients to what we were trying to do. We needed topicality, music, audience participation and celebrity, the four elements which would form the backbone of the programme. There was no long-term strategy to take us into the far future and we sculpted the programme as we went along, reacting to what was available. We worked all hours in the office, in pubs, hotel lobbies, everywhere and anywhere we needed to, contacting agents and anyone else who could help us with guests for the programme.

We really weren't sure what we wanted to do in those early days or how to go about doing it. We were unashamedly modelling ourselves on the *Late Late Show*, but obviously differed in screening material relevant to Northern Ireland. In the beginning we were working twenty-four hours a day to get the new show up and running. We were innocents abroad and knew very little about the territory we were entering. In programming terms among the showbiz fraternity, we were nobodies. We needed personalities known throughout Britain and Ireland and it didn't help that nobody outside Northern Ireland had ever heard of the KELLY show or its host Gerry Kelly. 'Gerry who, did you say?' they would ask wearily, followed often by, 'And where did you say the show goes out from? From Belfast? No, er, I don't think so.'

The KELLY show had no track record, and track record counts for everything. Underlying all these problems was the Belfast or Northern Ireland factor. We were asking personalities to travel to Belfast at a time when the city was being compared with Beirut, then engulfed by a ghastly civil war. The year before, P. J. O'Rourke, the celebrated American political satirist, journalist and humorist, had published his book *Holidays in Hell*, subtitled 'Our Intrepid Reporter Travels to the World's Worst Places'. Belfast had a chapter all to itself. It was a bitingly funny book, but its premise was not all that humorous for our researchers trying to entice guests into the province. Belfast was most definitely not a place that showbiz personalities came to or wanted to come to for that matter. Another basic problem lay in finding speedy ways to contact the celebrities and personalities. Many of the television shows featuring these people engaged the services of celebrity bookers, self-employed specialists whose specific job is contacting famous interviewees and booking them. But we didn't have such an animal and we didn't know who to contact even as a first step. If you wanted Cliff Richard, for instance, how did you get his phone number? How could you make contact with Tom Jones? We had no idea. We didn't know any of their agents and they certainly didn't know us.

On Friday, 22 September 1989, one week after our first show, the Provisional IRA exploded a bomb in Deal Barracks in Kent. Ten soldiers were killed. There was widespread disgust, not least in the heartland of England, which made invitations to come to Northern Ireland for a light-hearted chat show all the more difficult. On the last day of that year, 1989, an opinion poll in the *Observer* estimated that 51 per cent of the British population wanted the British Army withdrawn from Northern Ireland. It was not the backdrop we would ever have chosen to launch a chat show, but we constantly made the point that the violence was not all there was to Northern Ireland.

GK: Did any of your Big Brother *contestants react badly when they heard you had once been a man?*

Nadia Almada (post-operative transsexual): I was never a man. I just had male genitalia.

GK: My apologies.

Chapter 5 ～
| FROM DREAM TO REALITY

Now that *KELLY* had progressed from a dream to reality and a date for the opening programme had been set, all our focus began to concentrate on the studio and studio design. Ideally we needed a large space sufficient to accommodate a fair size audience, an interview area and a performance area. The studio should have a high ceiling to accommodate the lighting and good ventilation with air-conditioning to carry away the heat from the powerful lights, all of which act as heaters. Those are the basics. But there was a problem. At the time UTV had only two studios, a small one and an even smaller one. We were allocated the bigger of the two, so our immediate problem was how to stuff a quart into a pint pot. Frankly there were people with bigger front rooms than the space we had, though admittedly they might be denizens of north Down.

What we needed was the best studio designer we could lay our hands on, somebody who might in his spare time be amusing himself with a mixture of origami and putting ships in bottles. As luck would have it, we found a superb freelance designer who happened to be working in UTV during that year and we told him what we needed, trying not to betray whether by expression or body language that in the recesses of our hearts we doubted if anyone could manage the task. Unless we got what we needed in that studio, the *KELLY* concept would be crippled from the start.

One wall of the studio contained large scene dock doors, used to move pre-built scenery in and out, much like what happens backstage in a theatre. For most of the time it was wasted space as these doors could not be blocked by seating or other such hindrances. And so the designer came up with the highly unusual idea of straddling the doors with a form of scaffolding, allowing an audience to sit above the doors with a bird's eye view of the studio. However, the only drawback to this plan was the close proximity of the audience's heads and the extremely powerful lights only a matter of feet above them. As anyone who has ever sat in those seats will tell you, it did get extremely warm over the course of the evening.

With additional seating squashed in around the walls, we finally managed to accommodate about 100 people in the audience. The interview area was large enough to fit myself and a sofa which would take up to four guests at a time. This area became affectionately known as 'the tulip' due to its final shape.

This meant we had very little space left for the performance area. In fact it was so tight that on one occasion I remember introducing Tom Jones, and as I reached out in that theatrical way we have of introducing guests, I hit him on the shoulder with my hand! Now that's tight.

To add to our design woes even further, most of the set had to be dismantled after every show on a Friday night because the studio was also needed to house UTV's nightly news programmes Monday to Friday. The props guys—Big Isaac, Bobby and Davy—used to hate weekends, striking the KELLY set and replacing it with the news set. All in all though, it was a miracle of design and it got us up and running. Obviously nobody would choose to present a light entertainment show like KELLY in such cramped conditions, but we had to work with what we had. So rather than moan about it, we set about using it to our advantage.

Believe it or not there were some plus points. For example, as those who have been to the show know, with the audience practically sitting on my lap, a certain intimacy was immediately created. No one was more that nine or ten paces away from the guests, which created a feeling of involvement with the action and interaction happening in front of them. They could see the whites of the eyes of the performers and this had the effect of bringing people right into the show. Our guests liked it too and very often they would turn and talk to the audience directly, which allowed for a more inclusive interview.

On the other hand, I know that first-time visitors in the audience entered Havelock House with the expectation of a large studio with seating stretching into the darkness and the distance. It was precisely that impression we were striving for and through the skilful use of television direction, deft camerawork and the copious use of the wide angle lens, I think we managed to achieve that illusion.

Now that the studio audience was in the mix, our next task was to design ways to get the audience at home involved. Obviously we would have competitions and so on, but we needed more. We wanted to know what people at home actually thought. We wanted to hear those thoughts and we wanted to provide a platform through which those opinions would be heard on a larger scale. We hoped that the Northern Ireland public would take ownership of the programme and feel that KELLY was every bit as much their programme as it was mine and that their views would be heard and reflected on the show. The only way we could do that back then was to open up phone lines and allow people to have their say.

But with the paramilitaries causing murder and mayhem on the streets and passions consequently easily inflamed further, you can imagine that we had to be very careful with the live phone calls into the programme. It could be argued that in a place like Northern Ireland, live calls should have been used very sparingly, but the use of the telephone had brought about a minor revolution in broadcasting.

Commercial radio was a telephone pioneer and when Downtown Radio began broadcasting in 1976, it used the phone extensively to bring its audience into programmes. The ubiquitous phone was, and remains, a cheap and effective outside broadcast point. When Downtown began, the only other local radio was BBC Radio Ulster, which was on air only a few hours a day. BBC engineers of the time regarded themselves as the guardians of the technical standards of broadcasting. They believed phone microphones could not give the required technical standard and there-fore restricted its use. It was used mainly for news and current affairs programmes at the BBC, and usually pre-recorded. The standards regulator for commercial broadcasting at the time was the Independent Broadcasting Authority (IBA), which until 1991 owned and operated all commercial transmitters in the United Kingdom, television and radio. The IBA was not quite so finicky about the technical quality of phones, but they did worry about what ordinary people might get up to if allowed to broadcast from their own hallways, which is where the first phones, usually single installations, were normally sited. UTV had to take these concerns into account, and while embracing the telephone with gusto, had to put safeguards in place.

Radio broadcasters use a 'delay' system whereby phone calls are delayed by up to four seconds before broadcasting. This gives the presenter time to abort a call should anything untoward be said by the caller. However, this is not a foolproof system and the industry is riddled with stories of how many a delayed phone call got through to air mistakenly. RTÉ radio listeners are only too aware of one particular phone call after the presenter asked her audience to tell her where they would like to be buried. I didn't even know who BiBi Baskin was at the time!

The only story I will repeat here concerns Michael 'Hendi' Henderson when he was presenting his weekend show on Downtown Radio in the 80s. He had asked a simple question for a little competition he was running and began taking the phone-in answers. The first caller through was a Belfast woman.

'And what part of Belfast are you from?' enquired Hendi.

'The Shankill Road,' came the reply.

'And do you have any children?'

'Four,' said the lady.

'And what are they?' said Hendi.

'Oh, they're all good Protestants like myself,' she replied. Innocent enough but believe me there are worse stories.

UTV could not use a delay system. It was far too cumbersome, so we decided to use the phone-back system. We had six operators manning phone lines throughout the programme. People would phone in and give us the gist of what they wanted to say. If we had room for their comment or question, we would phone them back. From the programme's point of view, this was a much simpler system and had several advantages. First, in those days phone calls were expensive enough and we didn't want people wasting their money hanging on, waiting to go on air. Secondly, it gave us the security of being able to put some production effort into the phone element of the show; and thirdly, it was a security measure, knowing the contributor's phone number. During the troubles there was always a wariness among broadcasters that some people might possibly use live phone access to a programme to say something inflammatory, defamatory or profane. That slight worry still persists, but I must say from our experience over the past decades, when the phone became an indispensable component of broadcasting, that only on the rarest of occasions have members of the public abused the trust put in them by saying something unacceptable live on air.

Believe it or not, we have had the very opposite problem. During that first series of KELLY we found the Ulster audience shy, retiring and reticent, and this was equally true of the studio audience. People did not want to stick their heads above the parapet to give an opinion, so when we put the roving microphone in front of them, they tended to play safe, holding to Seamus Heaney's notable line, 'The famous Northern reticence, the tight gag of place and times' from his poem 'Whatever You Say, Say Nothing'. I used to regard with envy the animated Gay Byrne audience on RTÉ, where people almost climbed over each other to bestow opinions on every topic under the sun.

But Northern Ireland was different and there was an understandable reason for what was happening with the KELLY studio audience and with other audience broadcasting programmes. In those days a very large proportion of regional broadcasting in Northern Ireland dwelt upon the troubles and their effects. The television screens were alive with a multiplicity of opinions, but to a large extent they emanated from those who were accustomed to giving opinions in public. These were 'experts', people from various authorities, from government, government agencies and senior civil servants, from the police, army, the political parties, the trade unions, the paramilitaries, community leaders, activists, charities and the like. And as soon as such people gave an opinion, as often as not the broadcaster or journalist would follow up with a probing and searching question. The opinion formers, if we can call them that, were generally able to handle a thrusting interview. It could be seen as part of their job to do so.

But that was not where the ordinary man or woman in the street wanted to be. They were conducting their lives adhering to as much normality as they could manage in those bad times. A common and perfectly logical survival technique was to avoid confrontation almost instinctively because there was enough controversy going on all around them blighting their lives. Inevitably, the microphone in Northern Ireland became associated with altercation and dispute, an attitude which permeated through even to the fun atmosphere of the KELLY studio.

We did eventually break down this resistance to giving an opinion. Slowly people began to see that the KELLY show was coming from a different quarter. We were not, except in the gentlest manner, going to rebut or confront them. We wanted to tease out opinion, usually on topics far removed from politics and combat. They saw that we were not seeking out the extremes, that we would never try to embarrass anyone, that we did our best not to sensationalise. However, getting this message across to our audience, inside and outside the studio, took a good year. Only then did people begin to trust us and begin opening up about what was on their minds.

———

GK (addressing Chris Eubank, the boxer, who arrives on the Kelly set on a small foldable scooter): Do you go everywhere on that?

CE: Everywhere in the world.

GK: And have you brought that over with you today?

CE: Absolutely.

GK: Would you describe yourself as slightly eccentric?

*CE: No, I'm just me. I'm a normal guy who just hap-
pens to talk too much about common sense.*

———

I keep reminding myself that our programme did not begin in
a television multi-channel era. Television was special. If you
appeared on the box and you came from Dromara, Lisnaskea,
Randalstown or Sion Mills, any place away from the limelight,
your neighbours would stop you in the street the next day. It was a
special event. Our audience ratings at the beginning were colossal,
partly because we enjoyed the tail end of a shared communal
experience which television could still provide. If we did something of note on the programme, practically all of Northern
Ireland shared it. Those days have gone, perhaps never to come
again. Nowadays I think you could walk for twenty miles and not
meet someone who had watched the same programme as you did
the night before. They could have been watching channel 103
while you might have been watching channel 503.

But for the studio audience, KELLY was a big night out, somewhere safe to enjoy such an experience. Places of public entertainment suffered greatly during the troubles. Hotels, bars, even dance
halls and theatres were being bombed and finding secure public
places to go in the evening could be difficult. You did not pop into
a strange pub for a drink. Coming to the KELLY show was a piece
of welcome escapism. Entrance to our studio was by ticket only
and very soon there was a nine-month waiting list. Our tickets
were held in the same regard as tickets to the Grand Opera House.

For the studio audience it was a special kind of theatre, one where they saw a little of the back stage as well as a front-of-house view. It wasn't just myself, the guests and the performers; there was the whole exciting ambience of a television studio with the harsh lights and microphone booms. There was the studio set, which perhaps looked a bit more flimsy and dull than on screen. It was a new world even though a surprisingly small one, where the cameras and cameramen would, at the behest of an unheard instruction, swirl and snake about the studio floor, feverishly lining up a new shot. The studio audience loved watching the floor manager, whose job was to be the eyes, ears and mouth of the programme director, who was out of sight in front of a bank of controls and screens behind a glass wall. But for the audience, the floor manager was the controller of all the action and they watched enthralled as he or she passed instructions to me, ordered both objects and people to be moved about the studio floor, and signalled to me or the performers to start or stop. Turning on his heel, the studio manager told the audience when to applaud and when to stop, if that was needed. In fact the audience hugely enjoyed all the paraphernalia and choreography involved in getting through a live television show. Unlike a recorded show where the action stops and starts, sometimes very tediously, the live show must go on, warts and all. The adrenalin flows on and off stage.

For the first few shows I used to do my own audience warm-up. Warm-up is an indispensable part of any audience participation show. You really do need to get the audience accustomed to you and the surroundings, otherwise they can be cold and inactive during the first part. So I would go out on to the studio floor thirty minutes or so before the show was due on air and have a bit of craic with them. Not being a comedian I struggled with this, but then it was my good fortune to discover John Linehan, alias May McFettridge.

Eamonn Holmes was still presenting *Good Evening Ulster* at the time. When he heard we were looking for a warm-up person, he suggested a relation of his called John Linehan. John is married to Eamonn's first cousin Brenda and he used to liven up the Holmes family gatherings with his wit and repartee. I had never heard of him. Eamonn was just beginning to branch out from the journalism upon which his distinguished career is based by doing disco work round and about. This led to him being asked to fill in for a scheduled absence at Downtown Radio, the local commercial radio station.

At the time Steve Wright was featuring spoof phone calls in his BBC Radio 1 show and they were working very well. Eamonn thought he could put a sort of Belfast twist to this idea and so he asked John, who was earning his living as a motor mechanic, to try out for the radio show. Thus May McFettridge was created—May, after his mother-in-law and Eamonn's aunt and McFettridge after an Antrim Gaelic footballer he randomly chose from a sports report on the back of the *Irish News*. Those phone calls from May into Eamonn's show were the first outings for this wonderful character and her rude and sometimes abrasive banter.

'I'm going to try out a relation of mine tomorrow on the radio show,' Eamonn said to me one day. 'Have a listen and tell me what you think.' I listened and then dreaded the inevitable phone call from Eamonn to ask what I thought. Should I tell him the truth? Of course, I had to. 'It's pure crap,' I replied. 'It's been done a hundred times before. George Jones [BBC Radio Ulster's afternoon show] is doing that make-believe woman Sadie as his sidekick and this sounds just the same. And anyway James Young did the whole thing a lot better decades ago. I'm sorry, but he's not funny.' That said, I duly forgot about May McFettridge.

Then about a month later, UTV was staging a concert at the Grand Opera House in Belfast and I was master of ceremonies. As fate would have it and unknown to me, May McFettridge had also been booked to work with me as a filler between the acts. The production needed time to change from one act to another, so my role was to clown about with May in front of the curtain, mostly ad libbing. I looked at the plan with dread. I was horrified that John Linehan may have been told by Eamonn, if not my actual words about his Downtown performance, then a good summary of what my opinion had been. I was not looking forward to being on stage with him.

The first night arrived and out came May with a mop and bucket, pretending to clean the stage, supposedly oblivious of the packed audience. We hadn't really put a script together and so we just began to wing it. I can honestly say that within minutes I found myself laughing at some of John's off-the-cuff remarks. He was quick witted, sharp, very funny and unique, not at all an imitation of James Young. My too-quick initial assessment of him had been well and truly rammed down my throat and I have to say nobody was more delighted about that turn of events than myself.

So at the end of that week in the Opera House it was time for a good dollop of humble pie. Of course he knew what I'd said when I first heard him and now he tells the story as an exposition of my abilities as a talent spotter. But so impressed was I with him that I asked him there and then if he would like to act as warm-up for the *KELLY* audience. He agreed immediately and continued in the role for sixteen wonderful years. John had the audiences eating out of the palm of his hand and although he was not seen on screen, he was integral to the success of the show. In fact there were times I thought he was too funny, leaving the audience with faces so stretched with laughter that when the show actually started, they could scarcely laugh for me and the guests. As he reached the end of his patter each night he would introduce me. 'It is now time to meet the star of the show, Gerry Kelly.' That was my cue to walk on to the set and for him to leave. And each time as we passed I would whisper hoarsely, 'Funny?' and roll my eyes heavenwards. To this day that's a line we still use and laugh about. We became great friends and nobody was prouder than me when he was deservedly awarded an MBE in the New Year honours announced in December 2006.

By the end of the summer of 1989 we had as many bases covered as we could. Considering the woefully low number of people working on the programme and the fact that we came from a standing start, we were now confident that we had the infrastructure and the concept of a product that could go to air. All we had to worry about now was the content of that first programme.

Chapter 6 ∼

FIRST SPIN ON THE
MERRY-GO-ROUND

We needed to make an impact with the first programme. As you can imagine, in any television series the first programme is vitally important. If it doesn't grab attention, if it bores people, if it doesn't stand out, then viewers will be less inclined to tune in to the next one. The history of television is littered with examples of series starting off on the wrong foot, disappointing audience expectations and consequently being shelved quietly after a month or so. So the first one had to be good.

We needed to stick to our self-designed recipe for success—something of local interest, something of wider importance, good music, big names, good chat and audience involvement.

For our main item on that first show we decided to major on the controversy that was surrounding Scotland's Maurice 'Mo' Johnston, the football striker who had just signed for Rangers FC in Glasgow. It was a big news story at the time. Johnston had started his career in 1981 with Partick Thistle and then moved on to the English club Watford. After a season and a half with Watford, he had signed with Scottish team Celtic, scoring fifty-five goals in his three years there. In 1987 he had moved to the French club Nantes, from where he suddenly announced that he would re-sign for Celtic at the end of his contract with Nantes.

However, in July 1989 Johnston decided against returning to his old team Celtic and instead went to Rangers where Graeme Souness was player-manager. It was one of the few indirect transfers from one Old Firm club to the other. Shock horror!

Although Johnston was not the first Catholic to sign for Rangers, this move made the headlines. It was a deliberate action by Souness, who wanted to end Rangers' policy of avoiding signing high-profile Catholic players. The sectarianism between Celtic and Rangers was very strong and lives on to this day.

The resonance of the Johnston situation for a Northern Ireland audience could not be ignored and it was a gift for our first programme. Northern Ireland was awash with supporters of Rangers and Celtic and the Johnston saga had managed to antagonise many supporters of both clubs. It had been a conscious move on the part of Souness, who wanted to be able to select players on ability and nothing else. He was laying down a marker. And it was a calculated move on our part to include this story to attract an audience and create some kind of response from the public.

Try as we might, we couldn't get Mo Johnston himself to come to Belfast for the show, so we settled for his agent, Bill McMurdo, a straight-talking Glaswegian who brokered the deal. It was to be the beginning of a long personal friendship between Bill and me, not least because Bill was also to become George Best's manager. But back then Bill was a complete stranger to me and I was unaccustomed to his dark sense of humour.

Up in the green room, where guests are entertained before and after a show, I was very nervous and Bill sensed as much when I went to meet him. He knew this was our first show and he realised I was a little uptight.

'How are you feeling?' Bill asked me.

'Terrified,' I replied truthfully.

'It's all going to be fine. You introduce me, I'll walk on and I'll open up with something witty.'

'Like what?' I asked.

'I'll tell them that I have seen you before, beating a big drum in an Orange parade.'

I blinked at his straight face. I was now in an even more agitated state. What was this man going to say on a live show? And did I have the experience to cope with and rein in someone who goes off on a rant away from the subject matter in hand?

———

Melanie Chisholm (Mel C of the Spice Girls): It's a bit different with the babies. We do want to do more live stuff but it won't be so manic because we're all getting a bit old for that malarkey.

GK: Talking about the babies. You all started out Spice Girls. One's left, two are married, one's getting divorced—and two babies.

Mel C: It's like a soap opera, isn't it?

GK: It's like the Spice Women.

———

On the music front, local man John Anderson was dominating the British charts in 1989. Under the name of Jive Bunny and the Mastermixers, he had three No. 1's between October and December by joining together several old songs from the 40s to the 60s to create a megamix: 'Swing The Mood' topped the charts for five weeks from July, 'That's What I Like' for three weeks in October and 'Let's Party' for one week in December. In fact John's Jive Bunny became only the third act ever to have their first three singles reach No. 1 after Gerry and the Pacemakers and Frankie Goes To Hollywood. For our purposes, Jive Bunny was a godsend.

On the personality front, we turned to the soap stars of the day. The cast of these nightly mini dramas are very familiar to television viewers and grist to the mill for chat shows. Few if any had ever paid a visit to Northern Ireland, so it would be a major draw if we could encourage a few to come over.

I remember Andy Crockart asking me what I knew about the soaps. 'Bugger all,' said I. 'I never watch them.'

Well, Andy went apoplectic. 'That attitude ends right now,' he ordered. 'It will be part and parcel of your job from now on to know these characters, to be familiar with their settings and know where their story lines have reached. A large part of your audience are soap fans and they'll expect you to know what you're talking about when you interview their idols. So watch them!'

It was good advice and just another part of the steep learning curve I was on. Andy was right of course. From now on not only would I need to watch the soaps—and practically every other TV show—but also to read as many newspapers as I could, read as many books as I could, and know what was going on in the world far beyond what had been my interests in life up until then.

We spent days on the phone trying to secure the services of these actors and eventually came up with our final selection. We had Nigel Pivaro from *Coronation Street*, Kate Fitzgerald from *Brookside*, Ross Davidson from *EastEnders* and Fiona Corke from *Neighbours*.

Now just in case you have forgotten, Nigel Pivaro played Terry Duckworth, the wayward son of Jack and the late Vera Duckworth. Kate played Doreen Corkhill, wife of Billy. Ross Davidson was part of the original cast of *EastEnders* and played nurse Andy O'Brien. Sadly Ross died from a brain tumour in October 2006 at the age of 57. Fiona Corke played Gail Robinson, the recently divorced spouse of Paul Robinson. It was a good line-up with each character having a major storyline at the time.

We also booked the hugely popular twosome, Foster and Allen, one of the very few Irish acts who had appeared on *Top of the Pops* and who I'm delighted to say are still going strong after over thirty years in the business.

Our local discussion was based on the newly formed charity Northern Ireland Mother and Baby Action (NIMBA), which had been established the previous year to work towards reducing the premature birth, illness, disability and death of babies.

And finally, we would have Bacaan, two local musicians, Paul McAree and Eugene Dunphy, who would write and perform a topical song for the show each week, a bit like the late Jake Thackeray who used to do a similar job on programmes like the *Frost Report*, the *Braden Beat* and *That's Life*.

That, for good or ill, was the line-up for the opening show. As a team we had come a long way. We had worked flat out for months to prepare for this and, on paper at least, we were satisfied we had done the best we could.

At 10.30 pm on Friday, 15 September 1989, the opening titles rolled, our signature tune began and for the first time KELLY hit our television screens. Time for me to make my entrance. Deep breaths, head up, smile and say hello. Not as easy as it sounds, but this after all was what I wanted. This was the dream turned into reality, not a time for second thoughts. I walked out into the spotlight and the audience began to applaud—instigated entirely by the floor manager I hasten to add! 'Good evening and welcome to the first show in a brand new series called KELLY.' I can remember saying the words, but to be honest the opening minutes of that first programme passed in a blur. Trying as hard as I could to look relaxed on the outside, the butterflies were doing triple somersaults inside.

When the time came to introduce Bill McMurdo, I was dreading the little joke he had threatened. I hadn't worked out a witty response. But of course it didn't happen. Bill was an exemplary guest, talking informatively and entertainingly about Scottish football and the need to keep sectarianism out of the sport. But the central topic was Mo Johnston, Rangers and Celtic.

When we opened the phone lines to allow the viewers at home to give us their reaction to the Mo Johnston decision to sign for Rangers rather than Celtic, wow! Every light on those telephone consoles lit up immediately and our six operators never lifted their heads for the next hour. We had been right. It was a topic that caught the Ulster imagination and boy, did people want to vent their feelings. Mind you, only a few were keen to express their opinions live on air, most wanting just to sound off anonymously. But that was OK. We had time over the series to work on that. For the present, we were just glad that large numbers of people seemed to be watching the programme.

I tried to encourage the studio audience to get in on the discussion at one stage, but I probably didn't make the most of it at the time because of my inexperience. As the show progressed, my nerves slowly eased and I began to settle in and actually enjoy the cut and thrust of live debate. And then it was time for the first commercial break, three minutes to regroup, refocus and concentrate on what was coming up next.

And that's the way the evening progressed: no major cock-ups, just as smooth and trouble free as you would want a first programme to be. In fact I couldn't believe it when the hour was up.

After the show we all retired to the green room where the champagne began to flow. Members of management were on hand to congratulate us, which augured well for a second programme at least.

Heading back to Ardglass that night, I was thankful that things went well, but in spite of the congratulations I knew there were a lot of shortcomings in my own performance. I needed to develop a style of interviewing and to settle into the rhythm of the programme, longer interviews, casual chats and the ability to make it look easy. If the presenter looks uptight, then so too will the audience. Even though my name was in the programme titles, I realised very quickly that I wasn't the star of the show. That accolade lay with the guests. My job was to ask simple, coherent questions, questions that the person at home would want to ask. I needed to develop the art of conversation, to turn what is after all an artificial setting among cameras, lights and a live audience into a close intimate conversation, one on one.

In the meantime, we were only seven days away from the next show. The merry-go-round was turning.

———

Bill Roache who plays Ken Barlow in Coronation Street:

Well, if you have a happy family it's no good. I mean, I got my current, Deirdre, and even though we've got married, it's a bit dodgy. There's my bigamist son, my baby-selling daughter and a mother-in-law like Blanche. Great! It's got to be good.

———

Chapter 7 ～

MORE THAN JUST LIGHT ENTERTAINMENT

The year 1989–90 was a baptism of fire for all who worked on *KELLY*. We had spent so much time and energy getting the first programme to air that we hadn't fully realised that this was to be our lives for the next thirty-nine weeks.

When one show finished, we were straight into the next. It was a never-ending production line. Friday over, it was straight back into the grind on Monday. Nowadays when a new television series starts, there is usually a post-mortem to review how it all went and to plan improvements. But there were only the three of us working on the show, so there was no formal internal review, which many of today's television practitioners would find perplexing, even amazing. The following Monday we just got stuck into the preparation for the next one.

Programme makers are responsible to the programme controller and at the time UTV was 'in between' controllers. Moore Sinnerton had left and there was quite a time lag before his successor was appointed. When one was finally chosen, we would look forward to working with an experienced professional who would advise and encourage us as we set out on this exciting journey.

Within a month or so the new programme controller was announced. Maurice Smyth, who had actually been a presenter with UTV in its early days and had then headed off to New Zealand to join the then New Zealand Broadcasting Corporation, was chosen for the position. We had hoped for a good working relationship with him, but I'm afraid my first official encounter with him left me somewhat bemused and just a little apprehensive about our continuing relationship.

To explain what happened at that first meeting I need to tell you the story of a young Dublin man called Paddy Doyle whom we had on the programme in early October 1989. His was a story from a forgotten Ireland, of a young boy abandoned to the institutionalised hell which in the 1950s was this country's way of dealing with orphans. It was a harrowing tale of brutal deprivation, both physical and emotional, suffered at the hands of the Church and the medical authorities charged with his care, an abuse which resulted in the severe disablement of Paddy.

It was a heavy interview to have so early in my career and I was determined to get it right. In his book, *The God Squad*, Paddy had revealed the full extent of his treatment at the hands of others. At the age of 4 his mother died from breast cancer and six weeks later he found his father hanging from a tree. He was sent to an industrial school in Wexford to be brought up by the Sisters of Mercy order of nuns. Paddy's experience at that school was to be one long catalogue of emotional deprivation and physical and sexual abuse. Beatings forced him to deny the memory of his father's suicide and so extreme was his distress that by the age of 5 he had developed a limp. By the time he was a teenager, quite a number of pointless operations had been carried out on his brain which were to result in the extreme contortion of his already twisted limbs. To this day Paddy is wheelchair bound.

Justin Keating, a former Irish Minister for Industry & Commerce under Liam Cosgrave, had reviewed the book, writing: 'Subjected to the same treatment, the vast majority of humans would have been driven mad, and would therefore have spent all their days in institutions.'

This was therefore an interview that needed great sensitivity and understanding. On the programme and to portray as graphically as we could to our audience the horrors of Paddy's early childhood, I read out extracts from his book, relating how he had been beaten by the nuns caring for him. I can remember the gasps of disgust and outrage from our audience as Paddy revealed one abuse after another. To this day Paddy Doyle remains firmly in my mind.

This was the first KELLY show our new programme controller had seen and on the back of it he invited me out to lunch in the Europa Hotel in Belfast. I was on tenterhooks. Normally programme controllers do not entertain lowly programme presenters to lunch, so this was a very new experience for me. I was pleased with that particular programme and was looking forward to Maurice's assessment. He said to me, 'I watched last week's programme and there are a few things I would have done differently.' I nodded and waited politely to hear his suggestions. He continued, 'When Paddy came on in the wheelchair, I would have made a fuss about lifting the wheelchair up the step on to the interviewing podium, with a couple of the props guys to do the lifting, and we should have seen this on camera.' I was gobsmacked. We had installed a ramp to ensure that Paddy and his wheelchair could have dignified access to the studio and his interview position. All I could do was nod dumbly at him, so he gave me his next suggestion.

'When you came to the point where Paddy was describing how the nuns beat him with canes, I would have had a stuffed dummy on a table and had a couple of people with sticks beating the dummy, showing precisely how it was done.'

By now I was almost speechless. My first thought was that this new programme controller must be pulling my leg, testing me in his own bizarre way. But he was the boss, so I limited my response to a calm 'Maurice, I don't think that would have been appropriate.' My raging instincts however were to tell him to go to hell. When I got back to the office and related what he had said, the others were equally flabbergasted.

So that was my first meeting with this new programme controller and from that point on I knew we could not approach him for support, still less for guidance. He didn't seem to understand the sensitivities or where the boundaries lay. We all immediately felt very exposed because in a television station the programme controller is next only to God. We could not complain to the managing director, because he had just appointed the man. We decided henceforth that we would simply keep our heads down and work away quietly. Mercifully, Maurice never ever came back to us after that, for which we were most grateful.

To be kind to Maurice, I believe he suffered from being away from Northern Ireland too long. Since he had left, the troubles had started in earnest and the whole nature of the place had altered socially, politically and even culturally. This gap in his knowledge surfaced persistently. As a result his time at UTV was short lived and he left to return to New Zealand in 1991. I'm not sure if he was pushed or returned of his own accord. I just know I was glad to see the back of him.

———

GK: Thanks for all the enjoyment you gave us over the seven months.

Male Guest: Thank you.

GK: And by the way, I hate telling you on live television. Your zip is undone.

———

That aside, the first year of KELLY was proving both exhilarating and exhausting. I had so much to learn about interviewing techniques, how to encourage flowing conversation and at the same time garner as much interesting information from the guest as possible. Of course I would have prepared my notes on the points I wanted illuminated, perhaps five or six key questions, but I was always willing to move down any avenue which my interviewees wanted.

The very first programme taught me that and I continued to learn the importance of listening. I am often asked what makes a good interviewer and I always reply: 'First and foremost he has to be a good listener.' Sounds logical, doesn't it, but you would be surprised how many interviewers are so wrapped up in their own performance and so hell bent on getting out their own carefully scripted questions that they just seem to ignore the responses from the interviewee or don't actually hear them.

A classic case of not listening is the often repeated chat of Jim Bowen, who was the host of ITV's *Bullseye* game show, with one of the contestants. Jim asked him what he worked at and the guy replied that he had just been made redundant, to which Jim responded: 'Super. Smashing. Great!'

Some of the techniques I developed in that first year stood me in good stead over the next sixteen years or so. I remember interviewing Michael Parkinson once. Beforehand we had been discussing little aids and tricks he used in his interviews. He told me that the first thing he wrote down in his notes was the name of the person he was interviewing. Regardless of who or what they were, regardless of how famous they were, regardless of them being a household name or not, he always wrote the person's name down on paper. He had learned this lesson the hard way. He recalled interviewing the Prime Minister Margaret Thatcher on one occasion and as he started to introduce her—'Ladies and gentlemen, please welcome the Prime Minister . . .' And at that instant he simply could not remember her name. He hadn't written it down and only for an alert programme director whispering in his earpiece was he able to continue with the introduction. I empathised totally with him because I too had already experienced a similar kind of embarrassing situation.

Like Parky, I tended not to write down the names of my more famous guests. One night I was introducing one of my musical heroes, Paul Brady. Normally I would have my introductions on autocue, but on this occasion I thought it better to go straight to Paul without a long, rambling introduction, so I had nothing in front of me. After all, who on this island does not know Paul Brady? And so I launched forth: 'Time for some music now and I'm delighted to welcome the brilliant . . .' My mind went completely blank. I repeated the word 'brilliant' just to give myself some time to think. I repeated it again and was only rescued when my director David Donaghy, knowing I was in trouble, shouted Paul's name in my earpiece. Lesson learned; only one of many as the year progressed.

There was another element of that first year which wasn't obvious to the public, but of which I was very aware. This might sound odd, but I had never met anyone famous before. There is an assumption that if you work in television you must be bumping into famous people all the time, but that was not the case, certainly not for me. I had met one or two personalities while working with Gloria, but very few. So at the start of KELLY I didn't know anybody famous at all and I was not accustomed to rubbing shoulders with celebs. I had to work out how to deal with them.

Don't get me wrong. I am not and never have been star struck, though I confess I could become wobbly at the knees in the company of a golfer like Tiger Woods. Right from the outset I believed that we were all out there doing a job. My role was to ask the questions; theirs was to answer them. For that one hour on a Friday night I had to believe I was their equal.

————

GK: Do you work off an allowance from Dad. Is that how you work?

Tara Palmer Tomkinson: My money is now what I earn. On my twenty-first birthday, when everyone else had a convertible car outside the house, I had something like an old banger from the farm. I said to my father, 'Look I'm not driving this thing up to London.' And my father said, 'If you want wheels, you earn them.' So my parents are down to earth. They were my saving grace through everything. The one thing I resent in people is flashiness. I think money can be so vulgar. Some people say, 'It's easy for you to say that because

*you've always had it.' Well I have always had it and
there's nothing I can do about that. What I can do is
put it to some good use instead of putting it up my nose.*

*GK: It must have hurt your parents a lot, that period
when you were using drugs.*

*TPT: Of course. My parents, between my sister and me,
have converted to Judaism and been through rehab.
(laughing) They're fine.*

———

My first encounter with anyone remotely famous came in the
second programme of that first year. We had managed to book
international singing star and actress, Eartha Kitt. How we got her
I cannot imagine. But she was a superstar, albeit from a slightly
bygone era, but a superstar none the less. Maybe her reputation
was on the wane, but I remember being absolutely terrified of her.

From the limited research material we had on her, I realised
that Eartha Kitt was not a lady to be trifled with. Her upbringing
had been harsh, having been ostracised at an early age because of
her mixed race heritage. When she was just 8 years old she was
given away by her mother and sent from the cotton fields of South
Carolina to live with her aunt in Harlem. It was when in New York
that her exceptional flair for show business was recognised and by
the end of the 1960s not only was she a big name on Broadway but
she had also appeared in movies alongside such legends as Sidney
Poitier, Sammy Davis Jr and Nat King Cole. She even had her own
star on the famous Hollywood Walk of Fame. Orson Welles once
described her as 'the most exciting woman in the world'. She also
had a unique singing voice and those of us of a certain age will
remember the famous Eartha Kitt growl.

She arrived at UTV, having been picked up in the biggest and
cleanest taxi we could find. Not wanting to appear too eager, I
waited fifteen minutes or so before I went down to the make-up

area to welcome her. First impressions were not favourable. She was exceptionally small, very gruff and not very welcoming. She demanded her own dressing room—not an unreasonable request, but for us it was something of a problem because UTV was not blessed with generous accommodation at the time. She had brought her own entourage of about five people, including a hairdresser, a make-up lady and a publicist. We quickly did a bit of reshuffling with the other guests, managed to settle Miss Kitt and her company all in one room and eventually, with a fair dollop of good old Irish bullshit, managed to get her to become almost human.

However, when the time came for her performance on the show, the audience was treated to a very different Eartha Kitt. Gone was the gloomy face, the surliness, the tight lips, the long pregnant pauses in conversation, and in their place a radiant film star full of anecdotes and showbiz smiles—even a little flirting, would you believe.

I chatted with her for ten minutes, showed two video clips of her singing and acting talents and looked forward to spending a little more social time with her in the green room after the show. Alas, as she left the studio floor during the second break, I wasn't to know that that would be the last glimpse I would have of the great Eartha Kitt. She gathered her entourage about her, headed for the front door and was back in her hotel practically before the break was over.

Mind you, the next week a little note on Europa Hotel headed notepaper arrived on my desk thanking me for my hospitality and wishing me well for the rest of the series, signed Eartha. Pleased as I was with that, I couldn't help but feel that if all so-called superstars behaved as icily as she did, I wasn't looking forward to booking many more big names. As the years went on, I was to learn that many are indeed like Eartha Kitt, but thankfully many more are not.

So by the end of my first month on the show, I was rocketing up a learning curve as steep as I could ever have imagined. No time to draw breath; upwards and onwards with relentless speed.

And then came the story of Brian Keenan. Brian came from a working-class family in east Belfast where he attended Orangefield School. He began work initially as a heating engineer, but his interest in literature eventually led him to take a degree in English and postgraduate studies at the University of Ulster. He subsequently took up a teaching position at the English department of the American University of Beirut, a move that was to propel him on to the world stage. On 11 April 1986, which was a bright sunlit morning, he locked the gates of the villa he rented in Beirut's Rue d'Amérique and began the ten minute walk to the university campus.

A vicious civil war was raging in Lebanon, especially in its capital Beirut. Western hostages were being taken. Suddenly four armed gunmen bundled Keenan into the back of an old Mercedes and drove him to the secret underground prisons of Lebanon's Islamic Jihad militants. For the next four and a half years Brian was held hostage in barbaric conditions and news of his captivity spread worldwide.

The KELLY team knew we should be getting involved in Brian's story and so we contacted his two sisters, Elaine Spence and Brenda Gillham, who were still living in east Belfast and who were running a fairly low-key campaign to try and secure their brother's release. We invited them on to the show at the end of September and that was to prove the beginning of one of the most rewarding episodes not only in my professional life but also in my private life.

Brenda and Elaine were two typical Belfast women with no experience of the media but who simply wanted the return of their brother. They spoke from the heart. During the interview they reminded me that I had actually known Brian because he and I had worked at the same time in City Hall. He was in a different department but our paths had crossed on a few occasions. I hadn't realised at the time that we were talking about the same Brian Keenan.

We set up a petition for people to sign demanding Brian's release and in the end hundreds of thousands of Northern Ireland people would add their name to that list. Brenda and Elaine were thrilled that so many cared about their brother's plight and I think they drew great strength from the fact that they were no longer fighting alone. I remember the *Irish News* printing each day the number of days that had elapsed since Brian's capture. Momentum was building and you could see Brenda and Elaine's commitment and pride swell, knowing that so much was being done to secure their brother's release. Over the coming months we invited the sisters back many times with updates on the international negoti-ations that were going on and how the petition was growing.

It was at this point, early in the programme's history, that we found ourselves dealing with such a diverse mix of issues that we began to realise that to be credible, KELLY had to deliver much more than just light entertainment. If we were to reflect the society in which we lived, we also had to deal with topics that would not normally come under that category.

My interests and strength have always been in what we in the business call human interest stories. Talking to ordinary people about important or personal subjects has always been something I enjoyed doing most. I have a great interest in people in general and I seemed to have the ability to make their individual tales interesting to those watching the show. It might take me three gentler questions to elicit some piece of information to Jeremy's Paxman's one abrasive question, but we are in a very different area of journalism.

I always liked to take a story such as the Keenan story, which would feature in political broadcasts and newspaper front pages, and bathe it in a different light. I would ask different questions and always in a conversational manner, just as if I was in some-body's front room. I could be tough when I needed to be and never shirked from asking the direct question, but I was a talk show host and therefore I had a different agenda to other hard-nosed journalists.

The campaign for Brian's release was relentless both at home and abroad. Eventually, on 24 August 1990, news filtered through that he had been released from captivity and was on his way to

Damascus. There he was handed over by the Syrian Foreign Ministry to the care of the Irish Ambassador Declan Connolly. Brenda and Elaine were flown by Irish government executive jet to Damascus to meet him and bring him home. I didn't see them before they left, but I could imagine their relief and total joy.

Having been actively involved in the Brian Keenan story, it was imperative to have him on the show at the earliest possible opportunity. Our first show of the second series was due to air in mid-September 1990, only three weeks after Brian's release. To arrange things I had gone down to Dublin Airport to meet the plane bringing Brian home and to hear his press conference. When he emerged to the throng of waiting journalists, who had come from all over the world, I was certain I was looking at a man turned utterly mad and deranged by his terrible experience. His eyes were wild and staring. He was totally emaciated and I thought to myself, this poor guy is off his rocker; they shouldn't let him out in front of a packed press conference. He can't be ready for this. I was standing at the back of the throng, not taking notes because I was only there to grab him if possible and book him for the show.

But that day I watched something remarkable. Keenan was far from mad. In fact he might have been the sanest man in the room. He spoke for over an hour with descriptions the like of which I had never heard before. It was an electrifying, enthralling performance before the world's press. Anyone who has read his book, *An Evil Cradling*, will have an idea of what I am talking about. At that press conference we were hearing what could have been the very first draft of his book, which is one of the finest I have ever read. Afterwards he did tell me that on that day he felt he might have been on the edge of a kind of madness, but it certainly did not affect his eloquence. He made that press conference into an event like no other. Here were journalists who had been around the world several times, who had seen some of the rawest events and reported upon them, and here they were with their mouths open and tears in their eyes.

I eventually had a word with Brian and he agreed to come north for the show. I was a little disappointed though because he felt he had to do the *Late Late Show* first on RTÉ. Because he had been travelling on an Irish passport he felt that he owed a public expression of gratitude to the Irish government for helping to release him and the *Late Late* simply had to be the first port of call for that purpose. Fair enough.

But when he did appear on the KELLY show on 21 September 1990, what a welcome he received. What a night! It was one of the most emotional shows I have ever been involved in. Brenda and Elaine were present, and on walked Brian. I remember him hugging me. The audience rose immediately in a spontaneous standing ovation. He was in tears. We had asked the folk group Barnbrack to come along and sing their own emotive song, 'Belfast', for him. We had also invited the Chieftains, Brian's favourite group. In fact that night Brian and the Chieftain's Matt Molloy struck up a friendship that has lasted to this day. Brian and his family are now next door neighbours to the Molloys in Westport, Co. Mayo.

Looking back on that evening, I knew Brian was still in a bit of a daze; things were happening for him in very quick succession. However, he had the personal resources to take stock of what was happening to him and to react with coherence, notwithstanding the intellectual and emotional deprivation of the last four and a half ghastly years. His sisters were generous in their thanks to me, but I felt, and still feel, that we didn't really do very much; they did all the hard work. Our programme offered support, but so did very many others. Brian later signed a copy of his book for me, writing a rather nice quotation from Shelley. And underneath his sisters wrote, 'You done it, Gerry', which I value greatly.

I have remained friends with Brian Keenan ever since, and in 2007 when I was preparing to interview him for the *Gerry Meets* series on UTV, I went to his home in Sligo. I talked to him—more accurately, I listened to him—for over two hours. He was still as fascinating as the day I heard him at that first press conference eighteen years ago.

It was the Brian Keenan story more than any other that proved to us beyond any doubt that we were not just an entertainment show. Of course the music and celebrity elements were always important, but within a matter of weeks the KELLY show was beginning to define for itself a direction, a purpose and a worth.

Viewing figures, the be-all and end-all of commercial television, were excellent right from the off. We were obviously beginning to worry the local BBC, who had also developed their own brand of Friday night entertainment with a programme called *The Show*. It was hosted by, among others, my former UTV colleague Eamonn Holmes.

The Show was billed as a late night satirical programme but ran into trouble on its very first night. Another of the programme's presenters, Rhonda Paisley, the daughter of Rev. Ian Paisley, left the programme in a blaze of publicity after a particular sketch about her father which she regarded as 'lewd and crude'. She claimed she hadn't seen the sketch in rehearsals. One week later Eamonn Holmes too walked out. The BBC switchboard was flooded with wave after wave of complaints especially from members of Ulster's bible belt who wielded huge influence back in the early 1980s. The programme limped on for some time after that and seemed to gather new momentum when veteran BBC newsman David Dunseith was drafted in, but irreparable damage had been done. It was finally taken off the air, much to the disappointment of many, it has to be said.

I was one of those who regretted its departure from the BBC schedule, even though KELLY was in direct competition with it. I thought it adventurous, ground breaking and with a touch of irreverence that was much needed back at that time to prick the pretentious bubbles of many people and organisations. But I suspect it was too adventurous for the establishment of the day, a little before its time, and it eventually fizzled out. If *The Show* was to be shown today, no one would bat an eyelid. The BBC's loss was UTV's gain and KELLY's viewing figures soared week on week.

We were riding high and were rewarded in March 1990 when UTV management asked us to extend the programme to one and a half hours. A mere six months after those first tentative steps, not only was the management happy with what we were achieving but the whole of Northern Ireland was giving us the thumbs up by tuning in in huge numbers each Friday night.

With the extended time, however, came additional production problems. It may sound silly to say this, but an hour and a half programme is not simply a half-hour longer. It wasn't just a matter of sticking two or three more guests on to what we were already doing. The whole shape of the show had to change. There were now four commercial breaks instead of two and running orders had to be altered to allow for that. Only rarely could you run an item up to the break and then pick it up afterwards. Each section needed to stand on its own. But far and away the biggest problem was our lack of people working on the show. With a further half-hour to fill, we needed more staff. Most particularly we needed to employ a celebrity booker, someone who had the contacts and who could provide us with a constant stream of top names who would make the journey to Belfast.

Fortunately, around that time a young Manchester agent, Paul Madely, had contacted us after seeing a KELLY programme to offer his services. He said he liked what he saw and wanted to be part of our future. Paul was already making bookings for a host of British television shows, most notably *This Morning* with Richard and Judy. We employed him and, to be honest, it was one of the best moves we made in those early days. Paul proved invaluable, opening doors previously closed to us and securing the services of a host of celebrities who all made the journey to Havelock House over many years.

The first year of KELLY had been an unmitigated success. Not only had we secured a loyal following in Northern Ireland, but there was more than anecdotal evidence to suggest that we were making inroads south of the border too. Of course the *Late Late Show* was the Southern audience's first preference. However, if an item on the *Late Late* was struggling, some viewers were inclined to flick over to see what else was on. KELLY was the preferred alternative.

We went for our summer break that year happy with what we had accomplished but knowing that the next series would provide even higher mountains to climb and it would require a thorough examination of the team's stamina, creativity and flair.

Doing it over one year was relatively easy. Repeating and maintaining it—well, that was the trick.

———

Patrick Kielty: When you run the marathon there are other problems that are a wee bit more personal.

GK: Care to share?

PK: Well … (hesitates)

GK: Maybe not.

PK: When you run the marathon what happens is that things start to rub together. (chuckles from the audience) … and the strawberries need a bit of cream. You have to grease all moving parts. I used to wonder why all these runners were dressed in black lycra like Spiderman at a funeral. It was to stop the chaffing.

———

Chapter 8 ∾
| FUN AND GAMES

As the new decade drew on, *KELLY* began to gain momentum. We had now become the 'must see' programme in the UTV schedule. To celebrate our success, UTV built a new studio for us which would more than double the space we had in the old one and would allow us to be much more adventurous with the items and acts we could book.

We now had specially installed seating which could take an audience of up to 130, a dedicated music area to accommodate all kinds of acts from choirs and brass bands to solo artists, and we had a proper interview area capable of seating up to six guests at any one time. It was sheer luxury compared to the cramped and restrictive conditions of the old studio. With additional money available for new sets and new opening titles, UTV were beginning to really feel confident about their investment in the show.

We also reached the dizzy heights of being named the highest rated chat show in the whole of the ITV network. The programme was picking up awards: the Entertainment and Media Award (EMA) in 1990, 1992 and 1993 for Best Local Entertainment Show, and I was twice voted TV Personality of the Year.

We were also beginning to break down the reluctance of guests to travel to Belfast attracting such stars as Tom Jones, Celine Dion, Dave Stewart, Hank Marvin, Barbara Dickson, Elaine Paige, Manfred Mann, Midge Ure, Bananarama, Jerry Lee Lewis, the Bay City Rollers, Chris Rea, Steve Harley, David Essex, John Denver and Sarah Brightman, all in 1992.

Among our interview guests around the same period we had Roger Daltry, Leslie Phillips, Malcolm Allison, Michael Parkinson,

Jacky Charlton, Peter Alliss, Sir David Attenborough, Terry Jones, Ossie Ardiles, Andrew Morton, Richard Wilson, Les Dawson, Sir David Frost, David Hasselhoff, Warren Mitchell and Phillip Schofield. So by any standards we had come a long way since those early days in 1989.

To have such TV icons as David Frost and Michael Parkinson sitting opposite me on *my* show was way beyond any dreams and expectations we may have had so early in the series. I can't remember much detail about either interview. However, I do recall a certain panic we had over David Frost even before he arrived. Frost is a cigar smoker and UTV, even in those days, operated a no smoking policy throughout the building. So it was going to be embarrassing to ask him to join the great unwashed and step outside if he wanted to smoke. I asked our MD if it would be OK to use the boardroom should Sir David want to smoke. He refused!

Sure as fate, within minutes of meeting Frost he produced a cigar and was about to light up when I explained that, regrettably, we had a strict no smoking policy in UTV, even for knights of the realm and would he mind going outside. 'No problem,' he said. 'Where do I go?' I instantly liked David Frost.

Parkinson was a dream interviewee, full of anecdotes and stories and extremely generous to me as the interviewer. I'm sure my questions were not of the highest order, but he answered with enthusiasm and interest. I have to say that having Michael Parkinson on the show was one of the early milestones in my career. He appeared a few more times over the years and if we bumped into each other at some awards ceremony or other, he was always gracious enough to enquire how the show was going.

Our reputation was rapidly spreading down south and while we welcomed the increasing number of viewers, we were always acutely aware that we were UTV, Ulster Television, and our first allegiance was to serve our viewers in Northern Ireland.

By this time we were getting a little more confident and adventurous with our content. Director David Donaghy had left to join RTÉ and was replaced by a young Dubliner, Phillip Kampf, who

had worked on the *Late Late Show* and Gay Byrne's radio programme. Phillip had some unique ideas and was always suggesting
ways of pushing the envelope. For example, in 1995 he decided we
would do a programme devoted entirely to the question of what it
was like being gay in Northern Ireland. A good and proper idea, I
thought. However, it would turn out to be one of our most hated
programmes of all time, if our postbag was anything to go by.

Let me explain why we attracted so much flak. Homosexuality
had never been on the Northern Ireland agenda in any meaning-
ful way at all. In 1995 we were still talking bombs, bullets and
death, but under the surface other debates were taking place and
one was about homosexuality. We decided to use *KELLY* to bring it
to the surface.

The invited audience was made up of gay people—our selection, who in my opinion were very brave in agreeing to appear. A
measure of their courage can be gauged from the fact that a coach
full of gay people from Derry, on their way to the studio to be part
of the audience, never arrived. Their vehicle was attacked by a
stone-throwing mob as it left the city. How they knew where the
coach was bound, it's hard to say. But once discovered, they were
determined to vent their hatred and ultimately prevented the
coach from reaching its destination.

The structure of the programme was to have a panel including,
on one side, Rev. Martin Smyth, a Presbyterian minister and a
former Grand Master of the Orange Order. Rev. Smyth was also a
member of the Official Unionist Party and an MP representing
Belfast South. He was vehemently opposed to homosexuality. On
the other side of the desk sat Senator David Norris, an openly gay
member of the Irish Senate. He was a former university lecturer
and the founder of the Campaign for Homosexual Law Reform in
the South of Ireland.

We asked our panel to listen to gay people as they talked about
their situation and what was happening to them in society at
large. At the conclusion I would ask if anyone had changed or
modified their views in light of what they had heard. It came as
no surprise that minds had not changed.

But it is what happened after the programme that sticks so vividly in my mind. The KELLY office and UTV in general was hit with an avalanche of hate mail. How dare I have these homosexuals on the show! Didn't I know that homosexuality was sinful and therefore we had been defending and giving a platform to sinners? The complaints ran into their hundreds. I reflected with some sadness how backward we had become. It wasn't just the prejudice against gays. It was the sense that after decades of violence we seemed to have lost the ability as a community to lift our minds in a spirit of openness to topics other than the conflict. What were we doing to ourselves? I have wondered on occasions whether the conservative nature of our society, which has benefits to bestow, can nevertheless imprison us within walls of prejudice and bigotry. For so many, the only valid debates had to be about Orange and Green—and even those were not to be real debates, merely platforms for sloganising. Old rigidities stood firm. Homosexuality was a sin, a status not amenable to debate. I heaved a sigh and reflected how badly we needed a period of relative normality to allow us to adjust our intellectual and moral compasses.

———

Dale Winton (self-styled King of Camp): I must thank you for this.

GK: *The Joe Dolan* CD.

DW: When your researcher asked if we could talk about my private life, I said my first crush was Joe Dolan who sang 'Make Me an Island'. That was thirty-three years ago. He was a big star in England. And she got me the CD *and (pointing to Joe's image on the* CD*) he still looks fabulous!*

———

A ray of sunshine was the attitude of the management of UTV. The company backed us. UTV never at any point tried to tell us not to do a programme on homosexuality. The sacks of complaints did not diminish in any way their support for the programme and they rode out the storm with us. It is worth stating at this juncture that throughout the seventeen years of *KELLY*, the company never ever wavered, no matter how controversial the topic. Nobody in a suit ever turned up in the office telling us that we should have avoided this or that topic. Far from it; we were constantly encouraged to scan far and wide. In my view this behaviour speaks volumes about the editorial integrity of the station and of the calibre of the people in it. This steadfastness, allied with competence, may lie at the heart of the reasons why the television audience in Northern Ireland has held a special place in its affections for UTV over the half-century of its existence. Mind you, I think Phillip Kampf got his eyes opened that night!

But of course the show was also about fun. Once again Phillip was a man who could introduce novelty and interaction while still preserving its ethos. He had many ideas in that direction, some of them aimed at me as the presenter. He challenged me often, forcing me out of my comfort zone into areas of presentation that I would probably have run scared from a few years back. And I thank him for that. I learned a great deal from Phillip. But he wasn't infallible. His worst idea came in the form of what we called on the show, the tub quiz.

The idea was to have a hot tub in the studio with two families, suitably attired, competing against one another by answering general knowledge questions. The family was to be made up of a mother, father and two children, and the prize was a week in a villa in Majorca. So after the first week the winning family jetted off to Majorca, and the following week they competed from there against another family in the hot tub in the studio. If the Majorcan family won again, they could stay on for another week; but if they lost they had to come home and be replaced in the villa by the new family. Old hat now but quite revolutionary in the mid-90s. In fact, Phillip took a new refined version of this game to London with him when he went off a few years later to produce Channel 4's new *Saturday Night Lottery* programme.

Meanwhile, back in UTV the tub quiz had been working extremely well for many weeks. Families kept coming and going and public reaction was positive. But then something happened, something awful. One night I asked the youngest member of a family a question, a little lad of about 6. It was an important question because if he got it right, his family would win the right to a week in the holiday villa. Get it wrong and the quiz would continue. I asked the question, a simple one designed for a child. 'What did Little Miss Muffet sit on?' His family waited with baited breath. When he gave the wrong answer, there were sighs of disappointment from the audience. The quiz continued. As I turned to ask the next question of the family in Majorca, I saw the little boy out of the corner of my eye. He had his head buried in the folds of his mother's clothing, sobbing inconsolably. Watching this knocked the heart out of me. This was no longer fun. This little lad felt he had let his whole family down and in the most public way possible. It was a disaster. We had probably traumatised this child for life because he didn't know where Miss bloody Muffet sat. After the programme that night Phillip agreed we should pull the tub quiz.

The tub quiz was of course only one in a long line of games we developed for the programme. My favourite was the coin game. The first time I saw it played was in the bar of the Stormont Hotel opposite the gates of Parliament Buildings. A group of us had been at some dinner or other and had retired to the bar for a few drinks. Somebody put a column of £1 coins on the table and told us all to post a £5 note. We had no idea what he was on about, but we agreed anyway. He then explained that with £30 in the pot, one of us could bet up to that amount on whether the next coin revealed, when the top coin was removed, was heads or tails. That was all there was to it. So if you bet £5 on heads and heads came up, you took a fiver out of the pot. If it was tails, you put a fiver in. It was then the turn of the next player. He could now bet up to the new pot amount of £35. Sounds simple; after all each call is a

50/50 chance, isn't it? But believe me, there's more to it than meets the eye. Try it for fun yourself sometime, though I have to warn you that one of our crowd lost £120 that afternoon!

I looked at what was happening, at the absorption of all those playing and reckoned that this was a game that could be adapted for *KELLY*. Back in the office I phoned Eastwood's Bookmakers to calculate the odds on someone guessing all ten coins correctly. They worked it out as 2 to the power of 10 which is 1,024/1. The chances of someone guessing all ten correctly are very slim, but if it was achieved a goodly prize was the reward. I got the OK from UTV to put up £25,000 should anyone be successful with all ten coins.

The way we worked the rules was as follows. If you called the first coin right you got £50. You could stop at any time, but if you went on and failed, you lost all that had gone before. So, if guessed correctly, it was £50 for the 1st coin, £100 for the 2nd, £250 for the 3rd, £500 for the 4th, £1,000 for the 5th, £2,500 for the 6th, £5,000 for the 7th, £10,000 for the 8th, £15,000 for the 9th and £25,000 for the 10th.

Now UTV is not a benevolent charity. They knew the chances of losing their £25,000 were remote, one of the reasons I suppose they allowed me to do it in the first place. And indeed their thinking was right and their money was safe for a long time. Some people had been guessing correctly up until the 4th or 5th coin and then would stop, unwilling to continue and risk losing £500 or £1,000—until Friday, 9 February 1996.

It's a day I will never forget for many reasons. The date is one many of you will remember as the day the IRA cruelly marked the end of their seventeen-month ceasefire by bombing Canary Wharf in the docklands area of London. Two people were killed and millions of pounds worth of damage was caused.

Around teatime on that Friday evening I was sitting in my office putting the finishing touches to that night's programme when news filtered through of the bombing. It was so depressing. For the previous year and a half the people of Northern Ireland were beginning to believe that maybe, just maybe, a brighter, peaceful future lay ahead. The IRA was on ceasefire and there did seem to be some political advances. Seventeen months was long enough for the people of the province to experience what life without the despair of constant conflict might bring. The Canary Wharf bomb blew all this apart.

Television schedules were disrupted all evening as more and more news filtered through about the bombing. All newsrooms moved into top gear and Northern Ireland was once more centre stage. Television executives rushed back to their offices to revamp evening schedules for special news programmes. They programmed by the seat of their pants. KELLY was pushed back in the schedule immediately and we didn't know precisely when we would go on air, if at all. ITN in London and UTV were mounting special programmes, ditching their normal viewing. Our earliest starting time that night was now 11.30 pm. Even then what would we feature? Could we run a normal programme after what had happened? I confessed to those around me that I really didn't feel like presenting a programme of light-hearted content after such deeply depressing and devastating news.

I wasn't looking forward to doing that show. My instinct was to cancel it and let news take over the remainder of the night. I consulted with Andy Crockart, the man in charge of programmes at UTV, and told him my concerns. Andy vehemently disagreed. He said, 'Gerry, one of the reasons for your programme is to provide an antidote to all this destruction and death. It's what we've been doing for years. We've got viewers out there who might be relying on us to keep asserting that there is another world, a better one of smiles and optimism. You go on to that studio floor and do what you've always done. We especially need to do that on a night like this.'

He was, of course, absolutely right. The dictum that 'the show must go on' was coined long before television and I learnt that night what the phrase could really mean. I began the programme by being honest with the audience, telling them that I had not felt like going ahead, that after such devastating news how could we possibly follow with a light-hearted programme. It didn't seem right. And then I paraphrased what Andy had said to me and a spontaneous cheer went up in the audience, confirmation that we were doing the right thing. And out of the awful darkness of that night a little light shone.

It was time for the coin game and our first contestant on the phone was David McConaghy from Lurgan. Being a few nights before Valentine's Day, we had converted the tails on the coins to a more romantic hearts, so rather than heads or tails, it was now heads or hearts.

David got the first six right without hesitation and without even thinking of stopping and claiming his money. He also got the 7th one right—and the 8th. The prize money was getting serious at this stage. He had now won £10,000 and to be honest, in my own mind I wanted him to quit. If he called the 9th and got it wrong, he would lose everything. But on he went. 'Heads' he called. I lifted the coin.

'Correct! You now have £15,000. Do you want to go on for £25,000?

'Why not?' said David.

By this stage the audience were on the edge of their seats. My hands were shaking lifting the coins and I so much wanted him to win. 'So, for £25,000, David. Is it heads or hearts?' Without hesitation he called hearts.

Hands trembling, I eased the second last coin off the pile to reveal what was on the 10th and final coin. It was a heart! Well, the audience went wild, I went wild and David went wild. What a wonderful bright moment it was in an otherwise depressing night.

We had other games over the years, most notably the mugs game. It too proved popular, as did 'The Dice is Right', 'Higher or Lower' and 'Stick or Spin'.

But one of the odd things about our little games was the hostility of television critics who used to ridicule them. I could never quite understand this. They were wont to compare the KELLY games with dedicated quiz shows such as *Who Wants to be a Millionaire?* or *The Weakest Link*. When they published comments along the lines of 'If you want to see UTV's version, watch

KELLY', they were missing the point altogether. Our games were for audience fun only and were never designed to be anything else. They were a vehicle for allowing ordinary people on the show to participate and I can tell you I had more fun on that phone with contestants than on any other segment of the show. Sometimes tears of laughter ran down my cheeks listening to the comments and yarns of our contestants.

———

GK: You said Steve looked like the serial killer Fred West.

Louis Walsh: He does look a little bit like him. Same smile.

GK: Well somebody said he murdered a lot of songs.

———

On another occasion we had taken the programme lock, stock and barrel to Vicar Street in Dublin. And even with guests of the calibre of Gay Byrne, Louis Walsh, Darren Clarke and Michael Ball, it was our little game that provided a hilarious three or four minutes. The game we were playing that season was called The Dice is Right, a simple formula where I would throw two dice and the contestant would gamble on whether the next throw would be higher or lower. Couldn't be any easier. Bruce Forsyth made an entire game show out of a similar theme.

On this occasion I had chosen a contestant from the studio audience by drawing a name from a hat, but I don't think the gentleman quite grasped the rules of the game. He came up to the stage, sat beside me and I had a bit of craic with him before the game. He was a charming and amusing talker. Eventually I rolled the dice and the two totalled six. He chose higher for the next throw, which I would have expected. I threw again and sure enough it was higher, a five and a six, totalling eleven, one away from the highest possible.

'OK,' I said. 'What's it to be next time?' spoken in a tone betraying that I thought he scarcely needed to answer. Logic dictated that he should choose a lower number.

'Higher,' says he.

I blinked. Surely he was joking with me and the audience, but then I noticed his face. He was perfectly serious. He wasn't joking.

'Now wait a minute,' says I. 'The only score that could be higher would be a twelve and you are sitting on eleven. You would be betting on two sixes coming up. So what do you really want. Higher or lower?'

'Higher,' says he without hesitation.

The studio audience was by this time rolling in the aisles and I dare say the home audience as well.

'No no,' says I, by now well perplexed. 'You've got eleven. You don't want to bet all you've won on getting two sixes?' I still thought there was a chance he was winding me up.

'Higher,' he persisted.

Well, by now the studio was in uproar. The nice man seemed intent on throwing away all the prize money he had accrued.

'Look,' I said, speaking slowly so I could not be misunderstood. 'Take a bit of advice. Go lower. If it's higher, I'll still pay you. So go lower.'

But he was looking at me as if I had horns. He didn't seem to understand at all.

'All right,' he eventually and quite reluctantly agreed, under some pressure from everybody in the studio.

I threw the dice, hoping against hope that two sixes would come up to bring this extraordinary game to a fairytale ending. But the odds prevailed and something under eleven resulted. I handed the contestant his money, but as I did so I could still detect traces of bewilderment on his face. I wondered afterwards if I had dreamt the whole thing.

These games were all just a bit of innocent fun and really if you were to analyse the time actually spent playing them, you would find that the greater part was spent chatting and laughing. Sure what would TV critics know?

———

Honor Blackman:

I had to have it explained to me what a swinger was. I know about orgies and things and I knew people did it but I didn't know they were called swingers. I'm such an innocent.

———

Chapter 9 ∽

THE GOOD OLD, BAD OLD DAYS

The Europa Hotel in Belfast is probably one of the most famous hotels in the world for the simple reason that it has the rather dubious reputation of being the most bombed hotel in the world. Some say it has had more than forty hits over the years, but as a former manager of the hotel once told me, 'Any time a bomb went off in the vicinity and the hotel windows were shattered, it was put down as another Europa bombing.' I tend to agree with him, but there certainly were at least five major bombing incidents causing huge damage to the hotel over the worst period of the troubles.

You would think that with such a reputation, potential guests would have chosen to stay elsewhere. Not a bit of it. Practically every programme guest we flew into the province actually insisted that we put them up there. It must have been a macho thing, good for the ego or street cred, to be able to say that they had risked life and limb to stay in the Europa.

Of course, the reality of life in the hotel was nothing like its reputation. We had built up a great relationship with the Hastings group who owned the Europa and since the start of *KELLY* we used it exclusively for our guests.

However, that was soon to come to an abrupt end. On Thursday, 5 December 1991, the IRA planted a huge 1,000 lb car bomb in Glengall Street which runs down the side of the Europa. The bomb exploded causing immense damage not only to the hotel but the blast also spread to the magnificent nineteenth-century Grand Opera House next door, causing millions of pounds worth of damage to the two buildings. Thankfully no one was killed, but twenty-three people were injured including thirteen police officers and two soldiers.

The bombing provoked a public outcry. After all, this was the Christmas period, a time when ordinary decent people deserved some respite from the troubles which had already claimed the lives of over 100 people that year. A Junior Minister with the Northern Ireland Office, Jeremy Hanley, said: 'The IRA are trying to bomb Christmas out of Belfast.'

And indeed that was how we felt in the KELLY office. We phoned the Europa and talked to the manager David Boyce for an update. Was the hotel going to close? How about all those Christmas parties that had been booked? Were they going to be cancelled? David's answer was heartening. No, they were not closing. The parties were going ahead. No one had cancelled. Come hell or high water the Europa was determined to have Christmas as usual.

We couldn't help but admire their attitude and we felt it would be only right for us to somehow try and support them on the show. With Friday's programme only twenty-four hours away, we had very little time to come up with a plan. Eventually we decided that the best way to show our disgust at what the IRA had done was for me to take a 'live' camera down to the Europa and present part of the show from there. Viewers would be able to see for themselves the devastation and damage that was inflicted, not just on a building, but on the population of Northern Ireland as a whole. I would open the show from the hotel restaurant, show the destruction, chat to guests and staff then return to the studio to complete the rest of the show.

But when I arrived at the Europa, I wasn't quite prepared for what I saw. Practically every window was boarded up; plaster was falling off the interior walls and ceilings; many of the rooms were lit with bare bulbs. The kitchens were only working on half power. Yet in the middle of all this chaos, dinner was being served and guests were determined that Christmas would go on. It was a resounding two fingers to the IRA. Commentators often refer to the resilience of the Northern Ireland people throughout the troubles. That night it couldn't have been more manifest.

I spent some fifteen minutes at the hotel, but it was now time to get back to Havelock House which was about a mile away and continue on with the programme. I linked back to the studio where the group Goats Don't Shave were ready to perform a song lasting four minutes. After that we would go straight to the commercial break for approximately two and a half minutes. That would give enough time for a fast car to get me back to the studio for part 2 of the show.

And that's what happened. I continued with my next guest who happened to be ex Avenger girl Honor Blackman and then on to the star of *Z Cars* and *Softly, Softly*, Frank Windsor.

But as I was about to introduce the next music act, the shrill ring of an alarm bell filled the studio floor. I knew without being told what was happening. It was a bomb scare. Obviously someone had been displeased with the way we opened the programme and our audacity to side with the ordinary people of Belfast against terrorism. What I didn't know at that stage of course was whether it was a genuine bomb scare or just a hoax.

On a regular basis the paramilitaries would phone into TV stations and newspaper offices with a code word. This was how you would know the difference between a hoax call and the real thing. If the caller gave the correct code word, you didn't waste any time evacuating the building.

A few seconds later my director David Donaghy came through on my earpiece. 'Its authentic, Gerry. Everybody out.' I linked directly to a commercial break

Nobody panicked, but it was UTV's responsibility to ensure that all employees and everyone in the studio audience evacuated the building safely. There was some confusion as to where the bomb was located. Police officers escorted us all to the back of the building when it became clear that the bomb appeared to be in a car in the car park at the front of UTV.

It was a cold winter's night. Most of our guests had already returned to their hotel—not the Europa, I hasten to add—and the rest of us huddled together in an alleyway at the back of Havelock House. We couldn't get to our cars so we just had to wait for the all-clear. As fortune would have it, the guests I was about to introduce before the alarm went off were the Fureys. They too had evacuated the building. Luckily, they left with instruments in hand. Within minutes, Finbar struck up the music and for the next hour or so we spent a very enjoyable time singing together. Having seen what happened live on television, a church in Donegall Pass—which we had access to without crossing the front of Havelock House—opened its doors for us, offering hot drinks. Some of the audience took refuge there while the rest of us continued to sing. After about an hour or so, the all-clear was given. There had been no bomb after all even though the call was properly coded.

As I drove home that night, I couldn't help but smile to myself. Yes, I was annoyed that we had had a bomb scare, but didn't it vindicate what we as a programme had set out to do? The programme had mattered; it had made a difference somewhere. It had got right up the noses of people who were destroying the fabric of the city; we had rattled their cages and I wasn't in the least sorry for that. We were determined to do our best to continue with life and if we had succeeded in conveying that message on behalf of the ordinary people of the province, I could derive some satisfaction out of all this mayhem.

We had riled someone or some organisation over the stance we took against those intent on bombing the city into submission. We sided with the public and we made our point. Their only answer was a puerile attempt to disrupt a live television show.

———

James Nesbitt (speaking after personal criticism for playing the role of civil rights activist Ivan Cooper in the film Bloody Sunday): *It devastates me to think that people would think I had turned against my background. I'm very proud of my background and very proud of Northern Ireland. It would certainly never have been part of my agenda to go against that.*

GK: You can step away from that. You are an actor and that takes you round the world. Your family is left here and they are getting hurt by it.

JN: They are … I have the support of my family. If you make this film for anyone, you are making it for the families. And the very fact that it was the families that we tried to make the film for shows you that Northern Ireland is like a village. It is very tight-knit and my family is very important to me. I told them I believed in the film and I still do. I think it is an authentic portrayal of the events of that day.

————

Naturally, they would try again. They had seen how easy it was to take a live television programme off the air. We were easy targets. I can't recall exactly how many attempts were made over the coming years, but thankfully most of them were hoaxes. The next authentic call came in February 1999. I had just finished interviewing Letitia Dean from *EastEnders* and was about to welcome Pete Conway, who is Robbie Williams's father, when the alarm broke through. No political reason this time, just a little reminder that we could be disrupted at any time. Incidentally, Pete Conway thrived on the whole situation!

Things got a little more personal in October 1992. I had invited the Rev. Ian Paisley on to the show along with Bob Jones, he of the Bob Jones University (BJU) in South Carolina, USA. This famously was where the Rev. Paisley was awarded his doctorate, the cause of much comment and speculation. We didn't talk politics, confining our discussion to the university and to whether there was any truth in the widely held belief that Paisley had bought his degree from BJU rather than it being awarded. Jones himself was a fascinating character and I believe the item made for a very interesting fifteen minutes.

The following Monday a message awaited me when I got into UTV. Would I please go and meet with the head of personnel. Wondering what on earth he wanted me for, I made my way to his office. There I was told that the newsroom had received an anonymous phone call saying that I was to be shot! Me! Shot! I couldn't believe it. In fact I think I laughed and asked if they were sure the caller got it right. Did they not mean Paisley would be shot? After all, he's the controversial politician. I'm sure he deals with threats like that on a daily basis. I'm a mere chat show host. Why would anyone want to shoot me? I wasn't that bad on television, surely!

Try as I may to laugh it off, the police had a different view. They were taking the threat seriously and even came around to explain to me about personal security and the importance of checking under my car each time I got into it, and about changing my route to work on a regular basis.

So for weeks I did as I was told, but thankfully nothing ever came of it. Ian Paisley himself, on hearing about the death threat, called me to say, 'Don't worry about it, Gerry. If they were going to kill you, they wouldn't phone and tell you. They'd just do it.' I think I took some comfort from his words.

However the next threat on my life was slightly more serious. Again a phone call came to the newsroom eight months later, June 1993. I had the Belfast boxer Wayne McCullough on the show in advance of his upcoming fight with Conn McMullen in Maysfield Leisure Centre in Belfast. Wayne had had a magnificent amateur career culminating in a Gold Medal at the 1990 Commonwealth Games in Auckland and a silver medal in the Barcelona Olympics of 1992. He was now being noticed in the professional ranks and this time he was set to fight Conn McMullen, the reigning Irish champion, in his home town of Belfast. During the interview I happened to say that I would be along to Maysfield to watch the fight and I wished him the best of luck.

The fight was scheduled for Saturday, 18 June. That day I had arranged to play golf at Malone Golf Club and then go on to the fights that night. Halfway round my game of golf I noticed two figures walking in the distance. They were wearing suits, so obviously not fellow golfers, and it appeared they were walking straight for me. All sorts of fears crossed my mind. Had some member of my family fallen ill or been involved in an accident or perhaps died? This was when mobile phones were not as plentiful as they are today, so naturally if something had happened somebody would have had to come out on the course to get me.

As they made their way to me, I could tell something serious was wrong. Introducing themselves as two detectives from the RUC, they asked if I was intending to go to the Wayne McCullough fight in Maysfield that night. I said I was. Why? Another phone call, they told me, stating that if I attended I would be shot. My natural instinct was once again to smile and shrug it off as some loony out to frighten me yet again. But as I looked into the eyes of the two detectives I could see they weren't treating it as a laughing matter.

After further discussion we decided that I shouldn't go to the fight as they felt there was some substance to the threat. No reason, but substance, whatever that meant. Once again I was informed of the necessity to review my own personal security arrangements. I asked if I should inform my wife and daughters of the threat—I hadn't the first time, simply not to worry them—and they told me they had already phoned my wife to find out where I was. So obviously Helena would be asking what the police wanted me for when I got home.

For the next few weeks I checked and rechecked under my car every time I got in. Helena did the same with her car and told the girls, who were 13 and 11 at the time, why we had to do this. They appeared to take it in their stride but no doubt were inwardly confused and bewildered as to why this should be happening to their dad. I was angry that someone was putting my family through all this for no reason whatsoever.

For the next three Friday nights, the police told me they would be following me home in an unmarked car after the show. I wouldn't see them but they would be there. It was an unsettling time for us all, one that we didn't deserve. As the weeks drifted by with no further scares, we were gradually able to put it out of our minds and resume our normal lives. It all seems so ludicrous now, but those were the times we were living in not so very long ago.

But, as you know, there can be a funny side to all stories. On the first of those Friday nights when the police told me they would be following me home to Ardglass, I was quite tense. I could see the white of my knuckles as I gripped the steering wheel. I kept checking my rear view mirror to see if I could spot the unmarked police car or if anyone was following me.

I was driving a Renault at the time which had a voice activating device. As I neared my home, I breathed a sigh of relief in the knowledge that I was safe, at least for that night. Suddenly a voice in the car boomed out, 'Low on fuel.' Well, I jumped a mile. I thought there was someone hiding in the back seat and was about to pounce on me. I'd forgotten that the bloody car could speak! That really was the end of the death threats. We had one more evacuation of the studio, but as the century turned, all that nonsense ceased.

Oh, I forgot. I had one more death threat in January 2008, one week after I decided to leave UTV. There was even a ransom note with it. UTV were told that if they didn't hand over £50 million, I would be shot. Honestly! £50 million. At least there's one eejit out there who knows my true worth. Maybe UTV paid up. After all I'm still alive.

Another surreal situation I found myself in, although violent in the extreme, had nothing to do with Northern Ireland. In September 2001, I was in Leeds on a three-day shoot making a special programme about ITV's nightly soap opera, *Emmerdale*. Emmerdale itself is on the Harewood estate, a few miles outside Leeds, not a real village of course but one constructed solely for the purpose of the TV programme made by Yorkshire Television. The houses are real enough though, solid stone constructions typical of so many rural villages in the Yorkshire area. But it is purely a film set. The specially constructed buildings are mostly used for exterior shots only. For example, the outside of the local hostelry, the Woolpack, can be clearly seen, but the interior of the pub is located four miles away in a studio warehouse at Yorkshire Television. So when you see Jack Sugden enter the Woolpack for a drink, he actually has to travel another four miles back to the studio before he gets it.

The actors spend two or three days a week on set in the village shooting the exteriors; the rest of the time they are back in the warehouse where every internal setting has been constructed. Having said that, though, a few of the buildings in the village are also used internally, among them the vet's surgery and his home.

On the second day of our shoot, we broke for lunch and joined the rest of the cast for a bite to eat in their specially constructed on-site canteen. I was sitting beside Shirley Stelfox who plays the ill-tempered spinster, Edna Birch, in the series. In real life Shirley was married to another actor, Don Henderson, who starred alongside Leslie Grantham in the award-winning drama *The Paradise Club*. Sadly Don died in 1997.

Shirley was telling me how much Don had enjoyed his visit to the KELLY show when he appeared just a few months before his untimely death. As we chatted, we noticed quite a large crowd gathering round a television screen. Wondering what the attraction was, we made our way across. Peering over their heads, I could just make out images of a plane flying straight into a skyscraper. Odd, I thought. Why are people so interested in a film at this time of the day?

But, of course, I soon realised that this was not a film. This was actual footage of a real event. This was the al-Qaeda attack on the World Trade Center in New York. It was 11 September 2001.

The rest of the day was spent trying to get on with our filming schedule while at the same time not wanting to miss any of the incredulous happenings in New York. Later in the afternoon, when the crew was off recording general shots of the village, I was glued to a television screen in the vet's house. With me was

Dominic Brunt who plays vet Paddy Kirk and Steve Halliwell who plays Zak Dingle. We sat in silence, not quite believing what we were seeing.

But if the images of 9/11 weren't surreal enough in themselves, watching these events unfold in the company of Zak Dingle and Paddy Kirk was plain weird. So when someone asks me today where I was on 9/11, I have a pretty unusual answer for them, don't you think?

Chapter 10 ∽

THE GOOD, THE BAD, THE UGLY

I f I had a penny for every time I was asked, 'What was your favourite interview?' I would be a rich man. It's a question almost impossible to answer. I have a different response every time I'm asked, probably because my opinion changes in the light of life experiences and more probably because of the poor quality of my memory.

Over the seventeen years of KELLY I presented over 570 programmes, representing almost 1,000 hours of live air time. I guess I must have conducted upwards of 3,500 interviews in that time and introduced over 1,500 musical acts. I have interviewed all classes of people, from paupers to presidents.

But the most inspiring and caring man I ever met came from County Fermanagh. His name was Gordon Wilson. Gordon was the father of Marie Wilson, one of eleven people killed in the Enniskillen Remembrance Day cenotaph bombing by the Provisional IRA in 1987. In addition to those killed, sixty-three were injured, nine seriously, when the three-storey gable wall of St Michael's Reading Rooms crashed down burying part of the crowd in several feet of rubble.

The Provisional IRA admitted responsibility the following day. Terrorist campaigns seek to justify themselves with lofty claims, but what justification could the Provisional IRA have hoped to achieve from the bombing of a religious service in memory of the dead of past and present wars except profound disgust? It was an atrocity in the full meaning of the word. Marie Wilson was a young nurse who died, buried in the rubble with her father,

Gordon, who held her hand and spoke with her during her last moments of consciousness.

I had been introduced to Gordon before when I was invited to sit with him as a member of the Spirit of Enniskillen Bursary Awards Scheme, set up after the bombing. The scheme was established to enable young people from both communities to see life in other countries and especially to see how other countries and societies manage their community relations. So I had met Gordon on several occasions and I genuinely thought he was the nearest I would ever get to being in the presence of a saint. I admired him tremendously. At first, I must confess, I thought this man is too good to be true. But the more time I spent in his company, the more I realised that every word he spoke was the truth—a deeply impressive man.

Gordon's description of that ghastly deed in November 1987 echoed to the far corners of the world. He spoke of the last words between himself and his dying daughter in a famous BBC interview:

> She held my hand tightly and gripped me as hard as she could. She said, 'Daddy, I love you very much.' Those were her exact words to me, and those were the last words I ever heard her say. But I bear no ill will. I bear no grudge. Dirty sort of talk is not going to bring her back to life. She was a great wee lassie. She loved her profession. She was a pet. She's dead. She's in heaven and we shall meet again. I will pray for these men tonight and every night.

These words may be among the most remembered from the decades of conflict in Northern Ireland uttered by an ordinary but yet extraordinary man, a man who until that fateful day had quietly run a family drapery business in the High Street in Enniskillen in County Fermanagh.

He expressed forgiveness to his daughter's killers and pleaded with loyalists not to take revenge for her death. He was honoured throughout the island and deservedly so. Although a resident of

Northern Ireland and a Protestant, he was invited to become a member of Seanad Éireann, the Irish Senate, in 1993, on the nomination of the then Taoiseach Albert Reynolds.

On many occasions Gordon met with members of Sinn Féin. He also met once with representatives of the Provisional IRA, seeking the reasons for the Enniskillen Remembrance Day bombing, but failed to get a satisfactory answer. He also met several times with loyalist paramilitaries in an attempt to persuade them to abandon violence.

Sadly, Gordon died of a heart attack in 1995, aged 67, some months after his son David had been killed in a road accident.

Also in the studio that evening was Mrs Noreen Hill, wife of Ronnie Hill, former headmaster of Enniskillen High School, who had been in a coma ever since the attack. What had happened to her and her family was also horrendous. She of course was forever hoping that with the breaking of each day her husband would open his eyes and greet the world again. Of course all the people who were hurt that day, just a fraction of the 100,000 or so injured throughout the troubles, deserve to be remembered, but Ronnie Hill's injury was a form of living death. As his poor wife talked about that fateful day four years previously, she must have been hoping that the ordeal for both of them would end soon. She wasn't to know that her husband would remain comatose for thirteen long years. Ronnie died on 28 December 2000 without regaining consciousness. The death toll for Enniskillen should now read twelve.

———

GK: Before we start, can I say that you are looking very well. You seem to have lost a bit of weight.

Mo Mowlam: Shame I can't say the same about you.

———

During my first ever visit to Cape Town, South Africa, I interviewed another remarkable man who, though small in stature, is head and shoulders above most of humanity. Only very occasionally do you meet someone in whose presence you sense greatness. Yet this happened to me on meeting Desmond Tutu, the Anglican Archbishop Emeritus of Cape Town and former Nobel Peace prize winner. Standing a mere five foot nothing, I towered over him by almost a foot and a half! But I was enthralled by the way he spoke, his old-fashioned use of language, its precision, its eloquence, and the profound and civilised concepts he expressed with it.

I sat in almost dumb admiration of the man who had seen, had endured and had triumphed over so much in apartheid South Africa. I naturally talked to him about Northern Ireland and its problems and I remember him vividly saying to me, 'We have lived through our nightmare. You will too.'

His status world-wide was reinforced in my mind as we walked with him through the foyer of the hotel in Cape Town where we were interviewing him. We had difficulty progressing towards the lifts because of the number of people, on this occasion mostly American, who wanted his autograph. No rock star, no film idol, no head of a G8 nation could have received more respect and regard as did this man. It was astounding.

I interviewed him on subsequent occasions, most notably when I returned to South Africa in 2005 to make a programme about the Niall Mellon Township Trust, a unique Irish charity dedicated to providing homes to the impoverished communities in the townships of Cape Town. Both Archbishop Tutu and Nelson Mandela have given their backing to this wonderful charity which continues to grow from strength to strength.

Another person who looms large in my mind is the American astronaut, Colonel James Irwin.

Back in the summer of 1969, I was working as a counsellor in a children's residential summer camp in the Catskill Mountains outside New York. Along with a fellow American, we were responsible for looking after a dozen or so highly precocious 12-year olds twenty-four hours a day seven days a week for eight weeks.

My mum, Kathleen.

My beloved Nana.

Nana, Mum, my sister Kathleen and me.

Outside our home in Ardmeen Green, Downpatrick, with my niece Denise.

Grandad and Grandma Kelly.

At the party for my sister Patricia's engagement to Tommy Lundy, 1958. I was only ten years old at the time.

One of the very few photographs of the siblings together. (*From left*) Danny, Stella, Patricia, Kathleen and me.

'Big Lord Fontleroy', taken for *Lifestyle*. That's not a wig!

What it's all about: the 'eight' of us. Sarah, me, Claire and Helena.

Gloria Hunniford and me (*back left*) with our live St Patrick's Day programme in New York, 1980.

Gloria on one of her appearances on *Kelly*, 1991.

A younger me and an even younger Eamonn Holmes, counting our golf scores, 1992.

With Brian Kennedy on one of his early appearances on *Kelly*, 1993.

Secrets of the Street. With the late Lynn Perrie and Frank Carson in 1994.

In 2003, when Westlife were five!

Happier days. Kerry Katona and Bryan McFadden with three-month-old baby Molly, Christmas 2001.

With Neil and Christine Hamilton (*above*);
Stephen Fry (*right*); with Phil Coulter and
Moya Brennan (*below*).

Opposite page
A young Boyzone (*top*); with Daniel
O'Donnell at his home in Tenerife (*left
middle*); with Jackie Collins in her Hollywood
mansion (*right middle*); with Cliff Richard
(bottom).

Alex and George Best in 2000, on the memorable *Kelly* special.

Talking to Northern Ireland boxer Ray Close before his 1994 fight with Chris Eubank in Belfast. Looking on are Barney Eastwood and Don King.

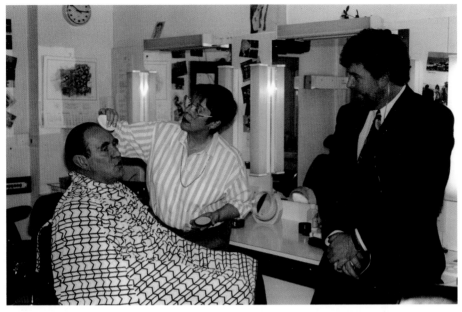

Secretary of State Peter Brooke in make-up before his appearance on *Kelly*, 1990.

A relaxed Secretary of State Mo Mowlam, 1998.

The wig exchange that never happened: May McFettridge, Mo Mowlam and TV Executive Phil Morrow, 1998.

In 2001, I was in the Woolpack in *Emmerdale* talking to Stan Richards who played Seth Armstrong, when the horrors of 9/11 struck.

With President Mary Robinson in Áras an Uachtaráin, 1995.

Enjoying the craic during rehearsals with The Dubliners and Phil Coulter, 1997.

With Michael Flatley in the Belfast Grand Opera House, 1996.

Honouring his personal commitment to me to play Belfast: Garth Brooks in 1995.

This was usually done through the medium of sports and social activities. These camps were unique to the States and still are to some extent, although I do believe they are now beginning to surface in Europe.

Those who remember the old Allen Sherman song, 'Hello Mudder, Hello Fadder', will understand something of camp life. The camp I was attached to was called Camp Sequoia. There are different levels of camps from charitable to very expensive. I happened to be in a very expensive one, run by a Jewish organisation solely for the sons and daughters of wealthy Jewish families.

The kids would arrive at camp in early July and remain throughout their entire eight-week summer vacation. Meanwhile their parents would take themselves off to Europe or some such place for their holiday, knowing that their kids were in safe hands.

After the first four weeks there was a Parents' Day, when the parents would return to check that everything was OK and then leave again to resume their holiday. By the time camp was over at the end of August, it was time for the children to go back to school. Who says the family unit is breaking down?

I have no idea how much parents paid to have their children at Camp Sequoia, but I do know that Parents' Day was financially very lucrative for me. As each father came up to thank us counsellors, they would reach forward for a handshake. And that's when the little surprise happened! Clutched in the parent's hand was a $50 note. As you shook his hand the note was quietly placed in your palm. Nothing was said, just a nod and a smile. Why they couldn't give the money to us in an envelope I'll never know, but it was a little ritual that afforded me the opportunity to stay on in America when camp was over to have a good look around for a week or so. Twelve $50 notes was $600, a fortune to a poor student in 1969.

As a result, I had a wonderful summer and also gained valuable experience working with young people that would stand me in good stead when I finally qualified as a teacher the following year.

On 20 July 1969, right in the middle of my time in the camp, an event occurred that would captivate my imagination for evermore. As part of the activities of that day, the entire camp was assembled in a large hall to watch live on television one of the greatest achievements of mankind in the last century.

Four days earlier, on 16 July, Apollo 11 blasted off on its three-day trip to the moon. At precisely 4.18 EST on 20 July—which because of the time difference was 21 July here—Neil Armstrong and Buzz Aldrin became the first humans to set foot on the moon while Michael Collins continued to orbit overhead in the lunar command module. It was a thrilling experience made all the more intense because here I was in New York surrounded by 400 Americans dripping with pride at their nation's achievement.

I too got totally caught up in the moment and can vividly remember NASA's final instructions:

'Eagle . . . you're go for landing.'

'Roger . . . picking up some dust . . . big shadow . . . contact light . . . OK, engine stopped.'

'Tranquillity Base here. The Eagle has landed.'

By the time Neil Armstrong stepped out on to the lunar surface with the words, 'One small step for man; one giant leap for mankind', well, I was almost ready to change my citizenship, such was the sense of pride among the assembled masses.

Since that day I have been fascinated by space exploration. So you can imagine my delight when American astronaut Col James Irwin was booked on the programme. He and fellow astronaut David Scott were on the Apollo 15 mission in 1971 and became the seventh and eighth men to walk on the moon's surface. They were the first to use the battery-powered lunar buggy to collect rock and soil samples over a wide area of the moon.

I was thrilled to sit opposite him in a studio in Belfast and to have the opportunity to chat to one of only twelve men in the entire history of humankind ever to have visited another planet. What made Irwin even more intriguing for a Northern Ireland audience was that he was an evangelical Christian. There were therefore many with similar beliefs in the KELLY audience.

We talked of religion and Northern Ireland. From space, he told me, Northern Ireland was a speck. And yet people on this speck were killing each other all because of a border which was utterly invisible from space. In the grand scheme of things, our problems here seemed so senseless.

He was also an inspiration to people who suffered head injuries. As a US Air Force colonel with war experience, he had thousands of hours' experience flying combat aircraft. Ten years before his Apollo mission, his plane crashed on a routine training mission, leaving him with two broken legs, a broken jaw and concussion that wiped out his memory. It required extensive psychiatric treatment and hypnosis to restore his memory and enable him to resume flying, which he managed some fourteen months later. While on the moon, he experienced a brief irregular heart rhythm, probably the result of extreme fatigue. Sadly, less than two years later, at the age of 43, he suffered a heart attack while playing handball, and after that he had a history of heart problems. It was a heart attack that eventually killed him at the age of 61 in 1991 only months after I had interviewed him.

In sharp contrast, certain other interviews stick out in my mind for very different reasons altogether. Take, for example, Oliver Reed, Alex Higgins and Reg Presley, lead singer with the Troggs. Now there's a threesome to conjure with.

Together they had recorded a version of the old classic Troggs hit, 'Wild Thing', so we thought it would be fun and just a little *risqué* to have them perform it on the show. We had called all three for rehearsal in the afternoon, but of course Alex didn't turn up. It was all a bit of a mess. But because it was a full mime—they wouldn't really be singing, just miming the words—we thought we would risk going ahead with it anyway on the show.

Reed and a few of his mates had begun drinking during the course of the afternoon, so naturally he arrived for the show in high spirits. Alex too must have been on the soup elsewhere because when he eventually turned up for the programme he was looking the worse for wear. Reg wasn't too bad. An hour before the show, all three were in the green room knocking back the drink. I know we shouldn't have allowed it, but you try telling Oliver Reed and Alex Higgins that the bar was closed!

For the performance the three lads donned leather bomber jackets and looked every inch the part of rockers. But there the similarity with pop stars ended. Alex was so drunk he couldn't remember the words and gave up even trying halfway through the song. Reed tried hard, swaggering and pointing, but he was bluffing no one. Again Reg wasn't too bad. After the débâcle of 'Wild Thing', all three came over for a chat.

Reed of course was an experienced television performer, drunk or sober, and so he dominated the chat. At times he looked at me as if he was about to hit me and followed that almost immediately with a wry smile. He was unnerving to chat to and totally unpredictable. Alex, on the other hand, hardly spoke. In fact he almost nodded off at one stage until Reed dug him in the ribs with his elbow shouting, 'Isn't that right, Alex?'

Alex woke with a start and attempted to join in the chat. Reg was twittering on about UFOS. Apparently he's a leading expert in the field and has some unique footage of alien aircraft. All very interesting to a point I'm sure, but it was fast dawning on all of us that this conversation was going nowhere. Anne, the floor manager, was giving me the '30 seconds to go' signal when Reed spotted her. Of course he knew what the sign meant so in true style and living up to his controversial reputation, he grabbed Alex by the hand and bawled, 'Come on, Alex. I've had enough of this crap. Let's go for a drink.'

And with that, he stormed off the set with Alex and Reg in tow. My immediate reaction was one of relief, because I wasn't sure how I was going to bring the interview tidily to an end anyway. But as I read the link into the next item, a terrible thought crept into my mind. What happens if they come storming back? Reed was unlikely to leave it there. But then I remembered we had engaged a couple of big props guys for duty on the studio floor in case of such a scenario. In the end it all fizzled out and the three boys headed off into the centre of Belfast in search of more fun— and drink, presumably.

Needless to say, alcohol and television appearances don't mix, a fact graphically illustrated when George Best gave that now notorious interview on the *Wogan* show. Up until then we had been providing guests with all kinds of alcohol, should they wish it, before the show. However, after George's performance, we reviewed our position and from then on only offered wine. We couldn't however guarantee that a guest wouldn't turn up slightly inebriated having drunk elsewhere. I remember Lynne Perrie, the actress who played Ivy Tilsley in *Coronation Street*. Lynne had a reputation for being over-fond of the booze and tranquillisers. In fact it was this addiction that ultimately led to her being sacked from the *Street*. We had her booked to appear on KELLY just after she had been sacked by Granada.

———

George Best: Unfortunately the FA*—we know what they're like.*

GK: What?

GB: Well, we know what FA *stands for ...*

———

Rather than risk her turning up drunk for the programme, we decided to send one of our researchers, Patricia Diamond, over to Manchester to baby-sit Lynne. Patricia flew out on Friday morning under strict instructions not to leave Lynne's side all day and to make sure she arrived in Belfast that night sober.

At one point in the afternoon, Patricia phoned me at the office with an update. In whispered tones she said, 'Hi Gerry. I'm at Lynne's house at the minute. She's upstairs having a shower. Now I can promise you she hasn't had a drink all day. I haven't let her out of my sight. But I have noticed that every time she goes to the loo she comes back looking just a little bit more glazed. I can't smell drink off her so I don't know what's happening.'

'Perhaps its pills,' I suggested.

'I don't think so,' Patricia says. 'I've been through her handbag while she was in the shower and I can't find anything.'

I don't think I've ever laughed so much. Images of Patricia rifling through Lynne Perrie's handbag were just too much. Talk about dedication to the job! When I met Lynne that night, I saw what Patricia was talking about. Let's just say she was in good form!

———

GK: Michael Jackson said one time that the Osmond name is not working, that you should forget the Osmond name.

Donny Osmond: He advised me to change my name. I advised him to change his clothes. I think he misunderstood me. He changed his nose.

———

These are just a few brief examples of the breadth of stories we covered on KELLY. Often we would have a particularly emotional story followed by something completely light-hearted and that, from a presenter's point of view, created its own problems—how to switch from empathising almost in a tearful way with one guest to suddenly talking to the latest heart-throb or sex siren to hit our screens. The programme was changing gear constantly. The mood was ebbing and flowing and that meant I had to change my approach without causing back-to-back interviews to jar. Good use of a commercial break or a music act to serve as a buffer or to punctuate the mood often solved the dilemma. I was also aware that TV commercials tend to be brash, fast moving and slightly louder than the programmes in which they are contained. So returning from such a break and going straight to a heavy or emotive interview tended to give the viewer, however subliminally, the impression that the programme was of a much slower, more laborious pace, something of an anticlimax, a bit of a downer. On those occasions, when we came back on air I would take a few moments with the audience and tell a little story or have a joke with them. This served to regulate the pace again for the viewer before going on to the next item. Having said that though, on a personal and professional level I never had any trouble laughing with one interviewee and crying with the next. After all it's what we all do in ordinary life on a daily basis.

I didn't want my own persona to change dramatically from my TV persona. Having met me, the biggest compliment anyone could pay me is to say that I am much the same person off camera as I am on it. Obviously the rarefied atmosphere of a television studio is somewhat different to real life. A studio interview with cameras watching your every move is not an ordinary conversation. But that is the challenge of a chat show host, to make an artificial situation look completely natural, to make an interview sound like two people chatting in a room.

I don't believe in having two Gerry Kellys, one for the camera and one for my personal life. I always believed that the nearest I could get on camera to my own everyday personality, the better the interviews would be. Unlike another famous guest of mine, Garth Brooks. During interviews, Garth would talk about Garth the performer as if he were another person totally. But more about him and others later.

| ORANGE AND GREEN

Bomb scares and death threats aside, the *KELLY* show never deliberately invited politics or political opinion into the programme. Throughout the 1980s and 90s the Northern Ireland public lived on a diet of news and current affairs detailing the latest atrocity perpetrated on a war-weary society. Reports on the latest killings or bombings were repeated on the hour, every hour, on both radio and television, making for a very depressing view of Northern Ireland indeed. No wonder visitors were frightened to come here.

As we saw it, our role at the end of a week was to provide some light-hearted relief, a break from the constant bombardment of bad news and an opportunity to show the other side of life in the province. What we didn't need was for some outsider to infer that *KELLY* had some kind of hidden agenda, that we used some form of religious or political bias when choosing our guests.

But that's what happened in the shape of no less a person than the deputy leader of the Unionist Party at the time, John Taylor MP, now the Right Honourable the Lord Kilclooney. In an article in the *Belfast Telegraph* he insinuated that the *KELLY* show was running an increasingly nationalist agenda. How utterly ridiculous, but his comments hurt the *KELLY* team. If Mr Taylor could have seen the groundwork carried out by the team each week in preparation for a Friday night show, he might have thought twice before opening his mouth.

Our week started on a Monday, clearing up some leftover business from the previous Friday and tentatively suggesting guests for the following Friday. On Tuesday mornings we held our first meeting with the whole team. This was when the bones of the show were put together. Researchers would come up with their suggestions as to who was available, who was suitable and who we should be chasing for the programme. These were detailed meetings and the researchers had to be on the ball. They were under huge pressure to come up with ideas and needed to have created for themselves a network of contacts and telephone numbers should the producer and I decide to run with one of their stories. When the final decisions were made, the team had until Thursday lunchtime to book the guests, have a chat with them before writing their research notes for me and organise their travel and hotel accommodation.

Come Thursday we would all sit down together and go through their notes, guest by guest, in minute detail. Following that, I spent all Thursday night writing introductions and questions for each interview. Nothing was left to chance. Very often I would ask a researcher how will such-and-such answer this question? There could be two or three possible ways in which the guest might respond and this I needed to know. I never wanted to be left exposed live on air. If they answered one way, I would have a series of questions as a follow-up. If they answered another way, once again I would be prepared for that alternative. So the initial conversation a researcher had with a guest had to be detailed yet broad enough to cover all angles. I could not afford to have an interviewee tell me something live on air that I had not anticipated. Of course, in the normal run of a conversation something new would come up that just couldn't have been foreseen. That was OK, but on the big questions, the kernel of the interview, researchers had to get it right. Sloppy research was the one thing sure to annoy me.

As you can see, the role of the researcher was vital. They had no time to dawdle and they certainly had no time, or even the inclination, to check a person's political or religious affiliations. Believe me, they had enough to worry about without that. Anyway, think about it for a minute. Let's face facts. KELLY was not the natural first choice for guests. Big names always wanted to do national television first. The *Late Late Show* was on a national TV station and of course it was based in Dublin, a city that enjoyed a real fashionable status. Parkinson, Jonathon Ross and so on also offered national exposure. But we, a regional show based in scary Belfast, were dipping into that selfsame well of guests as they were. Every week we were in there fighting with the big boys.

How ludicrous it would have been therefore if our researchers, having secured a guest in the face of all this competition, only confirmed his appearance if he was a Catholic. For John Taylor to have accused us of some form of political or religious discrimination was a gross and perverse inaccuracy. When a newspaper contacted me, I dismissed the claims as rubbish, and said they were not worthy of comment.

Nevertheless Taylor's remarks did harm us and I remember being somewhat angry with UTV for not entering the fray and defending the programme as publicly as it had been attacked. I'm still irate to this day at the accusation. However, management thought that the better strategy was to ignore Taylor's letter and let its sentiments wither away, as another politician once famously coined it, without the oxygen of publicity. The slur was to stick for many years.

I remember a former Mayor of Derry City Council presenting me with the city's Coat of Arms. In one corner of the crest is a skeleton. I asked what it signified and he jokingly replied, 'Oh that's a Protestant waiting for a ticket for the KELLY show.' Humorous though his answer was, I still felt a little pang of anger, not at him obviously, but at the fact that a few thoughtless words written years previously still reverberated around the province.

I always felt we should have faced the initial criticism head on and invited Taylor on to the programme to defend his stance. Regretfully, we didn't. However, we did invite other politicians, though not to talk about their political beliefs. For example, as each Secretary of State arrived, they received an invitation to appear. Peter Brooke, Patrick Mayhew, John Reid, Paul Murphy, Mo Mowlam and Peter Hain all accepted.

You have to remember these were politicians elected in another part of the United Kingdom but with the power to govern the people of Northern Ireland. We knew very little about them other than their political affiliation to either the Conservative or Labour Party. They flew in and flew out, usually heading back to their homes and constituencies at the weekends. The only time we heard them speak was on news or current affairs programmes condemning the most recent bombings or explaining new strictures to be set in place. It was time we learned a bit more. What kind of people were they? What makes them tick? That was the line we adopted, an attempt to put a human face and character on our lords and masters.

Of all the Secretaries of State, the one who stood out for me was undoubtedly Mo Mowlam. Having been a member of the Labour Party since 1969, Mo was elected Labour MP for Redcar, north Yorkshire, in 1987. It was a position she held for fourteen years until she stepped down from parliament in 2001. Tony Blair once described her as 'one of the most remarkable and colourful personalities ever to enter British politics', though Mo was to fall out with him over her opposition to the Iraq War. A few weeks before the May 1997 general election, she was diagnosed with a benign brain tumour and had to undergo radiotherapy and steroid treatment. As a result she gained weight and lost her hair but tried desperately not to let it affect her work.

For her first appearance on *KELLY* she was wearing a wig due to the effects of her illness. Her condition was not common knowledge in the early days and when she came to my studio it was only beginning to filter through to the public that she was suffering from a tumour. I first met her in the UTV make-up room. There she was, sitting on a chair, completely bald! Until that moment I hadn't known that she was bald and wore a wig in public. I confess I was taken aback. I hope I didn't show it too much. As it was, Mo couldn't have cared less what people thought. In fact I think she rather enjoyed seeing the surprise and shock on people's faces when they saw her without the hair. Just then, John Linehan came into make-up, preparing to change into May McFettridge for his warm-up spot. He too saw her bald head and couldn't resist some witty comment. John of course knows no fear. He'll have a go at anyone, Secretary of State or not. Mo laughed uproariously and the two of them immediately sparked off each other.

John then produced his May McFettridge wig and suggested that he and Mo swap wigs, an idea she thought was a great joke. She even wanted a photograph taken of the swap. It was at this point that the apprehensive Northern Ireland Office 'minders' stepped in, voicing their concern that this kind of frivolity might not be appropriate for the Secretary of State. So that unique photograph was never taken, which I feel sad about because it would have conveyed the fun that Mo grasped from life even in the face of her illness. It would have been a photographic testimony of her remarkable courage.

However, in defence of Mo's Northern Ireland Office minders in refusing to allow the photograph, there had been a previous horror experience involving a former Conservative Secretary of State and a chat show. What happened was every public relations person's nightmare.

On 17 January 1992 Peter Brooke agreed to appear on the *Late Late*. It was of course a live performance and the *Late Late* was doing exactly the same as *KELLY* with politicians. Gay Byrne was interviewing him as Peter Brooke, the person, rather than Peter Brooke, the politician. He was prevailed upon to sing 'My Darling Clementine' and did so with enthusiasm and enjoyment. Nothing wrong with that in isolation, but events intervened.

Earlier in the evening an IRA landmine had been detonated under a minibus at Teebane crossroads between Cookstown and Omagh, Co. Tyrone, killing eight Protestant workmen who had been working at a military base near by. They were travelling home when the attack occurred. It was by any yardstick a horrific multiple murder and stands out as one of the worst atrocities in the history of the troubles. There was a howl of protest and anguish from the Protestant and unionist community accusing the Secretary of State of gross insensitivity in agreeing to sing light-heartedly on the show in the immediate aftermath of the carnage. The damage to Mr Brooke's credibility had been major, even prompting him to offer his resignation. It wasn't accepted, but what seemed at the time a piece of uncomplicated amusement effectively ended this Secretary of State's tenure of office.

So RTÉ's *Late Late Show* loomed large in the history and collective memory of the NIO public relations people. It is probably now branded into the hide of every political office and parallel press office that a piece of fun in a television studio has the capacity to backfire spectacularly. Had they been asked, Mo's minders could not have explained how a bit of fun like a wig exchange could harm the Secretary of State, except to say that back in 1992 Brooke's minders had thought there was no harm in a verse or two of a song.

———

GK: You were big mates with Mo Mowlam.

Dawn French: Still am. I was over in Hillsborough. It was fantastic.

GK: How do you know her?

DF: Er ... ehm ... eerr ...

Jennifer Saunders: She doesn't know her. She gate-crashed.

DF: Oh yes—a friend introduced us. And she asked us to Hillsborough Castle.

JS: Are you sure she didn't think you were Caroline Quentin (of Men Behaving Badly *and* Jonathan Creek*).*

DF: No, I think she mistook me for Meg Ryan. A lot of people do.

———

But such strictures were never going to completely envelop Mo Mowlam. This woman was never going to be conventional or predisposed to stand on her dignity. She bounded into the studio and sat on the couch with her legs tucked under her. In all the seventeen years of KELLY, I believe she was the only interviewee ever to do that, certainly the only politician, and most definitely the only Secretary of State.

I told her that on air and she beamed. I looked at her, listened to her and thought, my God, this is a breath of fresh air. We had interviewed secretaries of state in the past who proved very conventional, staid even, but not this woman. Mo Mowlam's whole approach was to wrong-foot people. She reportedly called Martin McGuinness of Sinn Féin 'babe' during meetings. Her handling of the Drumcree marching dispute inevitably caused controversy across both communities, but some of her important risky gambles paid off. In 1998 she made an astonishing visit to the Maze Prison to talk to loyalist and republican prisoners. It produced political results. She succeeded in persuading loyalist inmates to give the talks process another chance. I'm aware that many unionists believed she was biased against them and they disapproved of her very unorthodox behaviour such as the visit to the Maze. They also disliked her tendency to come across as much more touchy-feely than previous holders of the office, who were, it could be said, all men who aren't naturally touchy-feely anyway. In my book, she deserves to be remembered in Northern Ireland every time we think of the peace we now have, however flawed it might be.

She last appeared on KELLY on 10 May 2002, shortly after the publication of her political memoirs, *Momentum*. By this time she was really beginning to look unwell. Her speech was slurred and her movements uneasy. Her temper was just a little frayed, finding fault with our researchers over trivial things. In the studio, however, you could still see that feistiness and devilment in her eyes. That night she wrote in my copy of her book 'To Gerry—a true friend.'

I treasure that book. Mo died on 19 August 2005, aged 55.

GK: How do you hope history will look upon you and your time in Northern Ireland?

Mo Mowlam: That I was somebody who helped the peace process along, that I worked with people across the board, that I worked with the community. This would only work if the people in Northern Ireland were for it ... if they enjoy the changes, the possibility of any party going back is very low.

I was always a little wary of inviting local politicians on to the programme. Much as I would have loved to, I knew we would have been heavily criticised for not talking politics. So it wasn't really a starter to invite Martin McGuinness of Sinn Féin on to the programme and talk about his love of Derry City football team without mentioning his involvement with the IRA. Or Peter Robinson from the DUP to drool over his passion for Japanese Koi fish without talking about his previous involvement in the Ulster Resistance Movement.

But when an opportunity did arise to talk to politicians about something else, we always took it. As early as 1992 we asked two of the founder members of the SDLP, Gerry Fitt and Paddy Devlin, to come on the show, two old warriors coming to the end of their political lives. They reminisced about their common trade union background and the byways their political paths had taken them. I remember looking at these two venerable men who had gone through so much and seen so much and thinking there goes the end of an era. I watched them departing the studio and knew that a new chapter was about to be written, based partly on what the two of them had achieved. They had been old friends and at the same time old rivals, and now they were just two old men. It was a time for the new boys and I couldn't help feeling just a

moment of sadness, because I knew it was the end of something—whatever it was.

One of the new breed was David Ervine of the PUP who came
to our attention in 1994. My producer at the time, Phillip Kampf,
asked me if I had heard of him and I replied, 'Very little.' We both
agreed that Ervine seemed to be articulating a new voice for loy-
alism, saying things in ways that had not been heard before. We
arranged an exploratory meeting with him in the Europa Hotel to
see what he would be like as a guest on the programme, a
completely informal gathering over a few pints of Guinness—
David loved his pint. That meeting stands out in my memory
because Ervine was an extraordinary person and for me, listening
to him for the first time, he represented a complete revelation. He
was naturally expounding a very unionist point of view but was
explaining its values and traditions in a manner that was very
refreshing. I distinctly remember thinking that this man will most
definitely be part of the future. So at the beginning of November
1994 we invited him on to KELLY. It was one of the first times
David was exposed to a mass audience.

His appearance caused quite a stir. As it turned out, I became
very friendly with David and we were to have many a drink
together over the years. I particularly remember a night in Dublin
when both of us happened to be at the same function. We slipped
away and spent the rest of the evening together discussing mostly
politics. We were in a public place and the Dubliners recognised
him, many going out of their way to welcome him. It was clear
from the Dublin street reaction to him that his message was being
well received in other parts of the island.

I was in New York when I received news of David's very sudden
and untimely death in January 2007 at the age of 53. Tony Blair
said he was a man who played a major part in trying to bring
peace to the North over the last decade, whatever his past. Bertie
Ahern described him as courageous and articulate. But he was
best summed up by his own brother Brian who said: 'David had
the guts and the courage to climb out of the trenches, meet the
enemy in no-man's land and play ball with them.'

In private, David Ervine was quite a guy, great company, and I think Northern Ireland will miss him for some time to come. I'm very pleased we put him on *KELLY* when we did.

Of course we had Seamus Mallon SDLP and David Trimble UUP as guests after the announcement of the first executive in Stormont when they became First and Deputy First Minister after the Good Friday Agreement. But it was another prominent peace builder in Northern Ireland who once rounded on me with some force after an interview I did on RTÉ.

I had been invited to RTÉ's radio studios in Dublin to do an interview with veteran broadcaster Brendan Balfe. In the course of talking about life in Northern Ireland, I had sounded off rather strongly about our politicians, describing them as happy to take their salaries but appearing not to be doing very much to carry things forward to try to end what was happening. They merely played party politics, I argued. They were bogged down in intransigence, unwilling to move whether they were Orange or Green. The remarks reflected a personal feeling I had long held that Northern politicians were always a step behind the thinking of the people through being too timid, preferring to follow the slowest moving elements of their electorate instead of undertaking the responsibilities of leadership and providing direction.

As it happened, John Hume was coming into the studios just as I was leaving. He drew me aside. He told me that he had been listening to what I had been saying on his car radio on his way to Dublin and took strong exception. He said that he himself—and he could only speak for himself—was dedicated to what he was doing, that he was not a fly-by-night politician, that he was in it for the long haul. He was an angry and offended man on behalf of all politicians. When he had finished tearing strips off me, I thought long and hard. His words made me feel somewhat guilty because I began to recognise that what I had said in the studio was painting with a broad brush. The blanket condemnation of all politicians, while excusable as an expression of the utter frustration shared by many in the province, did not justifiably apply across the board to all Northern Ireland politicians. In truth, I could see that there were indeed people in politics like John Hume who were sincere and hard working, a fact recognised by his award of a Nobel Peace Laureate shared with David Trimble.

In some ways I regret our early decision not to invite politicians on to the programme to account for their stewardship. After all, it could be argued that if we prided ourselves on reflecting the society we lived in, we left a gaping hole by not taking our political representatives to task. I also thought that without some reflection of politics, the full picture was incomplete. It used to annoy me considerably that Ian Paisley and Gerry Adams could trot off down to Dublin to be interviewed. But I also knew that if KELLY tried that, we would be accused of bias and/or comforting the harbingers of violence. That was the reality for us.

On only one occasion did I do what could be described as a purely political interview. By the end of 2005, life in Northern Ireland was virtually trouble free. People were confident about the future and the economy was on the up and up. A final settlement was within our grasp and appeared to be solely in the hands of Sinn Féin and the DUP. We decided to invite both leaders, Gerry Adams and Ian Paisley, to come on the show, on separate nights, to discuss the way forward. We made it clear we didn't want to talk about the past, simply how were they going to lead us into the future.

The invitation went out to their respective PR people and we waited for an answer. One week later we had an agreement with Sinn Féin that Gerry Adams would do the programme first. The DUP hesitated, wanting to hear what Adams had to say before committing their leader to the show.

On 28 October 2005, Gerry Adams appeared on KELLY and in a hard-hitting interview, he said something that was never said before, something that everyone wanted to hear but yet never expected to hear from his lips.

———

Former England striker Paul Gascoigne:

I remember one time on a Friday night I couldn't sleep thinking about the game on Saturday and I had about four bottles of wine, twelve sleeping tablets. I woke up at six in the morning and finished off the wine. Then I woke up at nine and had a triple brandy and then I went to the game. I went out and got Man of the Match three times.

———

Chapter 12 ～

| THE WAR IS OVER

Politically, 2005 was a momentous year for Northern Ireland. In the general election of May that year, Ian Paisley's Democratic Unionist Party won nine seats, half of the Northern Ireland total. The Ulster Unionist Party lost five of their six seats, which prompted their leader David Trimble's resignation following his own personal defeat at the polls.

On the republican side, Sinn Féin came second overall both in terms of seats and votes won, their best performance ever at a general election. The SDLP remained unchanged. All of a sudden the two parties on opposing ends of the political spectrum were thrust centre stage and became key to any political settlement.

Two months later, the IRA formally ordered an end to its armed campaign and said it would pursue exclusively peaceful means. It was becoming increasingly obvious that if Northern Ireland was to progress and pull itself out of the quagmire of over thirty murderous years, it's two biggest sworn enemies, namely Gerry Adams of Sinn Féin and Ian Paisley of the DUP, would somehow have to come together.

It was with this background that in October 2005, the *KELLY* show decided to break with its long-standing ethos of a politics-free zone and invite both leaders on.

Our agenda was very clear. We wanted both Adams and Paisley to appear on separate weeks. We had no wish to have them together, knowing that any attempt at an interview under such circumstances would only degenerate into the usual series of recriminations that we had all grown so sick of over the years. The thrust of the interview would not be what had happened in the past but what plans each party had to lead us into a new Northern Ireland and, considering their diametrically opposed views, how they could possibly ever work together.

We pitched the proposal to the PR departments of both parties and waited. Initially signs were good. Both came back to say that in principle they would agree, but would have to consult with their leaders personally.

Sinn Féin were the first to respond. Yes, Gerry Adams would appear and a date was fixed, Friday, 28 October. We relayed this message to the DUP boys, fully expecting they would respond positively and commit their leader to the following week. Again we waited . . . and waited.

At one stage we were told that Mr Paisley could not make it on the night in question as he had another engagement. We then offered an alternative date. Another week passed. Finally we were told that Mr Paisley would wait and see what Mr Adams had to say.

It was a major blow to our plans. Everything in Northern Ireland had to be a balancing act. We now had a dilemma. Should we give Sinn Féin sole access to the programme if the DUP refused to participate—which of course they wouldn't admit to. Any good political spin doctor would simply say that Mr Paisley was unavailable on the nights in question because of his huge work commitments. After all, you can't expect politicians to drop everything just because a TV programme wants them.

So we had a decision to make. If we ran with only one aspect of the overall picture, we would be open to accusations of discrimination and bias, a position that would completely distort our good intentions and nullify any real meaning to the debate. We thought long and hard over what we should do and in the end decided to go ahead with the Adams interview. At the same time, we would keep pressing the DUP in the hope that they would come round to the idea.

We repeatedly emphasised that this was not a news or a current affairs programme. Nor would it be a news or a current affairs-type interview. This was an opportunity for both political parties to talk to a wide cross-section of the Northern Ireland public. Ample time would be given for the leaders to expound and expand their political objectives, unlike the two-minute sound bite they were normally afforded on the evening news bulletins. I would be asking clear, non-aggressive questions. There would be no sabotage. We wouldn't be taking phone calls; nor would we be allowing any derogatory remarks from the studio audience. There would be no hidden agenda, no angles, no curve ball questions. Just tell us, gentlemen, what we all want to know. Now that the killings have stopped, how do you intend to lead us into the future? We couldn't have painted a more positive picture of what we hoped the two interviews together would achieve.

We informed the DUP when Gerry Adams would be appearing and told them we would be contacting them first thing the following Monday to see if they had changed their mind.

Naturally the interview with Gerry Adams worried me. I had never met the man before, didn't particularly like him and certainly did not agree with his politics of 'taking power in Ireland with an Armalite in one hand and a ballot paper in the other'. And yet I wanted to believe him. I wanted to believe that the IRA had taken the guns out of politics for good and that they were really committed to a peaceful way forward.

It certainly wasn't going to be an easy interview for many reasons. For a start I had never done an interview before that was solely about politics. Not only would the DUP be interested in my approach, but I also knew that every member of UTV's newsroom would have more than a passing curiosity about the interview. Some, I know, felt that *KELLY* was not the right vehicle for such a debate and that I wasn't the right person to be doing it. I should leave the hard news stories to them, seasoned news journos who knew the political nuances and were used to the cut and thrust of political interviewing. How could Gerry Kelly, a mere chat show host, possibly challenge such a controversial figure in a live debate?

But, you know, I couldn't have cared less what they thought. I knew exactly how I would approach the interview. Over the years I had earned a reputation for being able to gain the trust of interviewees especially when dealing with sensitive, personal issues. As a result they would often open up that little bit more, knowing that we would not sensationalise or ridicule what they were saying. This was a two-way conversation, not an aggressive inquisition. If I was to steer Gerry Adams away from his customary set of Sinn Féin stock answers to practically every question, I would have to engage him in real conversation. The questions would have to be succinct and to the point and at the same time reflect what the man in the street wanted to know. Having lived and worked in Northern Ireland all my life, I had a fair idea of what needed to be asked and answered.

Adams though was a seasoned campaigner, well used to tackling even the most antagonistic of questions. He wouldn't be forced into saying something he would later regret. He was measured in his answers and rarely lost his temper. At no stage did his press people ask for my list of questions, which slightly surprised me. They seemed happy to know just the general thrust of the interview and were not particularly interested in the specifics.

But Sinn Féin knew the significance of this interview. They were aware that their leader would be speaking to a different audience, that this would be a unique opportunity to get their message across to people who were not necessarily avid followers of current affairs.

I was surprised the DUP didn't also see the potential, from their point of view, of taking part. Still, we had time to work on them.

On the programme that night we would have our usual mix of guests. Chef Gary Rhodes was there, fresh from his culinary success in *Hell's Kitchen*. A rare appearance was scheduled from singer Rick Astley who had virtually disappeared from the pop scene after huge success in the early 1990s. We also had the Magee family from Larne whose son Philip was among the last ten contestants in the *X Factor* that year. So, along with our usual competitions and phone calls, this was the environment into which we would set Gerry Adams.

Adams arrived at Havelock House fifteen minutes before he was due to go on. The programme had already started so I didn't have a chance to speak to him beforehand. During the commercial break before introducing him, I spoke to the audience and told them who my next guest was. I also suggested that if anyone felt uncomfortable with that, they could leave the studio for the next twenty minutes or so and return towards the end of the programme. I didn't want anyone walking out live on air, so if the presence of Mr Adams would cause offence to anyone, now was the time to leave. No one left.

By way of introduction to Gerry Adams, I outlined our plan to interview both him and Ian Paisley about the way forward. I explained that we would not be going over old ground, that the interview was about now and the future and we would not be going down the whole 'whataboutery' route. I also explained that the DUP had not as yet given a definitive answer to Ian Paisley's involvement, but we were hopeful that he too would be appearing in the coming weeks.

Adams appeared cool but friendly, willing to answer any question put to him. I'll not repeat the whole interview in these pages except to highlight his response to one particular question—his answer would ultimately have far-reaching political significance.

He finished answering one question with the words, 'I don't know what else I can do to help.' To which I replied: 'I know what you can do to help, Mr Adams. If you said here and now that the war is over, that would be a huge help.'

Not expecting more than his usual dismissal of this question when asked on countless other occasions, I was gobsmacked when he answered. 'The war is obviously over.' Almost not believing my ears, I paused for a few seconds, taking in what the leader of Sinn Féin and the alleged leader of the IRA Army Council had just said. 'The war was over'—the very words that unionists and political journalists alike had been demanding from Gerry Adams for over a decade.

To have said it on KELLY was deliberate. I don't believe the words just slipped out accidentally. Most things that happen in Northern Ireland are well choreographed. I can only assume that Sinn Féin had agreed to this being said and at that particular time. Why he chose my programme to say it, I do not know.

Of course it was major news throughout Ireland and America. The *Belfast Telegraph* led their Saturday night edition with the banner headline, 'The War is Over.' Political parties debated the Adams statement and discussed its significance. It was surely another step towards ultimate peace in the province.

On a personal level, I was pleased that we had the bottle to have ventured into this area and was delighted with the general response to the interview. We silenced a few of our critics that night.

My favourite article about the programme, which included a few barbed comments but which overall made me smile, was written by the *Belfast Telegraph*'s feature writer Gail Walker under this headline:

ADAMS ON THE *KELLY* SHOW:
JUST LIKE BEING MUGGED BY YOUR GRANNY

If the latest *KELLY* show was anything to go by, Gerry Kelly has decided he has nothing left to lose and is going to spend his last series just slapping people about the face. His interview with Gerry Adams was so cold and clinical, it was like watching Basil Brush come out with a mouthful of expletives. It was an interview between a man of extraordinary menace who appeared by his ominous silences and cynical grin to be capable of extreme acts . . . and Gerry Adams.

Kelly's handling of Adams was forensic and funny. He asked questions Adams had never been asked, like who does he talk to when he talks to the IRA? And was there any single occasion over the years when Adams could have made just one phone call and averted a slaughter? These are things conventional political interviewers tend to steer clear of. It's almost as if it would be rude to ask.

Apparently Kelly is about to get a new UTV series of longer half-hour chats with people—and that can only be a good thing. Just let the biggest and shiniest suit in the business loose on the people he seems to like least. Drop the endless procession of C-list celebs with books to plug . . . and bring on Ulster's grittiest politicos.

The great thing about last week's show was that Adams was a man who turned up expecting a cup of tea and a chat about Falls memories and ended up getting mugged by his granny. More please.

––––

Political correspondent John Sergeant referring to Margaret Thatcher and her Cabinet:

There was that marvellous Spitting Image *sketch where they're all in a restaurant and she says, 'I'll be having steak.' And the waiter asks, 'What about the vegetables?'*

'They'll be having steak too.'

––––

True to our word, we contacted the DUP the following Monday to see if Paisley would now enter the fray and make his vitally important contribution to the way forward by appearing within the next few weeks. Sadly, he declined. I genuinely regretted the DUP decision and couldn't understand what they thought they would lose by Paisley's appearance.

Still, who would have thought that within eighteen months of that interview a new Northern Ireland Assembly would be up and running led jointly by two life-long enemies, Ian Paisley and Martin McGuinness, affectionately known in these parts as the Chuckle Brothers.

Sometimes fact is indeed stranger than fiction.

Chapter 13 ～

ABSENT FRIENDS

One of the biggest coups in the seventeen-year run of *KELLY* was attracting Garth Brooks to Belfast. Lest we forget, Garth Brooks was the best-selling solo artist in the history of recorded music. In the United States alone his albums had sold more than 100 million copies during the 1990s and over his ten-year reign he received virtually every accolade the record industry can bestow on an artist.

In Ireland he was hero worshipped. In May 1994 more than 80,000 people had flocked to his eight live performances at the Point Theatre in Dublin and then on his return in 1997, a further 120,000 went to see him over three nights in Croke Park, every concert a sell-out.

Not since the visits of JFK in the 1960s and Pope John Paul II in the 1970s had Ireland gone so hysterical over one man. Needless to say it was Ireland's top promoter, the late Jim Aiken, who was responsible for introducing Garth Brooks to Ireland and Ireland to Garth Brooks. I remember him telling me how the deal was struck.

Speculatively, Jim booked himself on a flight to the States and somehow managed to talk his way into meeting Brooks after he had tracked him down in Fargo, north Dakota. He had never spoken to the man before and Brooks had no idea who Jim Aiken was. Jim told him what he was there for, that Ireland wanted these concerts and that Brooks would have the time of his life. Now knowing Jim, I'm sure money was mentioned—although he said it wasn't—but be that as it may, Garth and Jim sealed the deal with a handshake there and then and, as they say, the rest is history. And that's a fact. The handshake was the two men's word.

When Brooks first came to Dublin for the Point Theatre shows, I took a film crew down to Dublin to interview him for our programme. We set up our cameras in one of the rooms of the Gresham Hotel in O'Connell Street in readiness for the interview.

Waiting on a major star like Brooks is always fairly nerve racking. Normally a TV crew like ourselves would be given a time slot. He will arrive at 4.15 and the interview must be over by 4.45, some press officer will tell us. Not a minute later. If you overrun, I will simply stop the filming.

Now normally, thirty minutes is ample time to talk in a filmed interview, but of course there is another dynamic at work in these situations. Using the Garth Brooks interview as an example, for a start I had never met the man before. So the first five minutes or so are taken up just introducing myself and the crew, indulging in a little small talk, all those things people do naturally when meeting for the first time.

For me, the initial few minutes are vital. Somehow in that short period of time I have to build up a rapport with someone I have never met before in my life. I need him to feel comfortable with me so that the eventual interview will look and sound as if it's just two old acquaintances chatting together.

And then of course there are all the hangers-on. Will he be surrounded by a bunch of lackeys desperate to please and accommodate his every wish? I've seen that before. Will he be cold and unwelcoming? I've seen that before too. Will he complain about where we want him to sit, about the lighting? That's a common one. Will he want Evian sparkling water instead of Ballygowan? I know one person who demanded that! Will he be tired and just want rid of us quickly? After all he has probably been doing interviews all day with radio DJs, other TV channels and the written press, answering the same old questions, giving the same old answers. You've no idea how boring that can be, I was once told.

So, I really didn't know what to expect, although I did trust the words of my old friend Jim Aiken who had simply told me, 'You'll love him.'

Anyway, Garth arrived on time accompanied by just one other person, his publicist! No entourage, nobody with a clipboard telling us when to start and when to stop, no make-up person, no hair stylist, no wardrobe mistress, no nothing as we say in Belfast.

After the introductions and the small talk, I asked if he wanted to start the interview. 'If you're ready, I'm ready,' he said. 'There's no rush.' In the end we chatted for over thirty minutes by which time the already burgeoning Garth Brooks fan club had increased by one—me! I found him welcoming, friendly, open, courteous, polite, well mannered, but most of all so very, very likeable. No wonder the people of Ireland took him so much to their hearts.

He did have one idiosyncrasy, however, which took a little time to get used to. Every now and then he would refer to Garth. I thought he was talking about another band member at the start, but eventually I realised he was talking about himself, not the Garth Brooks in front of me, but Garth Brooks, the performer on stage. He seemed to make a distinction between his two lives, the personal and the professional, and so when he spoke about his stage performance, he wouldn't use the word 'I'. He would say things like 'Garth wouldn't really sing a song like that' or 'Garth has many different costume changes.' It was a little confusing at the start.

Looking back, I sometimes wonder if this was an early indication and an explanation as to why, at the end of the 1990s, he took on the persona, the *alter ego* Chris Gaines. He even recorded under that name which only resulted, I believe, in bewildering his fans and ultimately poor record sales.

————

Ben Elton: … but it is also very funny.

GK: It would have to be.

BE: It's the first knob joke in an Andrew Lloyd Webber musical. After all it's about teenagers. It's the first time

anyone's ever offered Andrew affection rhymed with
erection and I'm not ashamed of it.

——

The next time our paths crossed was at the end of 1995. Garth was back in Ireland promoting his Croke Park concerts and I was determined to bring him to Belfast and to the KELLY studio for an interview. Once again, Jim Aiken was the promoter and he readily agreed to our request.

We gave practically the whole show over to Brooks that night, the only other guests being Robson Green and Jerome Flynn who starred in the TV drama, *Soldier, Soldier*, and who were also making a name for themselves in the music world.

By the time Garth Brooks arrived at Havelock House, word had got out that he was to appear on the show and hundreds of fans had turned up to greet him. His Point Depot concerts the previous year had, in the main, been supported by Southern Irish fans, but by the end of 1995 Brooks mania was sweeping Northern Ireland also.

The show that night lives long in my memory. Brooks brought his entire band along with him and they performed three songs, 'Fever', 'She's Every Woman' and 'If Tomorrow Never Comes'. I also spoke to his wife of the time, Sandy Mahl, and together they talked lovingly about their three daughters. It was a wonderfully happy night and it was evident that he and his people were enjoying the show as much as the audience.

As we neared the end of the interview, I remarked, 'The only negative in all this, Garth, is that you haven't included Belfast on your next tour. You are coming back to Dublin but not coming here.'

'The next tour has been set up a long time ago,' he explained, 'and we can't change it now. But I promise you, Gerry Kelly, that I will play Belfast. You have my word.' The audience applauded although I wasn't convinced just how practical that off-the-cuff remark was. Anyway, without labouring the point, I simply said, 'I'll hold you to that.'

Towards the end of the show, we sent a camera outside to see the fans who had been waiting patiently all evening in the hope of spotting Garth as he left the studio. It was a miserable November night and it had begun to rain. Garth suggested on air that we go and meet them and indeed that's how we finished the show, with Garth and me heading out the front doors to talk to the gathering crowd.

And there you might think the story ends, that when the red light on the camera finally goes out, Garth thanks everyone for coming, jumps into his limousine and heads off into the night. But that couldn't be further from the truth. For the next three hours he signed autographs, posed for photographs and at one stage, during a nasty downpour, invited those still waiting into his tour bus to shelter. Not until every last scrap of paper was signed, not until every last click of a camera, did Garth finally leave. It was 3.15 in the morning when he finally departed for Dublin. His good humour and his genuine appreciation of his fans is something I will always remember about him.

Fast forward eighteen months to those never-to-be-forgotten concerts in Croke Park. Garth paid an unexpected visit to Belfast to make a special announcement. The great and good of the Northern Ireland press gathered at the King's Hall for this special press conference. I went along to hear what he had to say. Flanked once again by Jim Aiken, he announced that he would be playing Belfast the following year, 1998—five concerts in the King's Hall.

When asked by one journalist why he had finally decided to play here, Garth answered, 'Well, I made a promise to Gerry Kelly on the *KELLY* show that I would do it and so I am now fulfilling that promise.' With those words he caught my eye and winked. The following September Garth played to almost 40,000 in the King's Hall, setting a new attendance record for both the hall and Northern Ireland.

Sadly, the next time I spoke to Garth Brooks was in a satellite recorded interview just after the death of Jim Aiken. Jim died in February 2007. No history of Northern Ireland would ever be

complete without a mention of the extraordinary contribution
Jim Aiken made to building a normal society here. Despite the
troubles, Jim succeeded in attracting some of the biggest names in
the entertainment industry to this island, bringing joy to countless thousands during some of our darkest days. Without him,
Northern Ireland would have become a complete wilderness,
devoid of any form of social entertainment and shunned by the
rest of the world.

Of course he will be remembered for those magnificent
concerts in Lord Henry Mount Charles's Slane Castle, especially
the night with Bruce Springsteen when almost 70,000 turned up
to see the Boss in 1985.

Along with Mo Mowlam, he came up with the idea of doing
open-air concerts in the grounds of Parliament Buildings at
Stormont in Belfast—a bold and adventurous decision considering
the political history of the place. Few could ever have imagined
rocking to the sounds of Rod Stewart, the Eagles or Elton John on
the neatly manicured lawns of Stormont.

But such was the drive and determination of Jim Aiken that he
would use all his charm, all his powers of persuasion and business
acumen to fulfil his dream of keeping Belfast and Northern
Ireland on the entertainment map. Jim's name was synonymous
with honesty and integrity—two rare commodities in the
business he was in. I was a friend of Jim for over thirty years. I first
met him way back in the 1970s when he was running weekly
dances in the Orpheus Ballroom in Belfast and then in the Boom
Boom Rooms in Cornmarket. Little did he or I think then that he
would go on to become the biggest and best concert promoter in
the British Isles and perhaps even further afield. Just for the
record, here are a few other names he brought to Ireland, north
and south: the Rolling Stones, Tina Turner, Justin Timberlake,
Shania Twain, Andrea Bocelli, Willie Nelson, Tom Jones, Kylie
Minogue, Roy Orbison, Dolly Parton, Johnny Cash, Luciano
Pavarotti, Kris Kristofferson, Waylon Jennings, Shirley Bassey, Take
That, Michael Flatley, Cliff Richard, Cher and Glen Campbell—
not a definitive list by any means, but a very impressive one.

In February 2008, in recognition of Jim's outstanding contribution, he was honoured posthumously with the Industry Award at the 2008 Meteor Ireland Music Awards.

Just after his funeral in February 2007, I put together an hour-long programme for UTV in tribute to Jim—'Gentleman Jim'. It was one of the most poignant programmes I have ever been involved in, with contributions from Christy Moore, Cliff Richard, Michael Flatley, Ronan Keating, Paul Brady and Garth Brooks. And then there were Jim's other friends, those not involved in the world of showbiz, of which there were many—people he grew up with and people he worked with. All said the same thing: Jim Aiken was a giant among men.

Jim's death at the start of 2007 was a real downer for all of us who knew, respected and loved him. Indeed, the year was to end on a similar note of despondency with the death of yet two more good friends, singer/songwriter Christie Hennessy and my old golfing mate, the legendary Joe Dolan.

Over the years Christie and I had built up quite a friendship. He was first booked for the KELLY show back in the early 1990s and I think we had him back at least a dozen times since then. He also came down to my home in Ardglass when we were recording a New Year's Eve show there. But from that first meeting I knew there was something very special about this gentle man from Kerry. Not only was I intrigued by the sheer beauty of his music and the eloquence of his lyrics, but I was also fascinated by his quiet, unassuming yet captivating personality. He was never one to seek fame or the cult of celebrity. He was first and foremost a family man who happened to have a remarkable talent for songwriting. He believed implicitly in God and in the power of healing. He himself was a healer. Over the years I was to have many a long chat with Christie away from the glare of cameras and microphones.

Christie left school at just 11 years of age and got a job as a messenger boy. As a result of his poor educational background he suffered badly from dyslexia and struggled with literacy throughout his life. Surprisingly, in later life he learned to treasure books and would often find himself in bookstores browsing the shelves, fascinated by their contents.

Each Christmas I would receive a card from Christie. One of his daughters, either Amber or Hermione, would write 'Happy Christmas, Gerry' and Christie himself would write his own name in what was a very childish scrawl. Thankfully I have kept all those cards.

By the age of 15 he had set out for London to seek work which he found on the many building sites throughout the city. It was a hard, tough life only eased by his love of playing the guitar and writing songs. He would play in jazz clubs at night just to earn a few extra quid. Christie was in his 40s before his talents were truly acclaimed when he was named Best New Act at the Irish Music Awards. He was 43.

One of his songs, 'Roll Back the Clouds (I Am A Star)', holds a great deal of significance for me personally. When I asked him about the origin of the song, he told me it was about his daughter Hermione. She was an actress and singer and would go to countless auditions in the hope of landing a job. Time and time again she would be rejected. He recalled one occasion when she had queued for hours and came home to tell her parents that she nearly got to the theatre door, but still a long way from the stage!

The reason the song strikes such a chord with me is because my older daughter Sarah also trained as an actress. Having attended university, she enrolled in the Gaiety School of Acting in Dublin, now widely regarded as Ireland's premier training academy. After two years of intensive study, she emerged full of hope and optimism about landing that first acting part. But over the following months and years she learned just how difficult and unforgiving her chosen profession can be. For every thirty or forty auditions attended, maybe, just maybe, an actor will land one job. Even then it will probably be only a bit part in some obscure show or film. It's soul destroying. Not only do you not get the job, but you're not even told that you didn't get it. There is no phone call to say you were unsuccessful, no feedback as to how you could improve. If your phone doesn't ring within the week, you can assume they've chosen someone else. So it's off to the next audition.

Just like Christie felt about his daughter Hermione, I too felt the same way about Sarah—that those people conducting the auditions missed someone special.

On the sleeve notes of his CD, *The Definitive Christie Hennessy*, Christie has written 'For his constant and never-ending support, I'd like to dedicate "Roll Back The Clouds" to Gerry Kelly.' Needless to say I treasure that CD.

Christie's death came as a huge shock to me. I had not seen him since he played the Grand Opera House in March 2007, when he seemed in the best of health. I spoke with him briefly after the show and he was in his usual good form. We parted with Christie's customary hug, promising to catch up with each other later in the year.

When the phone call came through informing me of his death in December, I couldn't believe what I was hearing. I was truly devastated and felt a huge sense of loss. Knowing that I will never hear Christie sing live again or listen to his uniquely humorous little anecdotes between songs will be a regret for ever.

Five days before Christmas, the Hennessy family held a private ceremony near their home in London, to which I was invited, and afterwards people gathered at the Merton and Sutton Crematorium for a private committal. As his coffin was being carried out of the church, Christie's recording of 'Roll Back the Clouds' began to play. The small congregation wept openly, including me.

Two days after Christmas, Christie's ashes were brought back to his home town of Tralee, where Requiem Mass was said for him. I wasn't able to be there, but I was content in the knowledge that I had already said my goodbyes in London. Christie was one of nature's true gentlemen, and it was my privilege to have been his friend.

And as if the end of 2007 wasn't sad enough, word came through on Boxing Day that Joe Dolan had also died. I knew Joe hadn't been well but when I phoned him at the end of November, he assured me that everything was all right, just a little blood disorder. But after Christmas he would be back playing golf and he would take me for a 'nifty' (£50) anytime.

That's how I got to know Joe—on the fairways of Ireland. He and I, both avid golf fans, played a lot with the Links, a charitable, celebrity-based golf society based in Dublin which has raised literally millions of pounds for good causes since its formation back in 1966.

Of course I had danced to Joe Dolan and the Drifters on many occasions in my formative years, but that Joe Dolan was a major singing star, way out of my circle of friendship, not the Joe Dolan I got to know over recent years.

'There's no show like a Joe show' was the popular slogan throughout Joe's illustrious career and anyone who ever saw him perform would testify to the veracity of that. But I knew Joe Dolan as one of the most generous and kindest people I have ever met. He did more for charity in his own private way than people will ever know. And that's the way he wanted it. However, Fr Brian D'Arcy let the cat out of the bag, so to speak, during his emotionally charged eulogy at Joe's funeral Mass in Mullingar. Fr Brian told the congregation that every Christmas Joe would thrust a cheque into his hand and say, 'You're in the business, Brian. You know who needs this.' And as Fr Brian explained, what was thrust in his hand wasn't just a few quid. It was in the thousands. Joe's secret charitable donations are now known by all, something that would embarrass him immensely if he were still alive.

Joe was great company, never down and always wanting to hear the latest joke. If you couldn't think of one, he always had two or three of his own that he was itching to tell you. He also loved a good argument, not in an aggressive way but on an intellectual level. He was exceptionally well read and often expressed to me a deep interest in the events of Northern Ireland. He totally threw me one night when I discovered he was an expert on the British royal family! He won that argument.

I don't think Joe ever fully recovered from the hip operation he had a few years back. After that I felt he began to look his age and even though we had a few rounds of golf together since then, they were few and far between.

Joe had many good friends from within the showbiz fraternity and equally as many from without. His funeral Mass in Mullingar on 29 December 2007 was filled with many of them.

Three good friends lost in the same year. Three good friends, each of whom excelled at what they did; each of whom gave immense joy and pleasure to millions of people across the generations.

We will probably never see their likes again—Jim Aiken, Christie Hennessy and Joe Dolan.

Chapter 14 ∿

COCK-UPS, CLANGERS AND CHAOS

Until Denis Norden came along with his programme, *It'll Be Alright on the Night*, at the end of the 1970s, cock-ups and clangers from actors and presenters were rarely seen by the general public. Today, of course, watching normally word-perfect performers mess up in front of the camera is such a popular format that TV schedules the world over are littered with many imitators.

It was a Belfast man, Paul Smith, who came up with the original idea. I first met Paul when he was working in UTV as a freelance producer in the early days. But it was his creation of *It'll Be Alright on the Night* that initially propelled him along the path to becoming one of the most influential men in the modern television industry.

Paul went on to become chairman of Celador Productions, the company which created the world-wide phenomenon that is *Who Wants To Be A Millionaire?*

Some of the very first clips on Denis Norden's programme came from UTV. Who will ever forget Charlie Witherspoon's famous interview with the fast talking George Cunningham from Strabane or the time wrestler Giant Haystacks, weighing in at a massive 45 stone, who threw the sylph-like sports reporter Jackie Fullerton awkwardly on his back.

I was in the studio the night of the Haystacks v Fullerton confrontation and saw the whole event for myself. The two didn't seem to be getting along, so when the time came for Haystacks to throw Jackie in a well-rehearsed 'slam', he added a little venom to the manoeuvre. Instead of landing Jackie square on his back, which shouldn't have hurt, he twisted him slightly causing Jackie to land on his shoulder. Believe me it was painful. Jackie wasn't pretending when he completed the interview with a groan.

The final chapter of this rather strained relationship was written some years later when we reunited Jackie with Giant Haystacks on *KELLY*. Sad to report, there was no kiss and make up. Giant Haystacks, whose real name was Martin Ruane and whose family came from Kiltimagh in County Mayo, died in 1998 aged 51.

Thankfully, I have only appeared once on *It'll Be Alright on the Night*. That was the time I ripped my trousers bending over to pack Easter eggs. I think it was for an item on *Good Evening Ulster*. In fact, the same clip was shown again when I was a guest on Gloria Hunniford's *This Is Your Life* in 1982.

But if Mr Norden had been looking for clips to put on his show in 1997, he could have taken the entire *KELLY* programme of 16 May from start to premature finish. This was the night my worst nightmare became a reality.

That week we decided to do the show live from the North West 200 motorcycle race, one of the biggest annual sporting events held in and around Coleraine and Portrush. It's a hugely important event both in terms of the sport and the money it generates through the 100,000 fans who support it. UTV covers the two-day meet in one of the most complicated television shoots imaginable.

It is very expensive to cover the racing circuit for television because it is about eleven miles long over public roads. Most motorcycle racing is on purpose-built racing tracks constructed with spectators in mind. They snake and double back on themselves, a bit like spaghetti on a plate, so that a circuit miles long can occupy a relatively small area. These circuits make televising easier because one high camera position can usually cover several bends, which are the points of special interest to the audience and spectators alike. But the North West circuit is nothing like that. It is a very long triangular course which doesn't double back on itself anywhere. To transmit the race, UTV needed to put more than twenty broadcast cameras at multiple points around the circuit. They even had a camera in a helicopter for those magnificent aerial shots.

Because KELLY decided to gatecrash the party, even more cameras were required as well as a mobile control room for the programme. And because both events were happening simultaneously, this created a mammoth operation, stretching UTV to the limits of their resources. More hardware was needed, so equipment had to be hired. We had set up a marquee to act as the KELLY studio, which required power from a generator rather than from the mains. We hired the generator from the BBC. What happened on the day was a television shambles.

All the ingredients for something going wrong were present. Understandably, UTV was overstretched trying to combine the race coverage and the KELLY programme. Indeed one of those tasks would have been a big enough operation on its own.

We were broadcasting live from alongside the start/finish line. The temporary studio really looked the part, even sporting an exhibition of motorcycles, old and new. The guest line-up was hot too, including the late Joey Dunlop, the greatest road racer of all time, and Phillip McCallen, the pretender to Joey's throne. My very first guests though were Katrina and the Waves, winners of the Eurovision Song Contest just two weeks previously. After the hello and welcome, I had a brief chat with the lead singer Katrina Leskanich and then invited her to join the rest of the band to sing their winning Eurovision entry, 'Love Shine a Light'. So far, so good. No sign of the impending disaster.

Now, Katrina was miming the song, as indeed were the musicians in the band. This was a situation we normally didn't tolerate on the programme, but because of the isolation of the venue and the lack of rehearsal time, we allowed it on this occasion. Normally it was permissible for the singer to mime if the band played live, and conversely it was acceptable for the band to mime and the singer to sing live. But this was a double miming whammy!

As the Waves were doing their thing, the lights in the marquee started to fail. They began to flicker for a time and then settled down again, but this was unnerving everybody, myself included. I had forebodings.

Suddenly, all the sound in the studio went down without warning, including the foldback. Foldback is the sound you hear in the studio and the foldback speakers are the low-powered units seen at the feet of performers facing back and away from the audience. Their purpose is to allow the performers to hear what the main speakers are pumping towards the audience and are vital for the purpose of keeping the singer and band in time with the miming track. So when these speakers failed, the band and the singers were left high and dry. They could hear nothing. Simultaneously all the microphones went down. So when Katrina couldn't hear the song, she and the band stopped miming. However, to compound the faults, the director and producer in the separate control van didn't know what was happening, because the backing track, unknown to the studio, myself and Katrina and the Waves, was continuing on air. Only the studio sound had disappeared. People at home therefore continued to hear the song while at the same time watching Katrina and the Waves standing shrugging their shoulders, looking around and wondering what on earth was going on.

Seeing what was happening, I gesticulated frantically to the floor manager and shouted in a loud whisper, 'Bring the cameras to me, bring them to me.' But the microphones had failed too!

As we grappled with all of this, the cameras then started to play up and the lights began to flicker again. It seemed an age before the technicians back at base in Havelock House realised there had been a catastrophic fault and it seemed to take ages before they took action and switched the screens to black. We at the outside broadcast unit cannot take ourselves off the air. It must be switched off where the signal enters the main control room, which for UTV is in Havelock House. The delay in removing us from the screen might have been only ten to fifteen seconds or so, but this is a long time in broadcasting, and to us in that accursed tent it seemed more like half an hour.

When we were finally taken off air, the station went immediately to a commercial break, which again can only be done from Havelock House. One of the advantages of commercial broadcasting is that at times of crisis you can always go to a commercial break and give yourself a few minutes to compose yourself. During that break we tried to fix the fault and thought we had managed it, so when the break ended we put the marquee back on air.

No sooner were pictures from the North West beaming back once more into the living rooms when everything started to go haywire again. Again we went to a black screen. We thought we had definitely fixed the problem this time, so off we went once more, but the technical problems just wouldn't go away. Clearly all we were doing was treating the symptoms of the malaise and not the real cause. We stumbled through the programme in this staccato fashion as best we could, but it was torture. We should really have abandoned it and substituted a Tom and Jerry cartoon. Perhaps the audience enjoyed watching someone else's series of disasters, but for me and our production and technical staff it was excruciating.

I had never seen a North West 200 motorcycle race and had arranged to stay up at the circuit all that weekend for the festivities. Instead, with expletives exploding from my lips, I threw myself into the car and drove straight home. I had never been so angry. At the time I blamed the UTV technical staff, but as it transpired they were blameless. The fault lay with the BBC generator we had hired for the show. No one of course could have known the hired equipment was going to fail, but that didn't salve my mood as I exited Coleraine that night.

Normally I watch a recording of the KELLY programme when I get home, not for vanity reasons but to check if I asked the right questions, was I really listening to what was being said or did I miss an opportunity in the conversation where I could have explored more. However, in the case of the North West 200 show I made an exception. To this day I have not summoned up the courage to watch what actually went out that night. I simply could not bear to do so. I should make the point that the hired BBC equipment going wrong was an accident. It was not sabotage, as someone once unkindly suggested to me. Television is technically complicated and even more so when you are making a temporary studio out of a marquee. There are cables and connections everywhere involving electronics and lighting, all of which has been transported and put together, usually against the clock. It does go wrong sometimes and that's life in television. But it certainly wasn't all right on the night that night!

The whole episode approached a recurring nightmare I used to have. I would be sitting in a television studio, but I don't know how I got there and facing me is a man waiting for me to introduce him. However, I don't know who he is, I don't know why I'm interviewing him and I have nothing written on my notes. That nightmare never happened in reality, but the North West programme is, I hope most earnestly, the nearest I'll come to that nightmare. Now, through no fault of their own, even the name Katrina and the Waves sends a shudder through me. Katrina was not a happy girl after the show and made her feelings very plain. She thought we were a bunch of amateurs. The band broke up a couple of years afterwards. Nothing to do with our programme, one hopes.

There was one further disaster, or near disaster I should say, but this time thankfully the television audience was not aware of it. It was the final programme of the tenth series. Now I know I have promised you that we always did the show live, but this night we decided to record. After all, it was the last programme of that year and we had arranged a huge wrap party in the Europa Hotel.

So that everyone would have time to change into their glad rags for the party, we started recording at 7.30 pm and hoped to be finished by 9.00 pm. That would give the engineers plenty of time to put the recorded programme to air at 10.30 pm while we were off partying in the Europa.

Everything was going fine. Part 1 was recorded, as was part 2. Time for part 3 and in this section we had Ronan Keating and Paul Brady. From *Emmerdale* we had John Middleton who plays the Reverend Ashley Thomas and young Kevin Fletcher who plays

Andy Sugden. I interviewed Ronan and Paul, after which they sang together. I also played the mugs game with two contestants on the phone and finally I interviewed the two guys from *Emmerdale*.

I said goodbye, thanked the audience for watching, hoped they'd have a great summer and that we would be back in September with our new series. With that the audience started to disperse. I went to wardrobe to change my clothes for the party, and that's when all hell broke loose. My producer Patricia Moore was frantically looking for me.

'Where's Gerry?' I could hear her shout.

'In here, Patricia,' I yelled back.

With that she burst through the dressing room door—luckily I was decent—and she said, 'Get your suit back on. We have to go back into the studio.' With that, she ran out shouting for the researchers to stop the audience from leaving and to find Ronan, Paul, John and Kevin and bring them back.

I soon learned what the panic was all about. One of our engineers had messed up the sound. Instead of recording all that was said in part 3, he recorded what is known as 'tone'—a long continuous beep. So we had to do this whole section of the programme again. The only problem was half the audience had disappeared and, even worse, Ronan Keating by this time was just hitting the M1 on his way home to Dublin!

After a few frantic phone calls we managed to get Ronan to turn round and come back. We even managed to recall most of the audience. This all took time and it was nearly 10 pm before we were in a position to record the third part of the programme again. Remember, the whole show was scheduled to be broadcast at 10.30.

So, I interviewed Ronan and Paul again. They sang again. I played the mugs game with the same two contestants. I chatted with John and Kevin and finally said my goodbyes once more. The time was now 10.24 pm. We had made it with only minutes to spare. Needless to say, the sound engineer was missing at the wrap party!

James Nesbitt: I got up very early this morning in London to do this Action Cancer thing. It was dark and I found that I had arrived here in my gutties.

GK: No shoes?

JN: My mother met me at the airport and nearly went through me. So they sent someone out to get me these, but they pinch me a bit.

GK: Show me the shoes.

JN: I think the price is still on them.

GK (pulling Nesbitt's shoe up to the desk showing the price tag): £39.99.

JN: Really, I was hoping to send them back but you've ruined that now.

In spite of our problems that night and at the North West, outside broadcasts played a significant and important part in the life of KELLY. It was always in the plan to take the show out of the studio at least once a year and the OB allowed us to do just that.

The first time we did it was in 1996 when we took over the Grand Opera House in Belfast for the night. This was a big technical step-up for us, a challenging break away from the comfort and familiarity of the studio. Instead of just over 120 people in the audience, we were now looking at over 1,000. We had other concerns. Would a chat show in such theatrical surroundings work? I mean, most of the KELLY show is designed around intimate interviews, so how would they work in a large space where voice projection was so important? Obviously we needed more visual items than usual, more music acts and to keep the chat to a minimum.

By that time Boyzone had been the biggest boy band in the country for over two years. They were booked. Belfast singer Brian Kennedy was also hugely popular. He was booked. Actor Jimmy Ellis, a native of Belfast and a man who knew all about theatre here was on the list. We would get him to do a poem— sounds like a Feis but he gave a most moving rendition of 'Dear Sarah'. Liverpool comedian Tom O'Connor was always a favourite in Belfast, so we booked him as well. Anuna and Eimear Quinn, who won the Eurovision Song Contest for Ireland in 1996 (yes another Eurovision winner) were also in the line-up. They of course were also part of *Riverdance*.

We were still looking for a star to headline the show, someone to put the icing on what was an already good line-up. As luck would have it, I bumped into him outside the Westbury Hotel in Dublin two weeks before the show.

I had met Michael Flatley twice before. The first time I interviewed him was when he was the lead dancer in *Riverdance*; the second time he had just left *Riverdance* due to what was described officially as artistic differences. He had told me he was setting up a new dance company and was in rehearsals for his own show which he was calling *Lord of the Dance*.

That evening in Dublin I had an appointment in the Westbury Hotel but found myself over an hour early for the meeting. To pass the time I decided to go for a walk along Grafton Street. I hadn't gone twenty yards when I bumped into Michael coming the other way. We exchanged pleasantries and I happened to ask him how rehearsals were progressing for his new show. As I asked the question, it suddenly dawned on me there was no bigger star in Ireland at the time than Michael. His acrimonious departure from *Riverdance* was all over the papers and the public was eagerly awaiting his new show.

I told him what we were planning for the Opera House in the middle of June and asked if any of his new routines were ready for public consumption yet. If they were, we would be delighted to showcase them. At once Michael became enthusiastic and told me that one of the men's dances was complete and that he would relish the opportunity of trying it out on a live audience. We struck the deal there and then. We had our headline act—Michael Flatley with the world's first glimpse into his stunning creation, *Lord of the Dance*.

The Opera House *KELLY* show was an unmitigated success. Flatley was a world star and when he flashed on to that stage for the finale of the programme, my heart leapt as high as he did. His performance was breath-taking. The 'Lord of the Dance' was back in business and about to take over the world.

Michael and I have remained close friends since that night. In 2001 he invited me to the south of France for a party in his exquisite villa in Nice. I forget the reason for the celebrations, but then Michael never needed a reason to party. After we touched down at Charles de Gaulle Airport in Paris, awaiting a transfer flight to Nice, I happened to switch on my mobile phone to check for messages. Unusually, I had seven missed calls and three voice messages waiting.

I had only left Ireland three or four hours ago, so what had happened in the interim for me to be so much in demand? The first and only message I listened to was from my producer. On *KELLY* the previous night I had interviewed Linda Gail Lewis, sister of Jerry Lee Lewis and a guest backing singer for Van Morrison on his recent tour. For legal reasons I cannot go over the conversation we had on the show. Suffice to say that Van Morrison had taken great exception to the interview and was about to sue me, the *KELLY* show and UTV. I couldn't understand what the problem was and decided to leave it until I returned home on Monday.

We arrived at our hotel just outside Nice and at 7 o'clock that evening limousines arrived to take us to Michael's home. As we drove up the mountain overlooking Nice, the French chauffeur told me that the higher up the mountain the houses were, the more prestige and money their owners had. Michael's was at the very top!

Surrounded by a security wall, the villa was amazing. Unfortunately, if you're looking for a detailed description of the décor and furnishings, I can't help. I'm really not into noticing things like that. I know, I'm useless—that's what my wife told me also when she started quizzing me when I got home. What I can tell you though is that the centre-piece of the whole house is a magnificent swimming pool that has direct access, not just from the living room, but from at least four bedrooms as well. On a balmy October evening in Nice, the views over the bay were dazzling. After feasting on the best of food and the very, very best of wine, many of the guests went in for a dip. I declined on the pretext that I hadn't brought my shorts! By this stage we were now into the wee small hours of the morning.

Michael was in the hot tub, on his own, having a quiet puff on his pipe. I sidled round to him for a quiet chat. Just like in 1996, I wanted him to appear in another of our outside broadcast shows, this time in the Opera House in Cork, not far from where he lived in his Castlehyde mansion outside Fermoy. As we chatted, I couldn't help but remark on his enormous change of fortune since that day five years ago when we met on Grafton Street just after he exited *Riverdance*. In that time he had become, deservedly so, a multimillionaire living the multimillionaire lifestyle with a yacht in the Caribbean, houses in London and Nice and a mansion in Ireland.

Michael was unattached at the time and I asked him if he ever felt lonely, that here he was surrounded by all this wealth but with no one to share it. He agreed that it would be nice to have someone and at times his fame could be a lonely place. I thought that if he agreed to do the Cork show, I would like to engage him in an interview like that.

At times, Michael came across in the press as being somewhat arrogant and egotistical. But I knew another side of Michael Flatley, the real Michael Flatley, and I wanted to share that side of his humanity with a wider audience. He did agree to appear on our show in Cork and as the interview developed I thought I would ask him that very same question I had put to him in his hot tub in Nice.

'Michael, you are now an enormously wealthy man,' I started. 'You have homes all around the world. And yet you have no one to share all this fame and fortune with. Deep down, are you truly happy?'

I sat back waiting for Michael to take it from there, to expose just a little of his innermost personality, to show that money doesn't buy happiness. He looked at me, paused for a while, smiled and said, 'Are you kidding, Gerry? Who wouldn't be happy with all this?' A showman to the end!

But I knew the truth and was delighted when Michael found and married someone with whom he will share his extraordinary life. On 14 October 2006, he married the stunning Niamh O'Brien in one of the happiest and most joyous weddings I have ever attended. Helena and I were guests when they tied the knot at St Patrick's Church in Fermoy, Co. Cork.

This was not the massive celebrity wedding many people thought Michael Flatley would have. There was no *Hello* magazine, no helicopters in the sky with photographers trying to get an unofficial snap of Niamh's dress, no heavy security barring people's way, just a simple ceremony where everyone was welcome. By the time Helena and I got into the church it was already three-quarters full of Fermoy residents who had been given an open invitation.

Michael and Niamh chatted with all the well-wishers before and after the ceremony and then it was off to the reception at their recently restored Castlehyde mansion on the outskirts of the town. For more than eight years Michael had set about restoring this magnificent Irish home at a cost of over 50 million euro. The result is stunning.

Michael's ability to throw a party is legendary, but for his wedding he pulled out all the stops. The 250 or so guests ate, drank and danced the night away right through until breakfast. Helena and I left just after we had our share of the four suckling pigs that came off the spit round 4 am.

Michael Flatley deserves every penny of the fortune he has amassed. He is one of the most talented performers in the world today and when you break through the bluster and smokescreen of showbiz, he's one of the nicest guys you could meet.

He also deserves his happiness, something he has at last found with his wife Niamh and their beautiful son Michael Jr.

But back to porridge. I did mention that Van Morrison wanted to sue me, didn't I?

———

GK: Have you got a day off this Christmas?

Ronan Keating: This was actually my day off. You've ruined it.

———

Chapter 15 ❧

WRITS, WRANGLES AND WARNINGS

Hearing the messages on my mobile phone in Charles de Gaulle Airport that Saturday morning, I was really alarmed. I had no idea why Van Morrison's people were threatening to take legal action against us. Throughout the Flatley party the thought kept niggling at me. That we could be sued by one of the biggest names in world music was more than a little disconcerting.

For the life of me I couldn't work out what I had done to upset Van Morrison. I never said anything against him on the programme, although admittedly the interview with Linda Gail Lewis was, in part, about an alleged affair she claimed she had had with him. But that was not a new story. We weren't trying to dig up dirt on Van. I had read about it in the newspapers months before and in fact I used those stories on which to base my interview with Lewis.

But when I arrived back in my office on Monday, I was to learn the full extent of just how offended Morrison was. He denied vehemently that any such 'affair' existed, saying the allegations were an 'outrageous fabrication', all part of Linda Gail Lewis's fertile imagination. He had instructed his lawyers to seek damages from UTV and had threatened to begin court action if he did not get a satisfactory response.

Unfortunately, the *Sunday Independent* reported on my interview with Linda Gail Lewis in their newspaper that weekend quoting almost verbatim what was said on the programme. The result was they too became part of the legal action.

Morrison released a statement that said: 'Ms Lewis makes these allegations knowing I am intensely private about my personal life and in the apparent belief that I would not engage in a public row and that her allegations would gain credence as a result. For a number of reasons I genuinely hoped that I could maintain a dignified silence in this matter but I now feel compelled to issue this statement.'

Morrison's lawyer said: 'My client has demanded that UTV and the *Sunday Independent* immediately issue a full and categoric retraction and an apology in relation to extremely serious defamatory allegations. Mr Morrison will also be seeking substantial damages and we have instructions to issue libel proceedings if we do not receive an immediate and satisfactory response.'

So, as you can see, this was heavy stuff, deadly serious.

UTV immediately called in their own lawyers. The interview was run and re-run in private many times, forensically going over what was said or not said and then it was left to the legal eagles to decide what we were to do. To be honest, I was sidelined at this stage. There was nothing more I could contribute to the discussion. It was now up to the lawyers to figure out the best way forward.

The matter was debated behind closed doors for many weeks. The only issue that seemed to have been decided early on was that we would not be giving an on-air apology anywhere in the near future. UTV's lawyers questioned Ms Lewis at length and at one stage it seemed we were to face Mr Morrison in court.

We had heard rumours, however, that the *Sunday Independent* had settled out of court, which meant that UTV was now fighting the case on its own.

The whole episode was personally very disturbing. I had no wish and certainly no intention of upsetting or falling out with Van Morrison. He was one of our own, a man to be admired, a man who had conquered the music world and he was from Belfast. He had appeared on *KELLY* before when he sang two songs on the never-to-be-forgotten George Best Special programme which rated as the most watched show we ever did. I was anxious therefore that whatever the outcome, there would be no lasting fall-out.

At the eleventh hour UTV was instructed by their lawyers that they should no longer pursue the case. To this day, I do not know the detail of that decision. But the company would not be contesting the matter.

Mr Morrison was paid an undisclosed sum by way of compensation by UTV and that was an end to the matter. Well, I thought it was the end.

At the start of 2007 Van Morrison and Terry George were to be honoured at the second annual Oscar Wilde ceremony in Los Angeles. This prestigious event is hosted by the US-Ireland Alliance and honours those Irish writers who have done most for the Irish film industry. It's held in the same week as the Oscars and, according to those who know these things, it is one of the hottest tickets to be had in LA during Oscar week.

The name Terry George may not be immediately familiar to you, but when I tell you that he was the screenwriter of *In The Name of the Father*, he was the script writer and director of *Some Mother's Son* and the co-writer, producer and director of *Hotel Rwanda*, you can see the calibre of the man. He's from Belfast but now spends his time between New York and Coney Island. Yes, Coney Island in Co. Down. He's my neighbour!

When I was planning a new series of programmes for 2007, some of which were to be filmed in America, it was thought that this was too good an opportunity to miss. As well as two Northern Ireland men being honoured, the ceremony was to be presented by Derry girl, Roma Downey. Roma of course is the star of one of the most successful series ever in America, *Touched by an Angel*. And to top it all, Al Pacino was to hand over the award to Van Morrison.

We immediately got in contact with the organisers and told them what we were planning, to make an hour-long documentary about the event and to interview all the main players. They were delighted with the potential publicity and agreed to do all they could to facilitate us.

With those assurances, we set about organising the trip. Luckily we hadn't gone as far as booking flights and hotels when a phone call came back from the organisers. An apologetic voice told us that Van Morrison had heard we were keen to film the awards ceremony and if that was the case, he would withdraw from the event. Unfortunately, therefore, the organisers could no longer accept our presence at the ceremony.

The only other legal hot water we got into concerned Daniel O'Donnell. Back in 1993 we had engaged a young local comedian, Bobby Christie, who had just won a national Comedian of the Year award. The young guy had rehearsed his material that afternoon and he was very funny—a little nervous perhaps, but then it was his first time appearing on live television.

Unfortunately, halfway through his act live on air that night, he lost his way and forgot his lines. Oddly enough, it happens more often than you would think in showbiz, but generally it doesn't worry the seasoned campaigners. For Bobby, though, it was sheer panic. In his distress he went off script and fell back on old jokes that were obviously running around in his head.

He resorted to telling an old Frank Carson gag about an Irish mother writing to her son in England. It goes something like this: 'Dear son, ever since you left home your father has turned into a sex maniac. He makes love to me at every available opportunity. P.S. Please excuse the wobbly writing.' Not the funniest joke in the world, but it usually raises a smile.

But instead of making it a random mother and son letter, Bobby unfortunately personalised the gag and named Daniel O'Donnell and his mother Julia.

Oddly enough, I remember that the joke didn't go down all that well with the studio audience at the time, but I didn't think any more of it after that. I was just wishing the young comedian would find his way again and get back to his scripted jokes which were funny. By way of encouragement, I laughed louder and longer than normal as I listened, hoping it would gain him a few precious seconds and give him a chance to regain his composure. Anyway he finished his act and I was relieved that he hadn't let himself down completely.

Little did I know then that the audience's cool reaction to that one joke was only an indicator of what was to come, because after the show the balloon went up with complaints by the score. Daniel fans all over the country were so insulted on behalf of the family that they phoned in to record their distaste at such an insensitive joke. Many phoned Julia herself to her home in Donegal and told her what the KELLY programme had just said about her beloved husband.

What few of us knew at the time, and certainly Bobby Christie didn't know, was that Daniel's father had died when he was quite young, leaving Julia to raise the family on her own. He was a much loved husband and father and so it was only natural that this joke was viewed as unfeeling and cruel. With this information, I could fully understand the hurt that had been caused and was adamant that we should speak to the O'Donnells, explain what had happened and offer our fullest apology. Before we could set that in motion, however, a solicitor's letter on behalf of Mrs O'Donnell arrived at UTV.

In an attempt to nip this whole sorry incident in the bud, our senior producer Andy Crockart immediately went up to Donegal to speak with Mrs O'Donnell. She wouldn't see him, but he did talk to Daniel's sister and through her conveyed our sincere apology to their mum. Legally, not much action seemed to be forthcoming, but we were still very much concerned at the hurt we had inadvertently caused and wanted to put things right.

That summer I was booked to host the finals of the Mary of Dungloe competition, which is held annually in Daniel's home patch of Donegal. Tradition had it that Daniel himself performed on stage at the crowning ceremony on the last night in the Dome, so I knew he would be there, as would his mum. This was my opportunity to talk to Julia and try to explain the circumstances surrounding the incident and to apologise.

I spoke to Daniel first and his reaction was one of understanding, but he did say it wasn't him I should be apologising to but his mother. She had been deeply hurt by the whole incident.

I eventually got to speak to Julia who listened politely but I could see she wasn't really accepting what I was saying. At one point she said, 'But you were laughing. You must have found it funny.' I tried to explain why I was seen doing that, but I don't think she understood my reasoning. Even though we left on fairly amicable terms, it was a long time before Julia fully forgave me.

Daniel on the other hand was OK about it. He knew that in the business these things can happen without anyone meaning anything malevolent. He knew it was patter gone wrong. At the same time though, it was quite a few years later before Daniel would agree to do the KELLY show again. I think he may have felt he would be letting his mother down had he accepted our invitation too soon. No further legal action was taken.

Thankfully, the unfortunate incident is now well behind us all. In the summer of 2007, I made an hour-long documentary on the phenomenon that is Daniel O'Donnell. We filmed a lot of the programme in his beautiful home in Tenerife and thoroughly enjoyed being in the company of him and his wife Majella.

GK (showing Daniel O'Donnell the CD featuring entertainer Caroline Aherne as Mrs Merton): Tell me, are you in love with this woman or she with you?

DO'D: I think she may have a bit of a fascination with me.

GK: I think she has indeed.

DO'D: She creeps up on you unawares.

Those two incidences aside, the KELLY show remained free of any other legal action—remarkable, considering we ran a live show for seventeen years. But although we managed to stay out of the courts, we did attract more than our fair share of controversy.

One of the most embarrassing incidents, which could have had huge legal implications, concerned a competition we were running that offered a car for first place and a second prize of a weekend in a hotel in Ireland. The ins and outs of this particular competition are unimportant. Suffice to say we had whittled the final entry down to fifty contestants. All that was left for me to do on the programme was draw out two winning names.

Confidently, I stood before the drum containing all the names and to heighten the tension I drew out the runner-up ticket first. I read out the name and gleefully announced that they had just won a fabulous weekend in a five-star hotel in Cork. Then on to the first prize. I reached in and picked out another ticket and, with a fanfare of trumpets, I announced the winner of a magnificent new car. No problems so far. We had our winner and we were trying to contact him by phone before the end of the programme to hear his reaction.

We eventually tracked him down and I had an excited conversation with him before we went off the air that night. I told him he could come to UTV anytime on Monday and collect his spanking new wheels. I always loved giving prizes away on the show and this occasion was no different. The winner was absolutely delighted. He duly arrived on Monday, collected his car and drove off into the sunset.

On Tuesday morning we took a phone call from a solicitor representing the runner-up in the competition. He told us that his client was refusing to accept the holiday in Cork because I had made an error in making the draw. According to the Betting, Gaming and Lotteries Act, I was in breach of the rules and regulations. The Act clearly states, he told us, that the first name drawn out must win the first prize. I apologised but added that there was very little we could do about it now. The draw had been made live on television, so we couldn't go back on that, and anyway the winner had already collected the car.

'You don't expect me to take it off him, do you?' I jokingly remarked.

'No,' he said, 'but I do expect you to compensate my client and present him with a new car too.'

I nearly fainted. The magnitude of my mistake was beginning to sink in. If this solicitor was right, then I had just cost UTV the price of another new car. I immediately told the programme controller who in turn contacted the company solicitors to check the Act. Sure enough he was right. The first name drawn out must win the first prize, the logic being that by removing the contestant's ticket—when he won second prize—he was not therefore in with a chance to win the top prize, the reason he entered the competition in the first place.

'So what do we do now?' I asked the controller.

'We have no option, have we?' he said. 'We'll have to present the runner-up with another car.'

And that's what we did. My little *faux pas* cost the company £16,000. So if you ever find yourself having to do a draw, remember that the first name out wins the first prize—an expensive lesson that I pass on to you for free.

———

Patrick Kielty: There was a ball in the hotel we were staying in and we gatecrashed it. Free drink—you know yourself. And suddenly the crowds parted, there he was—Daniel O'Donnell. And I said (going down on one knee), 'Bless me, Daniel, for I have sinned.'

———

In 1993, Annie Murphy was a guest on the show. Many people in Ireland will of course know the name instantly; others may have only vague memories. Surprising really, considering the Annie Murphy affair heralded the beginning of the end of the hitherto unquestioned obedience Irish people had for the Catholic hierarchy. Indeed it marked the beginning of the decline in the influence the Catholic Church had over its flock in Ireland, a downward trend that continues to this day.

Annie Murphy was a young American divorcee who was sent by her father to stay with his friend, Bishop Eamonn Casey, then just plain Father Casey, after she had suffered some emotional problems. In the early 1990s, it was sensationally revealed that Fr Casey had seduced the young Annie Murphy while in his care and had fathered a son to her some eighteen years previously. Murphy was now back in Ireland demanding that Casey publicly acknowledge the existence of his son and lend financial support for his university education. It was the biggest scandal imaginable in Ireland at the time.

Casey had fled to South America, while Annie Murphy was here wanting to tell her side of the story and seeking justice for her son. We invited her to tell that story on KELLY on 9 April 1993.

As you might imagine, the Catholic Church was opposed to the idea in general but even more so, because 9 April in 1993 happened to be Good Friday. What difference that made I'm not sure, but behind closed doors huge pressure was brought to bear on UTV management to make us drop the interview.

But doors are rarely completely sealed in Northern Ireland and the Catholic Church's objections soon leaked out. Now it wasn't in our interest to leak the story, but whoever did gave the *Belfast Telegraph* and other newspapers front-page headlines for three days. So instead of the story going away, as the Catholic Church wished, the publicity they brought upon themselves only heightened the level of interest and consequently increased the number of viewers of the KELLY show. Everyone now wanted to see for themselves the woman who would not be quieted.

To his eternal credit, the managing director at the time, Desmond Smyth, refused to be browbeaten and gave us the company's full backing to proceed.

The previous Friday, Murphy had appeared on the *Late Late Show*, which I watched, and for the first and only time I was disappointed with Gay Byrne's interview. Every utterance from Annie Murphy was greeted with scepticism by the interviewer. I didn't think she got a fair hearing. After all, who was most in the wrong, a Catholic priest who betrayed the trust placed in him, or an emotionally damaged young girl seduced and abandoned by a member of the cloth?

Ms Murphy also seemed to feel she was being poorly treated in the interview, so by the time she arrived with me she was very wary of all interviewers. I gave her free rein in the discussion. I saw no reason to disbelieve her. After all, the facts spoke for themselves. She was in Fr Casey's care, he seduced her, they had a son and he refused to live up to his responsibilities, denying for many years their very existence. That was it, black and white.

Today, such a story might not even make a chat show. But fifteen years ago it was the fattest, juiciest piece of scandal and shame ever to visit the Catholic hierarchy. I have not heard anything about Annie Murphy since, but I hope she and her son are doing well.

Oddly enough, on another occasion when I got into hot water, the *Late Late Show* was also involved. In 1995 the Irish Rugby Football Union unveiled the new anthem that would be sung henceforth at every Ireland rugby international. Called 'Ireland's Call', it was composed by Phil Coulter.

As the Ireland team is a mixed squad, North and South, Catholic and Protestant, it was generally viewed that the Irish national anthem, 'Amhran na bhFiann', was not the most appropriate song to represent the whole island, considering the political and religious sensitivities of the various players and fans. A new anthem was required, one that would galvanise both players and fans alike in one common cause. The answer was 'Ireland's Call'.

It was agreed with the IRFU that if the song was to be heard for the first time simultaneously by rugby fans throughout the whole of Ireland, then a link-up between the KELLY show and the *Late Late* would be the most effective way of doing it. It was further agreed that I would do the interviews with a few key players and administrators in the KELLY studio in Belfast and then go over to the *Late Late* in Dublin where Phil Coulter and a choir would perform the song.

Gathered with me in Belfast were Noel Murphy, a former player and manager of Ireland and the Lions; Ken Reid, secretary of the Ulster Branch of the IRFU; David Tweed, a player with Ireland in 1995 and a loyal Orangeman; and Willie Anderson, a former captain of Ireland from Co. Tyrone.

Not wanting a wishy-washy interview, I decided on a different tack, something slightly more aggressive. David Tweed was known for his staunch loyalist views and connections, so I started with him. 'Isn't it true, David, that you find it almost unbearable to stand to attention in Lansdowne Road in Dublin with the tricolour flying and the Irish national anthem being sung? This new anthem is solely to appease Protestants. It's not there to rally the team to greater achievements on the field of play. It's there for purely political reasons.'

Great question; wrong place, wrong time, wrong guest, wrong approach, wrong every bloody thing! Boy, had I misjudged the moment. The other guests looked at me in horror. What was supposed to be a friendly, celebratory chat, I had immediately turned into a political debate and they were having none of it. I was getting those come come now, Gerry looks and tut, tut, that's not what this conversation is about.

Within minutes I knew I had adopted a totally wrong tactic but was finding it difficult to backtrack. I manfully pushed on but was made feel like a recalcitrant schoolboy who was deliberately missing the point altogether. The discussion ended in confusion and then it was time to hand over to the *Late Late* to hear the song. As I did so, I could have sworn I heard Gay Byrne mumble something like, 'What was all that about?'

Sometimes you get it right; sometimes you get it wrong. I got it wrong and was publicly pilloried the following week in the press for my handling of the interview. To this day, every time I stand and listen to 'Ireland's Call' at an Ireland international rugby match, a little shudder runs through my body.

———

GK: Roger, I think you are due on stage at a quarter to ten and it is now a quarter past nine.

Roger Moore: They'll have to wait. I'm enjoying myself here.

———

Chapter 16 ～

A GOOD WALK SPOILED

y the mid-1990s my life was beginning to change quite
rapidly, not just in work but also in my personal life. *KELLY*
had become compulsory viewing for many people on a
Friday night and with it, of course, came instant fame. There was
nowhere in Northern Ireland I could go without being recognised
and increasingly the same was true for the South of Ireland.

In the beginning it was flattering to be asked for an autograph
or to be given the 'best seat' in the restaurant, but more and more
slices of my personal life were being exposed in newspapers and
magazines. For many years I lived in dread of some newspaper
man digging up pieces of my early family history, especially about
my father. I had never told anyone about him and I wouldn't have
known how to react if a journalist had confronted me with the
story. In some way my father's guilt became my guilt; his shame
became my shame. Stupid, I know, but that's how I felt. Most
times, newspapers have a knack of sensationalising such stories,
and at that time I didn't want that particular skeleton out of the
cupboard.

But it was in the more simple, mundane aspects of life where a
career in television can have its drawbacks. My two daughters, for
example, were still in their early teens and trying to live like
normal schoolgirls. It was only much later they told me that they
often got a hard time from other pupils in school simply because
I was their father. Helena and I tried very hard to keep them away
from all publicity surrounding me. After all, this wasn't their
choice. We would only agree to do family photo shoots, for
example, if they agreed and were comfortable with it. We were

determined to live as normal a life as possible and to do the normal family things.

When the girls were still in primary school, I remember on one particular occasion going off to Newcastle, Co. Down, for a Sunday family outing, something we had been doing for years. We would take them to an amusement arcade for a few hours, spend time on the beach, perhaps enjoy a meal together and then return home—an innocent day out but a family day, a special day, important time spent together.

On this particular day the four of us were walking down the main street in Newcastle licking ice creams. We hadn't walked ten yards when someone stopped me and asked for an autograph. I handed my ice cream to Helena and signed. Well, that was the last I saw of my ice cream! Others came up for autographs or asked me to pose for photographs. And something really popular at that time was to ask me to speak to their wife/mother/husband/granny/child on their mobile phone.

Now I would never refuse people who ask for such things; after all they are the same people who support me week after week on the show. They are always very courteous and polite, so the least I can do is respond likewise. If the truth be told, I thoroughly enjoy meeting the public. You tend to be told the truth in these circumstances because if they don't like something you did or said, they will tell you. I remember one old lady making a bee-line for me in Belfast. As she approached she asked, 'Are you Gerry Kelly?'

'Guilty,' says I.

'Well, you look better in colour,' she replied, and walked on.

Now whether she had only a black and white television set and I looked better in real life or she had a colour television set and I looked worse in real life, I'll never know. But then again you've heard the old maxim: 'The only thing worse than being recognised is *not* being recognised.' And I suppose there is a certain truth in that.

But that day in Newcastle, as I signed everything that was handed to me, I could see Helena, Sarah and Claire standing to the side waiting for over fifteen minutes to resume our family day out.

At that stage I decided we would head back to the car and go home. What was the point of continuing if I was going to be accosted every few yards and the girls forced to wait around until I had finished. That wasn't what we had come out for. I was quickly learning that recognition, even at my lowly level, came at a price. And I was beginning to resent it. I was determined that, in future, my family would be kept away from any publicity surrounding me.

Don't get me wrong. I know a certain amount of privacy is lost the minute you decide to put your face on television every week. That's OK. I was prepared to accept that, but what I didn't want was for my job to interfere and disrupt the lives of my children. That wouldn't be fair.

So it was now a matter of getting used to my new life and adjusting my family life accordingly. Sadly, it meant an end to local family outings. Even Helena, who used to like me going clothes shopping with her, decided she would now prefer to go alone. To be honest, I didn't object to that particular decision!

On the plus side, of which there were many, my financial standing with the bank was a little more healthy. Gone were the days when I used to cross the street my bank was on, terrified that the manager would run out, grab me by the collar and ask me in for a chat.

I remember the day of the final KELLY programme of the first series, when the management called me up to the boardroom, congratulated me on a successful year and gave me a cheque for £5,000 by way of a bonus. Later that afternoon Charles Hurst Ltd presented me with a new Jaguar for my personal use for an indefinite period, and just before the programme that night Chris de Burgh sent me up a magnum of champagne from his home in Dublin, tangible proof that the programme was working and that I personally was beginning to make an impact.

To be honest, it would have been easy to get carried away with all this new-found interest in me. Perhaps had I been a younger man, I could have been tempted, but at 40 years of age I had definite views of who I was and what I wanted. I was firmly rooted in the person I was.

_____

GK: If you'll forgive me for saying so, Tyne, you don't seem to have fallen into the trap of being the typical Hollywood actress. I mean the face lifts, the boob jobs, the botox, the detox. Have you assiduously avoided that?

Tyne Daly (detective Mary Beth Lacey in the TV *drama* Cagney and Lacey*) (laughing): I'm a very defiant person and it is really fun to defy what everybody is doing with these grey hairs. These hairs terrify people in Los Angeles. I go into rooms there full of people fully thirty years older than I and who are still preserving their looks from 1954.*

_____

Television is a fickle, unreal world, a place where the flavour of the month can fast become a bad taste in the mouth, a place where envy lubricates many people's attitudes and where jealousy can so confuse people that they begin to stab each other in the front! It was important to treat what I was doing as a job, like any other job, and not get caught up in the tempting tangents that automatically flow from a successful position in television.

One of the first things I did was to find a good agent, someone who would buffer me from the many requests I was getting to appear at functions or openings of supermarkets and so on. I found one of the best in Michael Magill, based in Warrenpoint, and for almost twenty years Michael advised and guided me through what I should be doing and, perhaps more importantly, what I should not be doing.

As a staff member of UTV, there are certain rules laid down concerning personal guest appearances. Basically, they frown upon news people aligning themselves too closely with commercial interests—common sense really, considering that a news journalist may be invited to open some company's new factory one day, and the next be obliged to quiz that same company over restrictive work practices or the like on the news. The two positions are not compatible; conflicting interests I think they call it.

However, I had left my staff job with UTV in 1990 and had gone freelance, setting up my own company. I therefore had a free hand in the personal appearances I made as long as I adhered to a clause in my contract which stated that I would not undertake any work that would conflict with the interests of UTV. Personal appearances can be a financially lucrative market. Paying a local celebrity to come along is one way for event organisers to ensure extra publicity and attract a crowd. For the celebrity it's extra cash, the icing on the cake.

It was something, though, that I did sparingly. I wasn't that keen on being out more than two or three times a month, so Michael would put a premium on my asking fee. He would do all the negotiating and I would only be brought into the equation when the deal was done. If a fee couldn't be agreed, Michael was the baddie, not me—I had nothing to do with it.

Charities were different. I never charge charities for any work I do for them, but that means you have to pick the charities you want to work with. Otherwise, if you accepted every request you could be out seven nights a week.

Each year Michael and I would nominate two charities that I would help. The most rewarding of these was my involvement with Concern Worldwide, an organisation dedicated to eradicating world poverty.

In 2004 I took a television crew out to Darfur in the Sudan to film the work of Concern there, and then in 2006 I visited Mozambique to see for myself the great strides, especially in education, that have taken place in that country because of this wonderful charity.

But it was Darfur that was to rock me back on my heels. I had actually never heard of the place and had no idea where it was when I was first asked to go. But what I bore witness to in that one week would change my life for ever.

Even though I had filmed the dreadful orphanages in Romania under the Ceaucescu regime and witnessed thousands of children abandoned and left to fend for themselves; even though I had visited and filmed the horrendous after-effects of the radioactive fall-out in Chernobyl, none of my life experiences up until this point had prepared me for Darfur. I remember referring to the situation as 'hell on earth'.

In 2004, Darfur was being described as the worst humanitarian crisis in the world and even though four years have elapsed and other tragedies have replaced Darfur in world headlines, to my mind it is still the worst humanitarian crisis in the world today. Armed militia, known as the Janjaweed, who are backed by the Sudanese government, are systematically cleansing large parts of the country. Killings, beatings, burnings, lootings and rape are all part of daily life in Darfur. The result is over two million displaced people, people who have been terrorised out of their homes and forced to walk hundreds of kilometres to find the relative security of a makeshift camp, set up hastily by agencies like Concern and Oxfam.

Even those who survive the violence and manage to reach a camp will still live in poverty and squalor. These camps can only offer the basics for living. Once a fortnight each child under 5 years old receives 20 grams of vegetable oil, 250 grams of CSB (corn Soya blend), 20 grams of sugar and two bars of soap. Everyone else had to fend for themselves.

I am no expert on the internal conflict that is raging in Sudan and obviously there is no simple solution. Some say it is Arab Africans against Black Africans, Muslim against Christian, North against South, but it's much more complicated than that. The Chinese government is involved because of the oil reserves in the country and it is their support of the Sudanese government that is exacerbating the situation. So, what is the international community doing about it? Damned little if you ask me.

But it's due to the efforts of such stars as George Clooney and Mia Farrow that the horrors of Darfur are being kept alive in the public mind. And earlier this year, when film director Steven Spielberg resigned his position with the Beijing Olympics in protest over China's involvement with Sudan, people began to talk about Darfur again. Sadly, it takes people like this to speak out and tell the truth.

The British government, the American government and, for that matter, the Irish government, are only heard through their silence. The lessons the world should have learned from the genocide in Rwanda just over a decade ago have not been learned. Darfur is the new Rwanda and the world doesn't seem to give a toss.

Believe me, once you've seen for yourself the extent of the horror that is Darfur, you begin to reassess your own set of priorities. And that was the case for me when I returned in December 2004 to a Belfast that was gearing itself up for a bumper Christmas season. The fairy lights, the decorations, the late night shopping, the Christmas parties, the turkey dinner, the seasonal good cheer were all tainted with the sights, sounds and smells of people suffering on the other side of the world. Christmas 2004 was not a good time for me. But human nature being what it is, and even though the images of Darfur still haunted me, I had to get on with my own life.

I still do work for Concern, going around the country talking to groups about my experiences there—at least that salves my conscience a little. As a young man I was into sport, being somewhat proficient at Gaelic football, soccer, badminton and table tennis, but then in my early 20s I discovered golf. This most frustrating of games has remained a lifelong passion and one of the best ways I know of escaping the pressures and rigours of everyday life. Golf, I am aware, is considered by many to be a middle-class, stuffy, male-orientated game played by men in checked trousers and loud jumpers. Mark Twain once described it as 'a good walk spoiled'. However, I prefer professional golfer Chi Chi Rodriguez's description that golf is the most fun you can have without taking your clothes off.

I have been a member of Ardglass Golf Club in County Down for over thirty years and was given the ultimate accolade in 2001 when I was invited to become captain of this historic club, an honour I treasure to this day.

Being a member of the local club and living in Ardglass have both been tremendously important to me over the years. Since I moved to the village after my marriage in 1976, I've grown to love the place. At the start I didn't quite understand the nuances of village life. I found it rather claustrophobic, with everyone knowing your business and all the locals apparently related. Take, for example, Helena's family, the Flemings, who are related to the Megraws, who are related to the Mulhalls, who are related to the Milligans, who are related to the Howlands, who are related to the Priors, who are related to the Willses, who are related to the Ewings, who are related to the Caseys, who are—get my point? It takes a few years to get to grips with familial relations. Mind you, I am still regarded as an import even though I've lived here for thirty-two years.

As for Belfast people who have settled here, well, they're treated somewhat more harshly. They are known as Frankies, a name that stems from the Second World War when many children were evacuated from the city to Ardglass. It was the custom for those children as they made the train journey to Ardglass to be franked on the arm with a number or name—hence the term 'Frankies', which has stuck to this day. All good natured, but still I'd rather be an import than a Frankie!

Throughout the troubles Ardglass was an oasis, a place where normal life existed and where it was safe to raise a family. Thankfully it was only on the very odd occasion when the mayhem of terror that was sweeping large areas of Northern Ireland impinged on life in Ardglass. The people of Ardglass have been very good to me and very protective. For example, I have heard stories of strangers coming into the village and enquiring of a local where I lived and being given all sorts of complicated directions more akin to a wild goose chase. I'm treated as one of the locals and I like that very much.

Most Saturday mornings I can be found on the local golf course playing in my regular four ball. It has been a tradition now for many years, and hopefully many more to come. Even though I have golfed all around the world and played in many star-studded tournaments with top professionals and celebrities, it's that four ball on a Saturday with my friends that I value most.

To have been captain of this 112-year-old club was a huge honour. And today when I look at the list of names on the captains' board, I feel a deep sense of pride that my name is among them. I continue to be heavily involved in the organisation of the club as both a council member and convenor of the marketing committee which helps promote Ardglass throughout Ireland and further afield.

The charitable Links Golf Society based in Dublin also honoured me by staging the Gerry Kelly Golf Classic for three years at both the Hermitage and Luttrelstown golf clubs. Over the three events more than £150,000 was raised for local charities.

One of the great advantages of working in television is that I get a lot of invites to play golf on some of the greatest courses in Ireland. Only golfers, I expect, can appreciate the thrill of stepping out on to the first tee at the likes of the K Club, Portmarnock, Royal County Down, Druid's Glen or Ballybunion. Whether you play off scratch or you are an 18 handicapper makes no difference. The fact that you can play on the same courses where some of the greatest professional golfers in the world have played is a buzz in itself.

I mean, your everyday Gaelic footballer may never get the chance to play in Croke Park, soccer players don't get to play in Wembley, tennis players don't get to Wimbledon or rugby players to Lansdowne Road, but ordinary golfers from any walk of life can play on the likes of the K Club where last year twenty-four of the greatest players in the world fought it out for the Ryder Cup.

I have always enjoyed the company of professional golfers. I wouldn't say I'm best buddies with many of them, but I have come to know some of the Irish players quite well. One, whose company is a delight, is Christy O'Connor Junior. Junior, of course, for all his world-wide success, will be forever remembered for his magnificent 2-iron approach shot to the 18th green in the 1989 Ryder Cup match at The Belfry in England. He was playing Freddie Couples in a singles match on the Sunday. The pair were tied going to the last hole. O'Connor's drive still left him 229 yards from the pin and when he lifted out a 2-iron from his bag to play his second shot, he knew he had to win the hole if Europe was to stand any chance of retaining the Ryder Cup. What happened next is the stuff of golfing legend. He rifled the 2-iron shot to just 4 ft from the hole, so close that Freddie Couples conceded the putt. Needless to say, it was the shot of the tournament, the shot that was to beat Couples and decide the outcome of the 1989 Ryder Cup. Europe retained the trophy. Well, that particular piece of sporting magic is part of Christy O'Connor Junior, the world golfing superstar, but there's another side to Christy.

In 1998, he and his wife Ann suffered a huge family tragedy, the nightmare of every parent. Their youngest son Darren was tragically killed in a car accident in County Galway. He was only 17 years old.

Weeks later I spoke with Junior who recounted to me a story that, simultaneously, brought tears to my eyes and a smile to my lips. Christy had agreed to play in a special Pro/Am tournament that Darren Clarke had organised at Portmarnock Links in Dublin. The proceeds of the day's golf, which was hoped would be somewhere in the region of £150,000, was going to the fund set up to help the families of the victims of the Omagh bombing.

Because it was so soon after the funeral, Christy told me he really didn't feel up to playing, but considering the worthiness of the cause, he decided to make the effort. As he was leaving his home, he noticed young Darren's golf clubs in the hallway. As he passed, he lifted Darren's putter and put it in his own bag.

During his round Christy decided to use Darren's putter. On the first green he sank a long putt causing him to lift his eyes sky-ward and smile. On the second, something similar happened, and then, he said, things got out of hand. On every green, no matter where the ball was, he sank the putt. He just couldn't go wrong. He couldn't miss the hole with his son's putter. I sat spellbound as Christy told me the story and a shiver ran through my body. Darren was obviously looking out for his dad.

In December 2004, I took a phone call from Junior telling me that his uncle, the legendary Christy Senior, was about to celebrate his 80th birthday a few days before Christmas. Junior had arranged for over 300 guests to attend a surprise party for him at the City West Hotel in Dublin and would I come down to act as host for the evening. What an honour! To be part of the great man's life, even for just an evening, was simply a thrill.

Christy Senior was probably the greatest natural exponent of the game Ireland has ever produced. He played in the Ryder Cup on ten consecutive occasions from 1955 to 1973, a record only surpassed by Nick Faldo at the end of the 1990s. For over three decades he dominated Irish and British golf. Even today that wonderful British commentator Peter Alliss considers Senior to be the greatest manufacturer of shots he has ever seen.

I knew Christy of course. He was a very active president of the Links Golf Society and I had even enjoyed a round with him on his beloved Royal Dublin course, where he was made an honorary life member.

On the night of his 80th birthday, Christy Junior had invited Senior out to the hotel for a meal on the pretext of a family celebration. Meanwhile all 300 of us were assembled in the Great Hall awaiting the entrance of 'Himself,' as he is generally known.

After their meal and with some excuse about going for a nightcap, Junior successfully steered his uncle towards the real party. As the doors opened and Christy entered, we all broke into 'Happy Birthday' and believe me, I have never seen anyone look so surprised. The secret had been well hidden and it was an emotional Christy Senior I invited on to the stage for a night of tributes and presentations.

Old film reels had been secured showing Christy playing in his heyday; tributes from fellow professionals, old and new, were paid; video links with some of today's stars were shown and presentations by the bucketload were made.

It was a night of huge nostalgia and a timely acknowledgment of the genius that is Christy O'Connor Senior. For me, to have been part of it was truly special.

I didn't get many opportunities over the years to chat to professional golfers on *KELLY* simply because they were usually off playing in some foreign land or other. But I do remember a night with Bangor golfer, David Feherty. David was one of the real characters on the tour and was never frightened to speak his mind. Today, of course, his devilish sense of humour and his quick-witted repartee is heard and enjoyed by millions of golf fans the world over through his on-course commentaries for CBS television in America.

I had known David for many years and he would often call into the little bar near UTV to meet up with a few of us when he was in Belfast. On this particular Monday there were about a dozen of us in the pub when David arrived.

During the course of the evening it was remembered that the All-Blacks were playing rugby at Ravenhill the following Saturday.

'Who wants tickets for the All-Blacks game at the weekend?' someone asked. 'I can arrange to get a few.'

There was an immediate chorus of 'Yes, Yes, Yes', as might be expected. But Feherty was silent.

'Don't you want a ticket, David?' I asked him, surprised.

'I've got a problem, Gerry,' he sighed resignedly. 'I'm playing in the Madrid Open this week and I fly out to Spain tomorrow, so I'll have to pass.' He looked genuinely crestfallen because he loved all sport. Then I saw him ruminating. Suddenly he came back to me.

'Look, Gerry, I've changed my mind. I'll never make the cut, so get me a ticket and I'll be back sometime on Friday night.'

Now for non-golfers, the cut in a professional tournament is made after the second day's play which is always on a Friday. Only the top sixty players or so make it through to the third and fourth days' play. So if you're not in the top sixty on Friday, you go home. David obviously felt he wasn't playing well enough to make the cut, so he could get a late flight back from Madrid on Friday night in plenty of time for Saturday's game in Belfast. Not the greatest mental attitude, I have to say, going into a major competition. Still, we would be glad of his company, so his name went down for a ticket. Payment would be collected on Saturday at the match.

Well, you've probably guessed the outcome. David did not show up for the game on Saturday. And why not? Not only did he make the cut but the so-and-so went on to win the bloody thing. David Feherty became the Iberia Madrid Open champion of 1992.

Months afterwards he brought the trophy back to that little bar in Belfast for us all to see. We had a huge celebration, so much so that everybody retired, including David, leaving the cup behind him. I'm not convinced it was ever recovered. And to cap it all, he never did pay for that ticket.

More recently, I was fortunate to get to know Ireland's latest golfing sensation, Holywood-born teenager Rory McIlroy. My first encounter with him was about ten years ago when he was only 9 years old. He had just won the World Under-10 Championships in America and even at that tender age was building quite a name for himself in golfing circles. We invited him and his parents, Gerry and Rosie, on to the programme to see for ourselves the extent of his talents.

At one point during the interview I asked Rory when did he get time to practise during the dark winter months. After all, by the time he got out of school, it was too dark to go to the course. He told me that each day he would practise by chipping a ball down the hall at home, through the open door of the kitchen and into the circular opening of his mum's tumble drier. It was such a visual and novel image, so we decided to put the 9-year old to the test. We laid a piece of carpet on the studio floor and set an open tumble drier fifteen yards away. He had four attempts at chipping in. The first just missed but the other three easily found the target—a remarkable feat. And if you don't believe me, try it yourself sometime.

Anyway, the interview ended up with me ruffling young Rory's hair and saying, 'Listen out for the name, Rory McIlroy. You'll be hearing a lot more about this young man in the years ahead.' I doubt if I've ever uttered more prophetic words. Rory went on to become one of the world's leading amateur golfers and in September 2007, at just 18 years of age, he turned professional. Today, this talented County Down teenager is viewed as the most exciting prospect in world golf.

As you've gathered, I like being around the professional golf scene and am very proud of the achievements of our Irish players.

On many occasions I interviewed the legendary Fred Daly, the first Irishman to win the British Open. In fact I made a documentary about him in 1987 when I accompanied him on a nostalgic trip back to the Royal Liverpool Golf Club in Hoylake on the fortieth anniversary of his celebrated victory there.

When he was presented with the famous Claret Jug in 1947, he jokingly remarked that the trophy had never been to Ireland and he hoped the change of air would do it good. Little did he know then that another sixty years would elapse before the trophy was to return when Padraig Harrington won it in 2007.

Talking of Padraig, I had the pleasure of playing with him in a charity tournament at the K Club just one week after he won the Open in July 2007. That day he was still walking on air. I don't think the magnitude of what he accomplished had sunk in. But when he repeated the victory in 2008 and became the back-to-back Open Champion, it must surely place him among the finest sportsmen this island has ever produced.

But it's not just their golfing prowess that draws me to these magnificent sportsmen. People like Darren Clarke, Paul McGinley, Graeme McDowell, Des Smyth and Christy O'Connor Junior are true ambassadors for their sport and their country. The inherent values of the game, integrity, honesty and commitment, all spill over into their personal lives, making them exemplary role models for any young people in this country.

GK: You spend your money wisely, don't you?

Darren Clarke: No.

GK: How many cars have you got?

DC: Too many.

GK: Six (writing the figure on a piece of paper). What cars do you own?

DC: A couple of BMWs …

GK (checking a list): Correct.

DC: A Mercedes.

GK: Correct.

DC: A Range Rover.

GK: Correct. And?

DC (after a delay and with a little smile): A couple of Ferraris.

GK: Correct. (loud cheers)

———

Chapter 17 ∾
| NEW YEAR'S EVE ON *KELLY*

New Year's Eve on UTV was traditionally a night when we linked up with our Scottish Television counterparts for their Hogmanay celebrations. We had never attempted to do a show in Northern Ireland for Northern Ireland. So, naturally, we on *KELLY* thought we should give it a go. However, our first attempt wasn't as successful as we would have liked, even though it looked good on paper.

We had been wracking our brains to come up with an idea which would encompass all the fun that viewers might expect on a New Year's Eve night. Without a strong tradition of our own it was difficult to identify the ingredients required for an end-of-year celebration. Going down to the pub and drinking your way into 1 January wasn't a viable option. So when we heard that the Europa Hotel was organising their own £100 per person bash, we decided we could piggy back their party.

They had planned the usual hotel evening of entertainment with a dinner dance and we thought we could give added value to the revellers by including a *KELLY* show over the midnight hour. We would have a ready-made audience, all in party mood, to give us that authentic New Year's Eve atmosphere. We would spice it up with a few well-known guests, some celebrated musicians and a bit of a laugh up to and through midnight.

The Europa was keen on the idea and we agreed that dinner would be over by 11 pm and then we would take over the entertainment at 11.15 through to 12.15.

All was going well until I arrived into the ballroom at around 10.30 and was greeted with a wall of sound, the sound of people in high spirits—alcoholic spirits! The party was really rocking. In fact it was rocking just a little too much which I thought could cause problems for us once the cameras started rolling. How were we going to quieten these party goers down for the programme which was due to start in just under three-quarters of an hour?

Try as we may, this particular crowd just wasn't interested. I spoke to them over the microphone explaining what we were about to do and was greeted with a good-natured cheer and a chorus of 'de de de de de. De de de de de. De de de de de de dee de—the first three lines of the *KELLY* signature tune, in case you didn't recognise it.

It was abundantly clear that they were out to enjoy themselves in the way they wanted and they didn't give a damn about the show or our entertainment. They simply would not shut up and the raucous noise throughout the hall was enormous. In retrospect I couldn't blame them. They had all spent a lot of money on this special night and if they wanted to talk, that's exactly what they would do. If they wanted to sing, that's what they would do, and if they wanted to drink, that's also what they would do. They let me know, not in an aggressive way, but in clear terms that this was *their* party, not mine. They weren't going to listen to instructions from floor managers, or anyone else for that matter.

In the end we managed to battle our way through the show, trying to keep the cameras away from the audience as much as possible and turning the audience microphones right down. The only time they really paid attention was on the stroke of midnight when the first few bars of 'Auld Lang Syne' were sung. I can honestly say that Robbie Burns's poem has rarely been executed with such gusto and passion as it was that night.

Not surprisingly, we never gatecrashed another party after that. If we wanted to continue with a New Year's Eve show, we would have to come up with a different idea for the following year.

I think it was our head cameraman David McBride who thought of it first. 'Why not do the show from your own house, Gerry,' he suggested. 'Isn't that what New Year's is all about, a party in a house?' Without thinking too deeply about it, I agreed that it was a good idea. David gave a wry smile, a smile that meant he knew that I had just given my permission for something that my wife could eventually kill me for!

When I told Helena of our plans, she asked what it would involve. I said the outside broadcast truck would be down for a day or two and we would record the programme in a few rooms around the house—no great disruption, just a little inconvenience for a couple of days. With that guarantee, she agreed to go along with it. How foolish! And how foolish was I for not anticipating what it actually means to have a full-blown OB in your home.

For a start, it meant having four huge vehicles parked outside for the best part of a week—not the two days I had suggested. It meant explaining to neighbours that they might have difficulty getting in and out of their driveways. But that was the least of the problems. Let me explain some of the other detail.

I knew that an outside broadcast needed lots of cabling for lights and cameras and such like, but until this particular New Year I hadn't quite realised the amount it would take.

'Ten miles of it?' said Helena in disbelief, 'and all of it has to come in through our house?'

But there was more. These cables had to go through doorways and of course there wasn't enough space under our internal doors to accommodate them. 'We've got the answer', said an engineer, as he started to unscrew all the doors off their frames. 'Don't worry, Gerry', he comforted. As I watched aghast, Helena stood in near disbelief as they fitted temporary plywood doors with an 18 inch gap underneath for the cabling. That solved the problem as far as the engineers were concerned. The cables could now go under the doors from room to room. But you couldn't do that with the doors leading to the outside, so the cables had to be brought in through the windows.

'How do we shut the windows now?' Helena asked the engineer mournfully. I dreaded the answer because I knew what he was about to say.

'You can't, Helena. They'll have to be kept open all week.' It was winter, so between the open windows and the gaps under the doors, the house was anything but cosy.

It took the best part of four days to set everything up, with upwards of two dozen people traipsing in and out of our precious home all day long. And all twenty-four of them had to use our lavatory! Nobody thought of bringing in portable toilet facilities.

Helena, like all home-makers, is house proud and had the place spotlessly clean for their arrival. But with all the work that was needed to set up, dust and dirt were inevitable. She would energetically remove it every time a dirty big footprint appeared on the carpet or when furniture was moved from its original spot. And indeed when transmission time came and the big powerful television lights were switched on, you could see the dust on every horizontal surface. So Helena spent most of her time frantically running about the place with a duster. I won't even mention the state of the bathroom!

Technically, lighting was a problem. You will notice that television studios are tall, usually about two storeys. This is necessary to accommodate the huge bank of lights that are required, suspended high over the studio floor for an even distribution of light. So because of the restricted ceiling height, lighting an ordinary house was a problem. We had oak beams in our lounge, so lights were glued, attached, screwed to, slung, wedged and any other way you care to imagine so that the room could be lit without a mass of shadows.

Added to all this was the problem of where to put the programme guests, to say nothing of the fifty or sixty friends and neighbours invited for the occasion. We also needed a room for make-up and for wardrobe—not easy to accommodate all this in a four bedroomed bungalow!

On the night, it felt like Dr Who's Tardis. It was a nightmare, just a nightmare. And yet it produced magic television. It felt like a real house party and not just a studio mock-up. Obviously, it would have been more sensible to build a 'home' setting in the studio, but we would have lost out on so much atmosphere.

My two daughters were very young at the time and they thought it was a great adventure. As for Helena? Well, when the last of the OB crew finally left the house twenty-four hours after the event, she was actually quite pleased. Even so, I waited a few months before I dared to ask if we could repeat the event for the next New Year. Unbelievably, she agreed—on two conditions. UTV would install portable loos and there would be some other area for make-up and wardrobe besides the girls' bedrooms. The deal was struck.

In fact we did four shows in all from our home, all of them hugely successful. One year I even managed to talk Helena into singing on the show 'The Spinning Wheel', accompanied by Phil Coulter. That's a precious moment in our family video.

Guests over the years included Christie Hennessy, Finbar Furey, Ronan Tynan, Ralph McTell, Brendan Grace, Roy Walker, Charlie McGettigan and Paul Harrington. We even cajoled many of Northern Ireland's most famous broadcasters to sing for us, among them Gerry Anderson, Jackie Fullerton, John Daly, Wendy Austin, Derek Davis, Candy Devine and Sean Rafferty.

Even though I say it myself, these were wonderful, wonderful shows, all the more so because we in Northern Ireland do not have a tradition of acknowledging New Year's Eve, notwithstanding our close ties with Scotland. Often we are at a loss to think about what you actually do, aside from going out drinking. A house party was quite a good answer. It was also gratifying to know that over 70 per cent of the television audience on New Year's Eve watched those KELLY shows. I believe it helped to forge a bond with our audience, to make us part of a huge shared experience, and it helped the name KELLY as a brand.

To this day people kindly and nostalgically say to me, 'Why don't you do your New Year's Eve programme from your home again?' They watch me smile, that smile our head cameraman David McBride had on his face when he first suggested the idea. Anyway, we've built a new house since then and there isn't a snowball's chance in hell that Helena would allow it ever to happen again. Party pooper!

And now for a confession—all the New Year's Eve programmes were recorded. Yes, I admit it. We had been bluffing the public for years. In fact, some of those shows were recorded in the first week of December! So how did we manage to convince the sixty or seventy house guests that Christmas had come and gone and that it was now time for 'Auld Lang Syne' three or four weeks before the event? Actually, it wasn't all that difficult. Everyone slipped into the mood very easily and treated it all as fun. However it felt odd and just a little fraudulent to be asking guests what they got for Christmas. I remember Paddy Kielty once going through a whole list of his presents without batting an eyelid. So, were we cheating the public? I suppose by recent television rulings we were, but it was an innocent lie, one I can certainly live with. We continued to do a *KELLY* programme on New Year's Eve right up to 2007 and I always felt it a privilege to be allowed to be part of people's celebrations, especially at such an emotional time of the year.

These were the only shows we recorded. All the others were live, something I am immensely proud of, not just for myself but for everyone involved.

———

Chris Tarrant, presenter of Who Wants to be a Millionaire?:

I hate it when people lose. I want them to win. I get no pleasure out of saying I'm sorry you've lost. These are huge sums of money. And there are times when I'm thinking, 'I can't believe you don't know that. How stupid are you?' And everybody does that. You all at home do that.

GK: You give nothing away.

CT: That's my job. I am good at a poker face. Of course there are times when I'm thinking, 'Just say it, just say it. And I will give you a quarter of a million or whatever.'

———

Live television is almost a thing of the past. Apart from the News, practically every other programme on our screens is recorded. Everything has been cleaned up in the editing process: the little missed cues, the stumble over a word or two, maybe a few bad camera shots or a glitch in the sound quality, all eradicated to make programmes and presenters look smooth and to my mind somewhat artificial. Performers, many of them very highly paid, will just not put themselves in a position where their fumbles and mistakes will be broadcast to the nation.

Producers and directors throughout the network would not even contemplate doing a show like KELLY live in front of a studio audience, a fast-moving show that on any given night includes five or six interviews, two or three live bands, perhaps a satellite link-up, videos being played into the programme and chats with members of the audience. They feel too much can go wrong and are prepared to stop and start, shoot re-take after re-take and spend four or five hours recording one programme. By this stage, of course, the audience is bored out of their minds and any spon- taneity from the guests has long since evaporated. The end result? A programme that looks flawless, a presenter who is word perfect and canned laughter dubbed over the lethargic applause from an already comatose audience. Either that or the audience has been so over-hyped and rehearsed that their reactions are totally over the top.

Early in my career I saw an example of the lengths to which some programme makers will go to ensure the presenter and his interviews appear witty and clever. Eva Herzigova, the Czech model who rose to fame through those sexy Wonderbra ads, was available for interview in London. In the 1990s she was one of the world's top supermodels and those rather evocative photographs of her in her underwear were causing quite a stir at the time. We decided to take up the invite and go to London to interview her.

Now what happens on a day like this, when obviously every tele- vision and radio station in the UK and Ireland has been invited, is we all turn up and are each allocated half an hour or so for our interview with her. Everyone is given a room in the hotel to set up their cameras and lights and then at a given time Ms Herzigova will appear for interview.

We were fourth in line that morning. Jonathan Ross, who was working for Channel 4 at the time, was first. As I had time to kill, I decided I would nip down and listen to Ross's interview to try and pick up a few tips for my own chat. I listened for twenty minutes or so and was pleased to learn that Ross had not uncovered any material or stories about Ms Herzigova that I was not already aware of. In fact I thought his interview was a tad boring and lacking his customary quick humour.

My own interview with her was passable. Let's just say she wasn't the most enthralling person I have ever chatted to, maybe the sexiest, but not the most captivating.

Anyway, that's not the point. As we were preparing to leave the hotel, I chanced by the room where Ross and his team had just done their interview. Four or five men along with Ross were hunched over a monitor watching the interview they had just recorded. I was to learn that two of the men were scriptwriters and what was happening was they were listening to the answers already given by Ms Herzigova to Ross's original questions and then rewriting new questions for him to record. With Herzigova's answers already on tape, the writers were able to script funnier and wittier questions for Ross to ask and then edit them into the original film. The result was that Jonathan Ross was seen to have maintained his cheeky-chappy, quick-witted reputation as if it was all done in real time and completely off the cuff. Clever but just a little disappointing, don't you think?

Our attitude on *KELLY* was always to go live. There was no tampering with interviews, no long days in the edit suites; show it as it is. To do so, we relied heavily on the expertise of our technical teams and were rarely let down. What we got in return was an authentic ninety minutes of television every week. Sure, there were little mistakes here and there, but these did not diminish the overall effect of the programme. Everyone knew that we had one, and only one go at getting it right. It heightened the tension in the studio, made everyone acutely aware of their role and responsibility and, to my mind, brought out the best in all of us.

I remember presenting a horse-racing programme from Downpatrick Racecourse with the exuberant Channel 4 pundit John McCririck. McCririck had never been to this particular race track before. He was more used to the manicured lawns and hospitality tents of Epsom or Ascot. But he loved Downpatrick. He told me, 'This is what real horse-racing is all about, not that pretentious crap you get at some race tracks. You can actually smell the horse manure here!'

Now it's odd I should remember that conversation and even odder perhaps that I should recount the story in the context of the *KELLY* show. But I always considered that what we did was real chat show television, not the highly edited, artificially produced content of some other similar UK shows. (By the way, forget the horse manure bit. That's the sort of line only smart-assed TV critics pick up on and then proceed to write a hilarious article for some newspaper or other.)

Live television is much more difficult to do and is much more risky to pull off successfully, and even though I can understand the reasons why people shy away from it, I found it exhilarating. I was never egotistical enough to worry that my mistakes would be seen by the nation. But I believed that if things did go wrong, be they mistakes of my own making or those of others, I had the confidence and the ability to cover for them. I wanted *KELLY* to be real. I wanted the audience to identify with the programme and with me. I was never the suave, slick presenter with the good looks and pearly white teeth. I was Gerry Kelly, a former teacher from Ardglass, an ordinary guy who did not believe in the pretentious air of mystery and intrigue that surrounds television and many television presenters. The show had to be accessible and be seen to be accessible. I too had to be accessible, not acting like some attention-seeker more interested in his appearance than the content of the show.

Critics often describe my style of presentation as 'homespun'. If by that they mean unsophisticated, that's their opinion. I would suggest another meaning and that's 'down to earth'. It's not a style of presentation that is everyone's cup of tea, I know, but it's who I am. It's not ostentatious, it's not a portrayal of something that I'm not. It's just me, I'm afraid.

Chapter 18 ~

SOME YOU WIN, SOME YOU LOSE

As the years progressed and as more and more guests were invited back for repeat appearances, I got to know and become friends with quite a few of them. There were others, of course, who could only be loved by their own mothers. One such notable, with whom I didn't see eye to eye, was Sir Clement Freud. He was booked to appear on KELLY on the same night as George Best which was exactly one week after Bestie's now infamous drunken appearance on the *Wogan* show.

Best was my first guest and I was determined to challenge him about his embarrassing television showing of the previous week. As usual with George, he was full of remorse and unreservedly admitted he was in the wrong. It was always hard to get angry with George and even though I had designed the interview around how much he had let himself and his family down, when George smiled apologetically—well, I simply backed off. For all his faults, George Best was so damned likeable. Anyway, after George's interview, we went to a piece of music and then it was the turn of Sir Clement. He had originally been invited over to Belfast by the Northern Ireland Tourist Board and that evening before the show, they had invited him out to dinner in Paul Rankin's restaurant, Roscoff's.

An hour before our programme was due to start, we took a phone call from someone in Roscoff's who wanted to mark our card. He told us that the former Liberal MP liked to be addressed as Sir Clement and if he ordered whisky and ice, it meant he wanted the whisky in one glass and the ice in another. Better to know these things in advance, I suppose.

My researcher had also informed me earlier in the day that Sir Clement didn't particularly want to talk about his grandfather, the famous psychoanalyst Sigmund Freud, and he most certainly did not want to talk about a TV commercial he did many years previously for dog food. In case you're interested, the commercial was for Minced Morsels and featured Sir Clement with a bloodhound called Henry. So these were two areas I was advised to avoid in the interview.

At the time, the 'George Best on Wogan' story had received massive publicity in every newspaper in the land for over a week. News programmes repeated *ad nauseam* various clips from the interview, so unless you lived on Mars there was little chance of not knowing what had gone on.

I assumed Sir Clement would at the very least have heard about the incident and because he had been speaking to George in the green room beforehand, I thought it a safe bet to open with his take on what happened. For such a renowned raconteur and newspaper columnist, his answer was surprising to say the least. He said he knew very little about the incident and therefore wasn't qualified to speak about it. Odd, I thought, but fair enough. Maybe he was on Mars that week!

The interview progressed, but within a few minutes I was getting the distinct impression that Sir Clement was not really in the mood to chat. Perhaps he was annoyed at being hauled away from Roscoff's before he had time to finish his dessert. Whatever the reason, I was getting nowhere and the interview had still six minutes to run.

In a final attempt to spark some reaction, I ventured into one of the taboo subjects. 'Can we talk a little about your famous grandfather?' I enquired.

'Which one?' he replied. 'I have two. Have you not?'

Well, bloody hell! What can you say to that? I was sorely tempted to ask him about the dog food commercial, but instead I politely thanked him for coming and came out of the interview four minutes early. Needless to say, Sir Clement didn't venture back to the green room to wait until the programme was over, so I never saw him again.

The following weekend, he wrote in his newspaper column a derogatory article about the night he spent in Northern Ireland and his appearance on the MURPHY show! As you can imagine, I was ever so slightly pissed off, but then I would never have to meet the man again, so what was the point of getting my knickers in a twist over him.

But then four years later, fate came knocking or should I say ringing. Sitting in my office one morning, I took a phone call from the producer of that wonderful Radio 4 show *Just A Minute*. He said that the BBC was planning to record a programme in Belfast as part of the Festival at Queen's and would I like to be a guest on the panel. I would be joining Paul Merton and Sir Tim Rice. *Just A Minute* has been airing on Radio 4 since the station was first launched in 1967 and enjoys a real cult following. It has a simple format: panellists are given sixty seconds to talk about a given subject without repetition, hesitation or deviation. Should any of the above occur, fellow panellists buzz in, state their reason to quiz master Nicolas Parsons and, if correct, continue on for what is left of the time. Whoever is left speaking when the minute is up wins the points.

As I considered it a rare honour to have been asked to participate in such an eminent show, I readily accepted. I heard nothing more for a few weeks and then the producer phoned me again.

'Gerry,' he said. 'You do know that Clement Freud will also be a panellist?'

'Why do you feel you have to tell me that?' I asked.

'Well, three or four years ago, I was a student at Queen's University in Belfast,' he said, 'and I watched you on KELLY interviewing Clement. You two didn't seem to get along. So I was just marking your card. Do you still want to do the programme?'

'Yeah, of course,' I answered, 'providing Sir Clement does.'

'Well, I have already asked him that question and he said he was OK about it if you were.'

'OK then, we'll do it,' said I. 'Just tell him my surname is Kelly.'

The night of the recording at Queen's was something of an anticlimax. I was all prepared to kiss and make up, but when someone introduced me to Sir Clement, he simply said, 'Yes, we've met.' We shook hands, recorded the programme and went our separate ways.

Thankfully, Sir Clement Freud was one of only a handful of guests to whom I took an instant dislike. Others included Judith and Alan Kilshaw, the British couple who in 2001 paid £8,000 over the internet to adopt 6-month-old American twin girls. It transpired that the twins' natural mother had already sold the two girls to another couple. The Kilshaws then snatched the twins, brought them to the UK and sold their story to the tabloid press. Eventually Social Services took the girls into care and following a bitter legal battle, they were sent back to foster parents in America.

Judith Kilshaw was a nasty piece of work, aggressive, loud, delusional and totally mad. Alan Kilshaw was meek and spineless, a pathetic human being really. I thoroughly disliked this vile couple and their sordid tale from the outset, and I think I made my views clear on the programme.

Others I expected to dislike but didn't were Jonathan Aitken, the Dublin-born, former British MP and Treasury chief secretary. In 1999 he was sentenced to eighteen months in prison for perjury and perverting the course of justice. At the time I remember thinking, you deserve it, you upper-class twit, but then when I interviewed him, I changed my mind. He showed genuine remorse and agreed that he deserved his punishment. When he told me how his work in prison included cleaning out the communal toilets and how he regarded this work as worthwhile, I was impressed. He came across as a reformed human being. Aitken is now involved with a task force looking into prison reform.

———

GK: Did you have to work in prison?

Jonathan Aitken (ex cabinet minister jailed for perjury): Yes, I was the lavatory cleaner.

GK: That's a come-down.

JA: Well, I didn't mind it and I'll tell you why. First, it was a job which had a point to it. Hygiene in prison is terribly important especially in showers and so on. It was better than other jobs because there was a point to it, unlike some jobs, like moving logs in a yard in the morning and back again in the afternoon.

———

Another person I was determined to dislike was American boxing promoter Don King. King is the larger than life character who promoted such legendary fights as the Rumble in the Jungle with Muhammad Ali and George Foreman and the Thrilla in Manila between Ali and Joe Frazier.

The more I read about this man, the more I grew to dislike him. He came across as a bully and a fraud, cheating many fighters out of their rightful winnings. Then there were the murder allegations, having been twice accused of unlawful killing and found guilty once. To my mind he was loud, brash and totally unsavoury.

And yet, when I met him I was like putty in his hands. He appeared on the programme with three other boxing promoters, Barney Eastwood, Barry Hearn and Frank Warren, and yet he stole the show. He was charming, sharp and very humorous. He called me 'K, E, double L Y' and sang a verse of 'Has Anyone Here Seen Kelly?' He said he wanted to act as my agent and told me we could make a fortune together. He ended up being a memorable guest and very affable—that is if you ignore his darker side. But then Don King is a television veteran, a master of self-promotion.

Another guest I was prepared to dislike was Paul Burrell, Princess Diana's butler and self-proclaimed 'rock'. My initial impression of him remained largely unchanged after the interview. He came across as much too suave, too good to be true. His over-inflated opinion of his importance in Diana's life was manifestly fiction. I just didn't believe him. And nothing he has done or said since, including his testimony in early 2008 at the inquest into the death of Diana, has persuaded me to change my mind about him. I don't like people rewriting history and I don't like people who live off the back or reputation of others.

But enough of this negativity. Let's talk about some of the greatest people it has been my pleasure to have been associated with over the years.

Top of the list is the late George Best. Just before Christmas 2007, when his sister Barbara McNarry asked me to be the guest of honour at the launch of her book, *Our George*, I thought long and hard about what I would say in my speech. I reckoned I had interviewed George on at least fourteen different occasions. And sadly I anchored UTV's funeral coverage of the great man from the grounds of Stormont on 25 November 2005.

First and foremost I was a fan. Many a Saturday back in the late sixties in Manchester, I spent large chunks of my meagre student grant to get into Old Trafford to watch George and Denis Law beguile and mesmerise the opposition. He was a god to me then and even though I was fortunate to get to know him over the years, he remained a god in my eyes. But it was a night, almost five years to the day before his death, that I will never forget.

On 10 November 2000, we had dedicated the whole *KELLY* programme in tribute to George and had invited many of his former Manchester United and Northern Ireland colleagues, his friends and family and many of his fans into the studio to make up the audience. His former wife Alex was also there.

One of the highlights of that show was the presence of Van Morrison who went out of his way to ensure that he would be there for George. It is remarkable to think that these two world renowned performers, Van the Man and George Best, were born and raised literally within a few hundred yards of each other in east Belfast. Not known for his eloquence, Van declined a speaking role that night, but there were many others prepared to make up for him including former Northern Ireland boss Billy Bingham and former NI team mate, the late Derek Dougan.

Scottish international and Liverpool star Ian St John had a few memories of his own to recall, as had boxers Barry McGuigan and Dave 'Boy' McAuley. But for me, the outstanding memory came from motorcycle road racer Robert Dunlop who was killed tragically while competing in the NW 200 in May 2008. Back in 2000, it was obvious that the death of his brother, the legendary Joey Dunlop, who was also killed, during a race in Tallinn, Estonia, was still weighing heavily on his mind. At that time, it would have been a natural reaction for Robert to consider his own position and think of his own mortality in this most dangerous of sports. When I asked him if he wanted to ask George a question, he thought for a moment and said, 'How did you replace the buzz, George? I mean when you gave the game up, what was there to take its place?'

I felt it was an extremely personal question from Robert. Indeed I think he was contemplating his own retirement but wasn't sure if the void his withdrawal from the sport would create could ever be filled. But if he had been hoping for a positive, upbeat response from George, then he would have been disappointed.

Honest as always, George told him he had tried everything, drink, drugs and women. He said, 'Nothing else works. Nothing replaces that buzz. When the whistle blows at 3 pm on a Saturday and 60,000 fans are chanting your name, nothing can replace that.' And perhaps that question and answer encapsulated the life of George Best. It may even be part of the reason why Robert decided to continue competing in the sport. Both Robert and Joey lived for road racing. I doubt if anyone or anything could have deflected them from their destiny.

George was an enigma, but his appeal was universal. His footballing genius spoke for itself, but it was George's weaknesses, his vulnerability, his imperfections, that caused people to so readily identify with him. The 'where did it all go wrong' story was one that George loved. That evening in the KELLY studio, the respect and affection in which he was held was palpable. The audience at home also thought so, giving us one of the highest ratings we ever achieved. Over 325,000 people in Northern Ireland alone watched George that night.

I remember on another occasion I went up to the green room to say hello to him before the programme. It had been widely reported that he had been off the drink at the time and indeed he was going to talk about his new-found abstinence with me on the show. Consider my surprise therefore when I saw him standing at the bar with a full glass of wine in his hand.

'I thought you were supposed to be off that stuff,' I said.

'What? Wine?' he came back. 'Sure that's not alcohol.'

Regrettably, I never mentioned the wine incident during the interview and perpetuated the myth that he was still off the drink.

The last time I spoke to George was in 2003 after his liver transplant. Although looking rather jaundiced, he was still hoping for a full recovery—as we all were. When he died in 2005, I was on a plane coming back from London. As I was making my way out of the airport, one of the security men asked me if I'd heard about George. I knew what he was about to tell me. I have to say it came as no surprise, but I was immensely saddened.

The day of his funeral, I presented UTV's coverage from an area just outside the main entrance of Parliament Buildings at Stormont, where the service was to take place. It was a wet, dismal November morning, but if proof was needed of the extent to which George Best touched the lives of so many people, one look at the throng of people gathered in the grounds would suffice.

There is a wall mural in Belfast that reads: 'Maradona, Good. Pele, Better. George, Best.' My feelings exactly.

They say it can be dangerous to meet your heroes, that often they don't live up to your expectations. I know that to be true of some, but in the case of George Best I consider it an honour and a privilege to have known the greatest football player in the world.

———

George Best: I've had one slip since I started and that's since February. I was ill.

GK: You did have a slip?

*GB: I had a couple of glasses of champagne and it set
me back. I felt really ill. Professor Williams put me on a
new drug which I have to take for six months … and
the actual craving has gone away.*

———

It is very satisfying to have been in at the start of something big. I
know the *Late Late* introduced the world to Boyzone with their
never-to-be-forgotten television debut, but we also played a part
in their early career. Likewise with Westlife. In fact I can remember introducing Westlife as Westside, the name they had chosen
originally but had to change. So that's how far back we go.

I've lost count of the number of times Westlife have appeared
on KELLY, but I always looked forward to their visits. I found them
extremely articulate, well mannered and totally professional.
Their appearances always caused a stir at Havelock House both
inside and out. From early morning, in all kinds of weather,
legions of young fans would be ensconced outside the building
when news leaked out that Westlife were on the show. They
wouldn't budge until the boys arrived and then remained until the
show was over that night. Some of them would have been there for
over twelve hours, just to catch a glimpse of their heroes. Inside,
all sorts of feeble reasons were given as to why office workers
needed to be in the studio during rehearsals. But nobody minded.
It was all part of the hype and atmosphere that permeated the
whole building every Friday. Westlife made a special effort to be
part of the last ever KELLY show in 2005. I was extremely flattered
and when they presented me with a fully functional mini motorbike, I had to laugh. You see, U2 had presented Gay Byrne with a
Harley Davidson on his last *Late Late Show*, but the boys said they
were not as rich as U2, so the mini bike was all they could afford!
Both boy bands, Boyzone and Westlife, became huge friends of
the KELLY show and even though I am a generation (or two)
removed from them, we got on extremely well.

Former Westlife member, Bryan McFadden, invited Helena

and me to his wedding with Kerry Katona in January 2002. It was a fairly glitzy affair with the reception at Slane Castle. It was the first time I had seen a real showbiz wedding up close and because *Hello!* magazine had paid for exclusive rights to the wedding pictures, no one was allowed to take a camera with them into the church or reception.

Kerry arrived at the little Church of the Immaculate Conception in Rathfiegh, Co. Meath, with a phalanx of security guards in tow. Immediately they threw a tarpaulin from the wedding limousine to the porch of the church in a bid to hide her and her dress from the hordes of waiting cameramen as she exited the car.

It was a strange day. I enjoyed meeting the McFadden family, a down to earth bunch of which there are many connections, but as for its billing as the 'celebrity wedding of the year', famous faces were thin on the ground. I remember having a drink with Louis Walsh, Ronan Keating and Brian Kennedy. That was about it.

Throughout the celebrations, I couldn't help but think that both Bryan and Kerry were much too immature to fully understand the significance of the day. They were treating it like another gig, just another opportunity to party. They were both just 21 and had a six-month-old baby, Molly. Bryan's career was just beginning to take off with Westlife and although Kerry had left Atomic Kitten, a career in television was beckoning.

Marriage and a baby seemed to me to be the last thing they needed at this particular stage in their careers. But who was I to judge? They appeared happy and in love and so the 250 guests drank long into the night toasting their future together. Sadly, as we now know, the marriage was not to last and was over within two and a half years. The split was bitter, hostile and very public, at the centre, two young children, Molly and Lilly-Sue, innocents caught up in the tabloid washing of their parents' dirty linen.

———

GK: How's Kerry?

Young Bryan McFadden with Westlife (embarrassed): She's fine.

GK: Have you phoned her today?

BMcF: About ten minutes ago, before I came on. (cheers)

Westlife member: About fifty times.

BMcF (more embarrassed): Shut up.

Westlife member: Aw, don't go all embarrassed, Bryan.

GK: This is serious, isn't it?

BMcF: Yeah, I love her. (aaah then applause from the audience)

——

But I suppose of all the guys, Ronan Keating is the one I know best. Over the years we have kept in touch either through TV and radio interviews or socialising both on and off the golf course. I have huge admiration for Ronan and indeed the whole Keating clan.

Each year Ronan, his sister Linda and the rest of the family organise the Marie Keating Golf Classic at the K Club in Kildare. It's just one of their major fundraising events for the charity which is named after their mother. When Marie died in 1998 from breast cancer, the Keating family decided they would do everything they could to bring an end to this insidious disease. Having raised literally hundreds of thousands of euros, they now have three purpose-built mobile units which travel the whole of Ireland providing cancer information and awareness to the general public, all free of charge. Now that's how you put fame and influence to good use. In the same way another Boyzone member, Keith Duffy, uses his celebrity to promote awareness of autism. Keith and his wife Lisa have two children, Jordan and Mia. Mia who is now 8 years old was diagnosed with autism at 18 months. As a result, Keith and Lisa vowed to devote a huge amount of their time and energy raising funds and promoting awareness of what being autistic really means. I listened to Keith speak at a fundraising dinner for his charity last year and I was bowled over by his passion and eloquence.

When I think back to those early days when five raw, un-coordinated, immature Dublin youngsters first appeared on *KELLY*, I wouldn't have given tuppence for their survival in the business. And I certainly would never have believed that two of them would have gone on to become so influential in charity work. Fair play to you lads.

When it comes to spotting raw talent, I have to say my track record is not that good. However, there is one Irish group I had no doubt would become international stars. It was the *KELLY* office sec-retary, Helena Gaffney, who first brought the Corrs to my attention. Back in 1994, long before they were widely known and long before any chart success, Helena had heard them in their home town of Dundalk and thought they would make good guests for the show. 'The girls are absolutely beautiful and Jim's not so bad himself,' enthused Helena. So on the strength of her recommendation, we invited them to Belfast. Being a family, and a young family at that, we also invited their parents Gerry and Jean to accompany them.

I remember nipping down to the studio to listen to them rehearse. My God, what a good looking family and what a sound they created. During their interview I also spoke to their mum and dad, which I suppose is a little naff, considering how big the group ultimately became. But they were very young at the time and only starting out on the road that was to take them to inter-national stardom, so to include Gerry and Jean was justifiable. Sadly, mum Jean died a few years later, making the Corrs' debut TV appearance in Northern Ireland all the more precious and poignant to the family.

Even after they hit the big time, the Corrs never forgot *KELLY* or their Northern Ireland fans, making regular appearances over the years. They paid me the ultimate compliment by pulling out all the stops to be part of the final *KELLY* show.

It never ceases to fascinate me how lives are intertwined. My youngest daughter Claire works with the Niall Mellon Township Trust in Dublin, a charity dedicated to helping families in the townships of Cape Town. Basically, what they do is bring upwards of 1,000 Irish builders out to South Africa each year and for one week have what they term a building blitz. Tradesmen from all aspects of the construction industry volunteer their services to work in the townships, replacing the corrugated tin shacks that hundreds of thousands of families are forced to live in, with proper brick houses.

A few years back I made a documentary about the Trust in a Cape Town township called Imazamo Yethu and I can honestly say it is one of the most worthy and life-changing charities it has been my privilege to see in action. It's hard to imagine the squalor and poverty in these shanty towns. And to see Irish men and women transform the lives of so many deserving families is both gratifying and humbling.

One of the volunteers I met on my trip was a Belfast barrister, Gavin Bonnar, who just happens to be married to Sharon Corr. Both Gavin and Sharon are huge supporters of the charity, each year rolling up their sleeves and getting stuck into the bricks and mortar. Sharon has even cajoled her sisters Andrea and Caroline and her brother Jim into getting involved through various fundraising events. Small world, isn't it?

Perhaps of even greater significance was the appearance of international megastar Celine Dion on the show in 1992. Back then she was only beginning to build her phenomenal career, although she was already a major star in her native Canada. She appeared with Peabo Bryson singing their award-winning hit 'Beauty and The Beast'. I have to say Ms Dion looked a lot different in those days to her meticulously groomed image of today. If I was being harsh, I could say the title of the song was an apt description of her transformation into the icon she is today. But I shouldn't say such a thing. Mind you, it's amazing what money can do for a person's looks!

Celine was not a complete stranger to Ireland even then. In 1988 she had sung the winning entry in the Eurovision Song Contest which RTÉ hosted in Dublin. In case you ever play Trivial Pursuits, the answer to the question: which country did Celine Dion represent when she won the Eurovision? is Switzerland. And for total nerds, the song was called '*Ne Partez Pas Sans Moi*' (Don't Leave Without Me). To my eternal regret, I did not interview her that night. Looking back, it would have been nice to have had an early-in-the-career chat with the lady, but then I don't think anyone could have imagined the heights to which Celine Dion would rise.

There is one other person closer to home whose career the *KELLY* show has been chronicling since his early days. I first met Coleraine actor Jimmy Nesbitt in 1991 just before his film debut in *Hear My Song*, the story of the legendary Irish tenor Josef Locke.

Incidentally, my mother once told me she knew Josef Locke when she was a girl in Derry. She said that his real name was Joseph McLaughlin and that he once asked her out on a date. I've checked and his name was McLaughlin, so I have no reason to disbelieve the other part of mum's story.

Anyway, Jimmy and another Northern Ireland actor, Adrian Dunbar from Enniskillen, who was also the co-writer of the film, played the two main roles and both came in for interview. That was the start of what proved to be a long relationship between Jimmy Nesbitt and the *KELLY* show. In fact I believe Jimmy holds the record for being the most often invited guest on the programme. He shares the dubious honour with Brian Kennedy and Peter Corry—sixteen appearances, one for almost every year.

It is not difficult to see why Jimmy is regarded as one of the most popular and talented actors in Great Britain today. From his sensitive role as Adam Williams in the TV series *Cold Feet* to his compelling dramatic performance in the film *Bloody Sunday*, the versatility and breadth of his acting talents can be appreciated. But Jimmy is also great fun to be with, and if he has an Achilles heel, it's because his ebullient, outgoing personality often gets him into scrape after scrape with the tabloid press. The paparazzi love pursuing him and in 2002 the *Sun* newspaper ran stories about his alleged affairs, stories that almost cost him his marriage. To counteract the damning publicity, he was a guest on the 500th KELLY programme, which we broadcast from the Millennium Theatre in Derry. He was full of remorse and apologies and described himself as being 'a bit of an eejit'. But that was then. Jimmy's hell-raising days have come to an end and he's now back on track.

———

GK: Just think that if you'd not flunked at Jordanstown.

James Nesbitt: I didn't actually flunk, Gerry.

GK: You did. You flunked after a year.

JN: I didn't, Gerry. I dropped out after a year before I had a chance to flunk.

———

I have always liked Jimmy. He is an immense talent. We have shared many a pint together over the years and hopefully there are a few more to come. Sure, he's done things he's not proud of, but then who hasn't? It's just that Jimmy's misdemeanours were written about in very large print on the front pages of every tabloid newspaper in the country—some of it true, a lot of it fiction. But that's the price he pays for fame and it's that part of his life which I do not envy.

Chapter 19 ～

| *KELLY* SHOW NUMBER 571

The build-up to the last ever *KELLY* was strange. Normally I would have wanted to know every detail of what was going on. For every other programme, my producer Patricia Moore and I would have spent countless hours each week discussing the line-up and the running order; what kind of approach I would take with the guests; what were the standby items should things go wrong, and so on.

But this time I was left totally in the dark, and what's more, I was told in no uncertain terms by producer and researchers alike that I was *persona non grata* when it came to assembling the final show. If I called in to the office unannounced, the conversation would stop abruptly. Papers and notes were quickly removed from desktops. Web sites were hurriedly closed down on computers and telephone calls were prematurely ended. Of course I knew what was going on, so rather than spoil the 'surprises' that were being organised, I would take myself off for a few minutes in search of a cup of coffee or some such pretext. I was told only what was essential for me to know.

Of course all this non-involvement meant that I had a lot of time on my hands that week. To be honest, I would have preferred to have been busy. Instead, the time weighed heavily on my hands and I couldn't help myself from drifting in and out of bouts of nostalgia. It's a vain state of mind to allow yourself to get into, I know, but when a hugely significant period of your life is about to come to an end, it's human nature to reminisce and speculate on the future.

It was a difficult week. I was receiving texts and messages from a host of friends and well-wishers, expressing their disappointment that the show was coming to an end and wishing me well in my retirement.

Retirement? Where did that come from? I had never even considered the prospect of retiring. Indeed I had agreed a whole new series with UTV called *Gerry Meets . . .* which would afford me the opportunity of doing something the KELLY show rarely did, and that was to have in-depth, one-on-one conversations with a variety of people. We were planning over twenty of these programmes, which would be shown in 2006 and a further twenty in 2007. So retirement wasn't even remotely on the cards. In fact I was probably going to be busier than ever.

Still, I was keen to quell any such notion that I was about to fade from the scene or that my career would end with the last KELLY show or, God forbid, I was planning to spend the remainder of my days in a pair of slippers or walking the dog along the sands of Coney Island. I don't even have a dog! I was still passionate about making television programmes and was excited at the prospect of the new series. Retirement, indeed!

The final show was the 571st in the entire seventeen-year run of KELLY, representing nearly a thousand hours of television programming. I presented 568 of them. On only three occasions since we began in 1989 was I forced to withdraw—one for a family bereavement, two through illness. For my first two absences, Eamonn Holmes was asked to step in, and for the third, Mike Nesbitt did the honours. Mike, of course, was a former presenter of UTV's nightly news programme before leaving a few years ago. Today he is one of four recently appointed Victims Commissioners, charged with the weighty responsibility of examining the legacy of the troubles in Northern Ireland and its impact on victims.

The more I was forced to twiddle my thumbs in a state of inactivity in that final week, the more I began to wonder what plans Patricia and the team were cooking up. The one thing I did insist upon was that the two-hour show had to be a spectacle, a show that would entertain and reaffirm why KELLY had met with such success over the years. It was not the time for self-indulgence.

To my mind, we needed strong guests, the best of music, good interviews and only a minimum dollop of nostalgia.

The final show should not be a tribute to me but rather a proud, final celebration of a local programme made in Northern Ireland by Northern Ireland people for an all-Ireland market, a programme that had broken all records both in longevity and in television ratings, a programme in which a loyal following of viewers had invested both their time and trust for over seventeen years, a programme of which we were all proud.

No doubt the evening itself would be a highly-charged affair, but I was determined to be as professional as possible under the circumstances, not to let the moment get to me.

The day before the programme, at our usual production meeting, I learned for the first time the names of some of the guests who had been lined up. I was thrilled and delighted with the list. But I also learned that there were large chunks of the programme about which I was told nothing. I would just have to cope with whatever and whoever came my way, I was informed.

At the end of every Thursday production meeting, I would always jokingly finish with the line, 'Bed early tonight. Show day tomorrow.' As we exited that final meeting, the only word I added was 'last'. It was a poignant moment in my life and indeed in the lives of the team, many of whom had been with me for years. As I constantly stress, the success of KELLY was never down to me alone. In the seventeen years of its existence there were six producers and over twenty assistant producers and researchers. All were invited back for the final show along with many of my friends in the business like Jackie Fullerton, John 'May McFettridge' Linehan, Peter Corry, Gerry Anderson, Sean Coyle, Eamonn Holmes and Gene Fitzpatrick.

As well as owing a huge debt of gratitude to all the production teams, the three people to whom I owe most were my special guests—my wife Helena and our daughters Sarah and Claire. Over the years they would only have been at the KELLY show on a handful of occasions. They always understood and appreciated that television presenting was my job and UTV was my workplace.

Their constant support was always in the background, never on public display.

————

> GK (*on being handed a soap on a string, a model of a shapely female lower torso*): What's this?
>
> Ricky Tomlinson (*Jim Royle in the* Royle Family TV *comedy*): It's my arse. I posed for that?
>
> GK: Did you?
>
> RT: Nooooo.

————

I remember on one of my birthdays, the girls gave me one of those coffee mugs with a message on it. It read, 'Behind every successful dad is a family who love him.' Without them, any personal success would have been hollow. They were as much part of the final KELLY show as I was, and I wanted the world to know that.

Everything was in place for the 571st and last ever show. I tried to treat the day much the same as any other Friday, sticking to my little routines, reviewing my notes for those I knew I would be interviewing, nipping out for the odd cigarette. As usual, at 8 o'clock I changed into my suit and went down to make-up. But that's when I had to admit to myself that this was no ordinary Friday.

The place was buzzing. Usually I would have make-up to myself at this time of the evening, but now it was crowded with guests and well-wishers. Even the green room was packed with those who had been connected with the show over the years and wanted to be part of the night. I was amazed and yet flattered that so many had turned up. With ten minutes to go, I made my way backstage, only to find that the entire camera crew had chosen to mark the occasion by wearing dinner suits and dickie bows! That made me smile.

As the opening titles rolled and the signature tune played for the final time, I entered the studio to thunderous cheers and applause that literally rocked me back on my heels. As I cast my eyes over the audience, I could see that the noisiest lot was the group of former KELLY producers and researchers who were seated together. Wherever I looked, I saw familiar faces, but the standing ovation was something I hadn't anticipated.

Knowing I had a two-hour show to present, I couldn't afford to allow the emotion to get to me, especially not in the opening minute! But believe me it was difficult. I searched out Helena in the audience and with an encouraging wink of her eye, I launched into the opening link. The two-hour roller-coaster journey had begun.

First up was Brian Keenan, the man whose story we covered back in the very first month of KELLY in 1989, and which defined the ethos of the show for the next seventeen years. After Brian the Corrs sang 'My Lagan Love' as a special request for me. Martin O'Neill, a footballing hero in Northern Ireland and even more so in Scotland where he led Celtic to unprecedented successes, was next, followed by Ronan Keating and Paul Brady, two long-time friends of the show, singing the aptly named 'The Long Goodbye'. Ronan presented me with a beautifully framed wall hanging of CDs recorded during his solo career and the time he was with Boyzone. An inscription read: 'Presented to Gerry Kelly in recognition of 17 years of great TV and the many years of amazing support. All the best for the future. Ronan'

Peter Corry, a personal friend and one of the most frequent guests, joined forces with Phil Coulter to sing 'Remember Me', my favourite Phil Coulter composition. Phil of course was the subject of a KELLY tribute show we did on him at the Waterfront Hall in Belfast in 1997.

The first of the surprises was Irish tenor Ronan Tynan, who flew in from America specially to be on the show. He arrived with a wicker basket full of drink for me—trust Ronan. His story was

the subject of a special *KELLY* St Patrick's Day show we did in 2004
when, among the guests we had asked for a contribution, were
President George Bush Senior and the former Mayor of New York
City, Rudi Giuliani. Ronan mixes in high circles these days, but
he's still the big, self-effacing, likeable guy he always was.

And still they came. Brian Kennedy, another personal friend
who appeared on the show almost as many times as I had. He was
followed by Carol Smillie, the presenter of *Changing Rooms*, and
Belfast girl Andrea Catherwood, now working as a reporter and
newsreader with ITN.

Up next, Westlife, who came in from Germany for the show
and who were heading back first thing the next morning. I was
truly flattered they had made such an effort to be there. But when
they presented me with the mini motorbike, complete with
helmet, I nearly cracked up, not with tears I hasten to add, but
with laughter. It was such an off-the-wall thing to do and a
brilliant parody on U2's present of a Harley Davidson to Gay
Byrne on his last *Late Late Show*. I never told the lads, but I eventually gave the bike to a charity who auctioned it off and made a
few thousand pounds. I knew they wouldn't mind.

Interspersed with the guests were video inserts from people who
wanted to be at the show but for one reason or other couldn't
make it. These included Barry McGuigan, Donny Osmond,
Pauline Quirke, Jimmy Nesbitt, Paddy Kielty, Marie Jones, Daniel
O'Donnell, Kieran McMenamin, Gloria Hunniford, Kieran Goss,
Zoë Salmon, Bernie Nolan, Cliff Richard, Dara Ó Briain, and
politicians Michael McGimpsey, Mark Durkan and Ian Paisley Jr.

And then the surprise to top all surprises. The only thing I was
told to say by way of introduction was, 'Behind the doors there's
another guest who has flown in especially to be with us. I have no
idea who he or she is, so mystery guest, come on down.'

I waited, wondering who on earth it could be. The doors
opened and . . . nothing. No one was there. Turning to the floor
manager to see what was happening, there, with a bottle of Cristal
champagne in his hand, stood Michael Flatley. I had been told
that Michael was in South Africa and wouldn't be able to make

the show. So to see him standing there, arms outstretched in welcome, was a particular thrill. Since those early days when he first appeared on the programme, Michael had become an international phenomenon. On that night he could have chosen to be anywhere in the world. That he chose to come to the last KELLY show was very special indeed.

As I began to wrap up the programme, Patricia came through on my earpiece to say that we had extra time and that someone was about to come on the floor to take the programme on from there. What on earth was she talking about? And then I saw Eamonn Holmes appear with a large red book in his hand, and for the next fifteen minutes or so, he conducted a sort of *This Is Your Life* on me with contributions from a variety of ne'er-do-wells.

And that was it, almost two and a half hours and it all went by in a flash. When I finally began to wrap up the programme, I asked for Helena, Sarah and Claire to join me and together we stood as the entire audience and all the guests sang 'My Way'. Then, and only then, as I stood in the embrace of my family, did the evening get to me. It took an enormous effort to fight back the tears saying my final goodnight.

No sooner had the programme's end caption disappeared from the screens when the party started. UTV had arranged for the studio to be cleared immediately. A bar was set up in one corner, food was served in another and over 200 people began to party the night away. I was on such a high, I refused to take a drink, worried about how alcohol would mix with the huge amount of adrenalin that was already coursing through my body. But I loved the evening. Not only had the show gone well, but I also thought it was an appropriate and fitting end to KELLY. The party ran on into the wee small hours of the morning. No speeches, no presentations, no egos, just the simple enjoyment of friends celebrating together in a common cause. As I left the building that night with my family, I mentally closed the KELLY chapter of my life and looked forward to the next challenge.

Christmas is always a joyous time for us at home and with the euphoria of the early part of December still lingering on,

Christmas 2005 was even better. But in the cold light of a New Year, my thoughts turned to a new and different working regime altogether. I had still retained the KELLY team who now set about the task of lining up a string of guests for me to interview in a series called *Gerry Meets . . .*

I was also working with U105, UTV's radio station, for which they won the franchise to broadcast to the greater Belfast area. It had opened six weeks previously, on 14 November 2005, and I was presenting a three-hour show every Sunday from 10 am to 1 pm. The station is housed in UTV and is filled to the brim with the latest state-of-the-art equipment. Needless to say it took me quite a while to master the required skills. But I got there eventually, I think.

This was a far cry from my days in Downtown Radio in the early 1990s when I presented a programme there called, rather predictably, *Kelly on the Radio.* In those days we were still playing vinyl records on a turntable and commercials had to be hand-loaded by the presenter throughout the programme. After each show, every detail of every song played had to be written up—the record number, the singer, the writer, the record company, the publisher and so on. In U105, there are no visible CDs, no advertisement cartridges, no forms to fill in. Everything is on computer. Still, the number of mistakes you can make, even though it's all done with the click of a mouse, is amazing.

I enjoy the radio and was fortunate enough to win a Sony Gold award back in 1993 for a programme I did with Downtown Radio immediately after the Shankill Road bombing which claimed the lives of ten people. So my return to radio via U105 was an old friend, but yet one of the new challenges that faced me after KELLY.

For a long time I had thought it would be nice to have the time to interview people at length. One of the problems with KELLY was that, because of the tightly produced nature of the show, interviews were of necessity short and sweet. We always crammed so much into a show that in-depth interviews were a luxury we normally couldn't afford.

Gerry Meets . . . was to be a recorded, one-on-one programme allowing me as much time as I needed for the interviews, which would be then edited down to thirty minutes. We still retained our prime time-slot on Friday evenings and though not as glamorous as *KELLY*, I knew there would be a sizeable audience for this kind of programming.

Throughout February 2006 we began to film the interviews, starting with one of my all time favourite people, best-selling author Maeve Binchy. Others lined up for the first series included the Taoiseach Bertie Ahern, Gay Byrne, Baroness May Blood, Majella and Daniel O'Donnell, Eamonn Holmes and former Secretary of State Peter Hain, all strong people with good life stories to tell. But as much as I enjoyed doing these programmes and as successful as they were, something kept nagging at the back of my mind, something unsettling.

It took almost a year before I realised what was wrong. In the end it was very simple. I wasn't happy. UTV was changing. Cutbacks were being enforced as ITV advertising revenue began to dip. New managers had been appointed and opportunities for new television formats began to close down. I sensed a wind of change sweeping through television in general and UTV in particular.

For the first time in almost thirty years, I began to think that maybe I should leave. Perhaps my time with UTV had run its course; maybe I needed a complete change. I hung on for the remainder of 2007, but nothing had changed. As the end of the year approached, I knew it was make-my-mind-up time.

———

GK: You know when you talk to world leaders, do you change your persona, put on a different suit? Or are you the Bob Geldof we all know?

Bob Geldof: Well I'm not as nice as I am here. I've said this before—and it is a disgrace—but there is a currency in celebrity. Any half-wit [of a celebrity] can voice some cliché of an opinion. And people go, 'mmm, interesting.' It's not interesting. You're a half-wit. We'll use that to get to Bush, to Blair and Schroeder. Bono and I are really the Laurel and Hardy of third world debt. He speaks of the panoramic vision and I'm there leaping over to grab their throats.

———

Chapter 20 ～

￨ NEVER LOOK BACK

O n the morning of Monday, 7 January 2008, I made the journey as usual from my home in Coney Island to my office in UTV. It was to be my first day back at work following the Christmas break, but to be honest, I wasn't looking forward to returning. Helena knew that all wasn't quite right with me over the holidays but we put off any discussion until Christmas was completely out of the way. As the New Year turned, I knew the time had arrived for me to make a career decision.

As I made the thirty-mile journey that morning, only Helena and I knew what I was about to do. A meeting with myself and UTV's heads of Television and Human Resources to discuss a new contract with the company had been postponed in December. This was the day of the rearranged meeting. As I entered the familiar surroundings of Havelock House that morning, I knew in my heart that the decision I had made would mean that this would be the last time I entered the building as a contract artist with UTV. I had made up my mind. I was about to sever my thirty-year-old ties with the station which I knew would come as a shock to both management and work colleagues alike. It was a decision I had wrestled with hard and long over the Christmas break.

2007 had been an uncomfortable year for me. Even though I was busy that year recording over twenty programmes in the *Gerry Meets* . . . series and four special shows based in America, I knew in my heart I wasn't fully committed. Somewhere inside me deep down, I was still missing the buzz of live television. In hindsight, it would appear that I hadn't quite got the KELLY show out of my system and was feeling that, whatever I was doing, it was a poor second to the previous sixteen years.

I hated the way I felt and knew that if I wanted to change, and I needed to, the only alternative was to step away from UTV and seek new challenges and opportunities elsewhere. Every person and everything in that building reminded me of the KELLY show. Over the years I had worked and had become friends with practically everyone involved in programme making in UTV. Even the studio was referred to as the KELLY studio. So, the only way to prevent myself from perpetually drowning in a sea of nostalgia was to shed my old skin and leave the familiar behind.

The meeting with the heads of department was short and to the point. I was not accepting a new contract and would be leaving UTV that very day. After the initial jolt, the two managers were very gracious and understanding. I knew they respected my wishes and I also needed them to know that I was determined to follow through on my decision. There was no point in trying to change my mind. Surprisingly unemotional, I left the meeting. My next stop was with John McCann, chief executive and my mentor during the 1980s.

I spent an hour with John explaining, laughing, chatting and reminiscing, and when it was time to go, we shook hands warmly, agreeing that we would keep in touch. The UTV door would always be open to me, he stressed.

I went off then to our publicity department to agree a form of words for the press release. I've always been a firm believer that honesty is the best policy, so no form of spin was required. We also agreed that the rest of the workforce should know of my decision so an email would be sent to everyone that afternoon. And that was that. All the t's were crossed and all the i's dotted. I was leaving UTV.

By this stage it was about 1 pm, so knowing that most of my colleagues, thankfully, would be at lunch, I made my way to my office. I really didn't want to meet anyone. It took me just under an hour to clear my desk. Carrying a large cardboard box full of memories, I headed for my car. As I swung out on to the Ormeau

Road, I forced myself not to look back. I spent the rest of the day at home helping Helena take down the Christmas decorations.

That night I took the first phone call, a friend at UTV enquiring after me and asking what had happened. As we spoke, another call was waiting, then another and another. Obviously the email had been circulated to the staff in UTV. And that was the start of what became a telephone marathon. It didn't take long for the newspapers to hear the story and by 8 o'clock it got to the stage where I was only answering those calls whose numbers I recognised.

To be honest, I was somewhat bemused and astounded at the media interest in my departure. Oddly enough, I was anticipating such a reaction back in 2005 when the KELLY show came off the air, but not in my private decision to simply seek other work outside UTV. But my exodus on this occasion seemed to be a bigger story than the departure of the KELLY show. I thought the press would have had much more to say about that decision rather than a freelance TV presenter deciding to seek out new horizons. All the papers carried the story over the next three days and it was even up for discussion on local radio stations.

The following weekend, Helena and I left to stay with friends in Spain for a week, just to clear our heads and give us time to assess the impact of my decision away from the interruption of well-meaning phone calls and the genuine concern of friends. It proved to be exactly what I needed. Within a matter of a few days in the winter Spanish sun, a wave of calm—for want of a better description—came over me and I knew I had made the right decision.

My timing was perfect and my optimism at an all time high. And even though I had done little in the way of seeking new employment outlets before I left UTV, my attitude was positive and I relished the year ahead and the challenges it would bring.

Of course, I miss UTV. It's not possible to walk away from a place in which you've spent thirty years of your life and not retain a special place in your heart for it. I made lifelong friends there and together we became part of television history in Northern Ireland. I am proud of what we achieved as a team in UTV, but you can't live on past glories.

Nothing stays the same: television has changed so radically that it is impossible to imagine a prime-time show today lasting seventeen weeks, never mind seventeen years. I believe I worked in the heyday of television, a time when television was important to people, when it represented worthwhile values and when it wasn't embarrassing to sit down with your children and view programmes together—even before the so called 9 o'clock watershed. Maybe Mary Whitehouse had the right idea back in the 1960s! (I'm only kidding.) Still, TV needs to clean up its act. But that's a matter for a new generation of broadcasters and decision-makers. In the meantime my life continues to be fulfilling. Most times it feels as if someone up there is looking out for me. I suspect it's my mother and Nana.

I have had the most amazing journey, a lifetime of privilege both in meeting people few have the opportunity to meet and more importantly being accepted into the living rooms of the nation for thirty years. It was more than I ever could have hoped for, further than even my imagination would allow. And what's more, I have still so much I want to do. The fun continues . . .

INDEX